D0114577

Warrior

Warrior

My Path to Being Brave

Lisa Guerrero
with Irene Zutell

hachette
BOOKS • New York

Hachette Books
Hachette Book Group
1290 Avenue of the Americas
New York, NY 10104
HachetteBooks.com
Twitter.com/HachetteBooks
Instagram.com/HachetteBooks

First Edition: January 2023

Published by Hachette Books, an imprint of Perseus Books, LLC, a subsidiary of Hachette Book Group, Inc. The Hachette Books name and logo is a trademark of the Hachette Book Group.

The Hachette Speakers Bureau provides a wide range of authors for speaking events. To find out more, go to www.hachettespeakersbureau.com or call (866) 376-6591.

The publisher is not responsible for websites (or their content) that are not owned by the publisher.

The views and opinions expressed by the author are her own, not necessarily the opinions of *Inside Edition* or CBS Media Ventures.

Print book interior design by Jeff Williams

Library of Congress Cataloging-in-Publication Data

Name: Guerrero, Lisa, author.
Title: Warrior: my path to being brave / Lisa Guerrero.
Description: First edition. | New York, NY: Hachette Books, 2023.
Identifiers: LCCN 2022019039 | ISBN 9780306829499 (hardcover) | ISBN
    9780306829505 (paperback) | ISBN 9780306829512 (ebook)
Subjects: LCSH: Guerrero, Lisa, 1964– | Women television Journalists—
    United States—Biography.
Classification: LCC PN4874.G7984 A3 2023 | DDC 070.92
    [B]—dc23/eng/20221003
LC record available at https://lccn.loc.gov/2022019039

ISBNs: 9780306829499 (hardcover); 9780306829512 (ebook)

Printed in the United States of America

LSC-C

Printing 1, 2022

The other kids felt sorry for me because
I didn't have a mother. But I felt sorry for
them because they didn't have my father.

TO WALTER COLES

"Guerrero means warrior, Lisita. Never forget that you were born to fight!"

—LUCY GUERRERO COLES
to her daughter, Lisa, in 1971

Contents

1

Justice for Juliette

As Dustin Chauncey waited to hear his verdict, he turned around and scanned the crowded courtroom until his eyes landed on me. He knew who I was—we'd met when he thought he'd gotten away with murder and I'd stuck my microphone in his car window to let him know he hadn't. A shiver raced through me as I returned his glare—it was like staring into the eyes of the devil. But I didn't look away.

I was part of the reason he'd been arrested and charged with the murder of two-year-old Juliette Geurts. For more than six years, he'd escaped justice. In a few minutes, he'd finally receive it.

As *Inside Edition*'s chief investigative correspondent for more than a decade, I've covered hundreds of stories—consumer scams, crooked politicians, corrupt televangelists, rapists and predators, child, women, elder, and animal abuse, and, well, the list goes on.

But I'd never solved a murder.

It began two years earlier when I received a message on Facebook from Monica Hall, Juliette's aunt. She'd grown frustrated with the incompetent police investigation of her niece's death and had reached out to the media for help. But her pleas to the networks, the cable news stations, and television personalities such as Dr. Phil and Nancy Grace had gone unanswered. It had been four years since Juliette had died, and I was her last resort. She begged me to look into it.

"It's been years of hell for our family. I don't know where else to turn," she wrote.

In the early morning of July 11, 2008, Juliette had been brutally beaten in her home just a few feet from her identical twin sister, Jaelyn. Juliette had suffered a lacerated liver from a kick to the stomach as well as cerebral hemorrhaging and a badly bruised lung. Even her crib had been broken during the assault. Yet none of the three adults—two men and Juliette's mother—who had been in the tiny ranch-style house that evening drinking rum and smoking weed had been arrested. The murder had not only remained unsolved, it had barely been investigated. Worse, the cops had bungled every aspect of it.

It had taken five days after the toddler's murder for the cops to seal the home as a crime scene. It was a year before her clothes were sent to a crime lab. The police never separated the suspects before they interviewed them—so they had time to coordinate their stories. The cops never charged anyone, even though they called Juliette's death a homicide. And when the principal witnesses and/or suspects left the state, law enforcement threw up its hands and just moved on. The more I read, the more furious I became. This was a little girl who had never had a chance, even in death. Juliette's aunt had been leading a petition drive that would compel a grand jury to be convened and a special prosecutor to be appointed to investigate the unsolved crime. But Juliette's story needed national attention to help Monica garner the necessary signatures.

I couldn't stop thinking about this tiny victim whose horrible death had been treated so callously by law enforcement.

"I have to look into this," I said to Bob Read, the senior producer for our investigative unit.

He told me what I already knew. "You have nothing to go on. There's no one to interview. There's no one to confront. The suspects have disappeared. There are no leads. This case is cold. What could we do that law enforcement couldn't?"

I wasn't sure yet. But I told him I'd like to meet and interview Monica and see where the story would lead. When Charles Lachman, our executive producer, gave it the green light, I headed to Gering, the remote town in Nebraska where Juliette had lived and died. I met with Monica, and we toured the home where Juliette had been killed. Then Monica played me the tape recording of her conversation with Doug Warner, the district attorney handling the case.

"I hope for Juliette's sake you will find justice for her," Monica pleaded.

I could hear the anger in the DA's voice when he replied, *"Don't give me that 'for Juliette.' Do you know how many dead babies I've worked on?"*

This recording was impossible to listen to without becoming emotional. As Monica and I talked about that awful conversation, about the sloppy investigation, and about the beautiful little girl who had been known as the louder, more rambunctious twin, my eyes welled with tears.

* * *

This is a book about bravery. I decided to write it because every day I receive messages from viewers asking me how I'm able to fearlessly investigate and interview bad guys. They want to know where my courage comes from. And my answer contradicts everything journalists have been taught. But I'm not a typical journalist—I was never trained in a traditional newsroom. I didn't receive a journalism degree. I didn't even finish college.

My route to journalism has been unconventional. I've been a cheerleader. A corporate executive. A Barbie doll. A sportscaster. A soap-opera vixen. A sideline reporter. A *Playboy* cover model. A Diamond Diva. A red-carpet correspondent. An investigative journalist. A disrupter. I made Dennis Rodman cry. I interviewed three presidents and hundreds of professional athletes in dozens of locker rooms throughout the country. I costarred in a viral video that has *one billion* views. I sued the New England Patriots—and won. I tracked down a murderer. I butted heads with Barbara Walters. I even played myself in a movie starring Brad Pitt.

But my proudest moments come from helping people find closure and seeking out justice.

My bravery stems from pain. I feel the victims' pain so acutely that I absorb their sorrow, rage, and frustration. Little Juliette was not another "dead baby." I felt as though she were my niece too. Monica's despair and anger were my despair and anger. I connect easily with survivors, no matter who they are and what they've gone through. Once that happens, I'm filled with empathy.

Empathy is what makes me brave.

Where does my empathy come from? I've been building it brick by brick during my lifetime. When I was a little girl, my parents—Dad, a social worker; and Mom, a Chilean immigrant—taught me compassion for others by taking me to homeless shelters and nursing homes. Then, when my mom died when I was eight, I was overwhelmed by a pain so fierce that it has helped me understand others' pain. When I became an actor, I was trained to channel the suffering, rage, and love that my characters possessed into my performance. And then when I was older, I endured harassment and abuse that led me into severe depression and suicidal thoughts. When I hear about someone's pain, I not only absorb their suffering, I remember my own.

I'm often approached by people who tell me they love my confrontational style. I race into dangerous situations, armed only with a microphone, and I demand accountability from those who hurt others. I've been struck by cars. I've had knives and guns pointed at me. I've been punched, pushed, kicked, and stalked, and I've received death threats.

But there are some who criticize me, saying a journalist shouldn't show emotion or take sides in a story. They'll tell me that I'm doing it wrong, that I'm not "objective." I reject the idea of being blindly unbiased. There are bad guys and good guys. A monster is a monster.

"I'll help you find justice for baby Juliette," I told Monica.

My producer, my cameraman, and I were relentless. We marched into the district attorney's office while he hid from us. I confronted Mel Griggs, the Gering police chief.

"Why has it taken so long to find the person responsible for her murder? There were only three adults in the house that night."

He paused for a long time. He stuttered and stammered. "That's true, and we have evidence that they were there, but none of them are talking."

It was infuriating that the police chief believed he'd done enough. We launched our own investigation, tracking down the trio's friends, acquaintances, former neighbors, and past landlords. We found the bars they frequented, the places where they'd worked, and the apartments where they'd lived. There were tons of dead ends. But we were obsessed with finding answers. We'd investigate other stories and then slip away for a day or so to work on some element of this one. Bob patiently allowed us to piggyback our trips.

Finally, after months of chasing leads, we discovered where the three suspects were living: Charyse Geurts, the mom, had moved outside Green Bay, Wisconsin, while her ex-boyfriend Dustin Chauncey (who wasn't the twins' father) and the third adult, Brandon Townsend, had relocated to separate towns in Colorado.

We found the apartment building where Charyse lived. When she returned from a night shift, I raced up to her car as she opened the door. I wedged my body in between her and the open door. If she decided to drive off, she'd have to take me with her.

"Get out of my face," she yelled.

But getting in faces is what I'm known for. Although I race up to my subject and pepper them with questions, I'm completely calm. My blood pressure doesn't go up. I don't breathe heavily. In sports they call it being "in the zone"—everything moves in slow motion, and you envision the outcome before it happens.

When I was promoted to chief investigative correspondent, Charles, my executive producer, said he saw me as a victim's avenger. I love that description. There's nothing more satisfying than demanding accountability on behalf of a victim. I never know how someone will react—they might tell me the truth or lie or run or push or kick me or my embattled, unflappable cameraman. But we're never going to settle for a "No comment."

I knelt in front of Charyse and asked her if she had killed her daughter.

"No!" She claimed she had taken a sleeping pill that night and didn't remember anything.

"Do you feel responsible for your daughter's death?"

"What mother wouldn't feel responsible?" she said, sobbing. "I don't want to talk anymore."

Most journalists would wrap it up there—she'd given me a "No comment." It really was enough for a good story. But it wasn't enough for the people who loved Juliette and were demanding justice for her. I continued to pepper Charyse with questions.

"Why did you run? Why aren't you helping police?"

Charyse sobbed harder. I wasn't buying it.

"Did Dustin kill Juliette?"

She paused and sighed deeply as though she knew the jig was up.

"Yeah, I believe that he did."

Oh, my God, she just pointed the finger at her ex-lover!

Next, we found Brandon Townsend, who said, "I think Dustin went in there in the middle of the night and beat her too hard."

This was astounding. I wasn't some cop in an interrogation room wearing down a victim after hours of questioning—I was a reporter with a microphone. I had two witnesses throwing

Dustin Chauncey under the bus. Townsend admitted on camera that Dustin had beaten the baby before.

We finally tracked down Dustin outside a suburban home near Denver. Since Juliette's murder, he'd been arrested a dozen times for everything from theft to violent assaults. As we approached him, I thought he might have a gun or a knife on him. When Dustin spotted us, he jumped in a car and sped off. My crew and I raced to our car and chased him through traffic. When Dustin's beater careened through a busy intersection, he was pulled over by a police officer. As soon as the cop finished writing a ticket, I rushed over to the open passenger window and thrust my microphone at Dustin.

"Did you hurt Juliette Geurts?"

He spit out his words. "No, I didn't. You guys can speak to my lawyer because I'm done. No comment."

"What do you have to say to Juliette's family?"

"I will speak to them on my own time. I'm done. Thank you."

As he sped off, I shouted one last question: "Did you kill Juliette Geurts?"

* * *

When we aired the first of our three stories, Monica was able to collect nearly two thousand signatures—more than double what was needed to convene a grand jury. There were rallies and marches for Juliette. There were signs demanding justice for the toddler on store windows and street corners. Messages about Juliette were scrawled on car windows.

With new evidence, such as DNA from Juliette's clothing and testimony from Brandon Townsend that had not been previously gathered, the grand jury was able to obtain an indictment. Dustin was charged with intentional child abuse resulting in death.

During the three-day trial, the evidence presented was truly horrific. Juliette's injuries were so severe that she must have suffered an excruciatingly painful death. DNA analysis of her clothing revealed that Dustin's semen was on it. The prosecution posited that Juliette had climbed out of her crib and gone into her mother's bedroom while Charyse and Dustin had been having sex. Juliette's crying had enraged Dustin. He had kicked and punched the baby before throwing her back into the crib.

The jury returned a guilty verdict in a little over an hour.

I was sitting in a row next to the family. They were grasping hands in nervous anticipation. Monica was near enough that I could hear her and other family members quietly weeping. As the verdict was read, the family gasped. When the court was dismissed, everyone spilled out into the hallway, embracing and sobbing. I was a journalist, but as I watched this unfold, I felt like a member of Juliette's extended family.

"Thank you for listening to me," Monica said as we hugged. "We did it! And we couldn't have done it without you and your team."

A few minutes later, I stood outside the courthouse, reporting on the latest development in Juliette's story (the final chapter would come when Dustin was sentenced to eighty years to life). Later that night, when I returned to my hotel, I sobbed as the enormity of the day hit me.

I'd tracked down a monster and helped put him behind bars.

This was the most gratifying moment of my career—and my life.

2

You Are a Warrior

At bedtime, when I was a little girl, I'd pull the top off my mother's lipstick and stare at the color. Metallic gold was her signature shade. She'd wear it to the market or a party or just around the house. I'd imagine her puckering her lips and applying it. Then I'd kiss the lipstick and tuck the tube under my pillow.

I was eight years old when Mom died. What she thought was a bad sore throat turned out to be stage four non-Hodgkin's lymphoma. Right after Christmas, my parents told my little brother, Richard, and me that Mom was sick and had to have surgery. She might lose her hair, and she'd probably stay in her room for a while, they said.

Six weeks later, she was gone.

I remember that moment like it was yesterday. My dad gently roused us from sleep early on Valentine's Day.

"Your mother's in heaven with God. She's no longer in pain."

While Richard sobbed, I sat on my bunk bed and stared at my dad, not really understanding his words. I didn't yet realize that this was the most devastating moment of my life. It took

11

me years to comprehend that my mother was really gone. I'd fantasize that she was away on a trip or on some secret mission. I'd even pretend she'd been kidnapped. Once her ransom was paid, she'd return to me. Of course she'd come back. Everyone had a mom. How could you grow up without one? It seemed impossible.

Every child believes their mother is beautiful. But even as a little girl, I knew there was something different about the way people would stare at my mom. With her full lips, high cheekbones, dark eyes, olive skin, and long brown hair, she stood out from all the other moms in the neighborhood. People would stop her on the street and say, "You look like Sophia Loren." I'd hold her hand and look up at these strange faces staring at her. I had an urge to protect her from everyone who gazed her way.

But Mom didn't really need my protection or anyone else's. I had this epiphany when I was seven and we were returning a purchase at Pier 1 Imports. Even though Mom was fluent in English, she was self-conscious about her heavy accent. The cashier had trouble understanding what my mom was saying. A line formed behind us. I could hear a woman mumbling under her breath as the minutes ticked away.

"Why don't you go back to Mexico," the woman complained, loudly enough for the entire line to hear.

The store became silent. I stood behind my mother and watched her back stiffen. She suddenly seemed much taller than her five-foot-three frame. She swung her head, and her long, shiny hair whipped around. Then she glared at the woman.

"I'm from Chile, not Mexico. That's not even the same continent, you ignorant woman!"

The woman's jaw dropped. She put her head down and didn't say another word.

Mom and I never spoke about what had happened. And maybe if she had lived beyond her twenty-nine years, the incident would have been just one of many stories about my fierce mom. But this moment has become how I remember my mom—beautiful, strong, and larger than life. She wouldn't let anyone insult her or her family. As we walked out of the store, I was overcome with pride for this woman whom I would lose in less than a year.

When she was sixteen, my mom moved from Santiago, Chile, to Chicago with her parents and four younger siblings. Her dad, Raul Guerrero, was a tailor who designed uniforms for bellmen, pilots, and the Salvation Army. Family legend has it that he sewed a costume for one of the Beatles when they were in Chicago for the Yellow Submarine tour.

My dad tells me that shortly after the Guerreros arrived, everyone at their local church was buzzing about the oldest Guerrero daughter. She was this exotic beauty bursting with talent. She always clinched the leads in the church's musicals and dramas. My dad would steal glances at her during church services. But he never imagined she'd notice him. When he finally got the nerve to ask her out, he was shocked when she said yes. By the end of their first date, they were in love. At that time, my mom spoke very little English, and my dad knew zero Spanish. "We spoke the language of love," Dad likes to tell me. They married a year later. Mom was twenty—my dad, twenty-five.

During the day, Dad went to The University of Chicago for his master's in social service administration. At night, he drove a city bus. They lived in a tiny studio apartment about a block from Chicago's Wrigley Field and slept in a Murphy bed that folded up against the wall. Their apartment was so small that when they pulled the bed down, they couldn't open the front door. When I was born, I slept in a dresser drawer lined with towels. My dad describes it as a wonderful but difficult time.

When I was five, we moved to San Diego, where my dad served as director of social services for the Salvation Army. My mom ran the food distribution center there. We lived in a tiny two-bedroom house next to an abandoned lot at the end of a cul-de-sac. My mother would speak her native language only when she was on the phone with her siblings. She insisted we speak English. But as much as she wanted me to fully embrace being American, she also wanted me to be aware of my culture.

"Do you hear the jungle drums, Lisita? Remember, you're a Latina too." She'd turn on the record player and we'd dance around the living room to Chilean music as well as the Beatles, Aretha Franklin, and her favorite, Roberta Flack. "You dance like a Latina," she'd say, laughing. "Always remember, you're a Guerrero." She'd explain to me that her last name, Guerrero, was Spanish for warrior.

"Lisita, don't forget, you are a warrior."

I'd nod and smile. I was part of a bloodline of brave and strong people. I loved being a warrior. It was like having a super-power Mom and I secretly shared.

After Mom died, I couldn't imagine ever feeling like a warrior again. I felt sad, scared, and lonely. I was also very angry. I was angry at God for taking my mom. I was angry at how unfair life was—why did everyone have a mom but me? I was angry that my brother and I were the kids whom people looked at with pity. And I was angry at Mom. Why had she left us? Why hadn't she said goodbye? Why hadn't she written me a letter? I searched her bedroom for a hidden note. I wanted some final message from her to tell me what to do, what to become. But there was nothing. I swiped her lipstick off the dresser and her pillowcase off the bed as keepsakes.

"Your mom didn't want to say goodbye to you. She was convinced she was going to get better," my dad explained years later. As much as I couldn't believe she'd leave me, Mom couldn't believe it either.

After the funeral, relatives volunteered to raise us. They said we could move to Chicago and live with one of their families, at least for a while. After all, my dad was devastated and in shock. At Christmastime, we were a happy family celebrating the holidays. Six weeks later, we were shattered. Dad was thirty-four and a widower with two small children. But Dad wouldn't hear of anyone taking us from him. "Absolutely not. These are my kids, and I'm going to raise them."

I remember eating a lot of McDonald's, Burger King, and pizza. Dad cooked us fried-egg sandwiches—that was the extent of his culinary skill. While he may not have been the best chef, he was the greatest, most loving dad. He was there for every recital, every play, every softball game. Occasionally, he'd hire a live-in housekeeper so he could get his work done. But Richard and I didn't want anyone else taking care of us. We wouldn't listen to these women, and we wouldn't eat their cooking (we'd rather have McDonald's anyway). If they spent the night, we'd put frogs in their beds. We were little monsters. Most of these women ran out after a few days. After three housekeepers quit, my dad gave up.

I adored my dad. He was my hero, and I wanted to be just like him. Since Dad loved sports, I did too. He'd spend a few hours on the weekends watching football, baseball, or basketball. I'd jump on the couch, cuddle with him, and watch the games. I liked all sports, but I especially loved football. It was fast, physical, and brutal. I'd ask Dad to explain every detail. Yes, I was that annoying kid who had hundreds of questions about everything—scoring, positions, strategy. I think Dad spent more time explaining the game than actually watching it. We'd read the sports pages and discuss the latest news. As I became more proficient in the game, he'd quiz me on football facts. "What's the latest quarterback controversy?" "Name all the starting quarterbacks in the AFC." When he had friends over, they'd be amazed that this little girl knew more about football than they did.

After the games, we'd go outside and toss a football. Dad spent hours teaching me how to throw a perfect spiral. A few years after Mom died, we'd moved to a house that overlooked Qualcomm Stadium (then known as Jack Murphy Stadium), the home of the San Diego Chargers. Their quarterback, Dan Fouts, quickly became my favorite player, and I begged Dad for a number 14 jersey. We could hear the crowds cheering during the games.

"When I grow up, I'm going to be the Chargers' starting quarterback," I told my dad.

"Keep practicing," he'd say.

When I look back at school photos, it's pretty obvious that there were no female influences in my life. My hair looks like I chopped it myself—which I did. When it came to fashion, I was completely clueless. Before school started each year, Dad would take us shopping for bargain clothes at Mervyn's department store. I'd try on outfits and ask Dad's opinion. It never dawned on me that my color-blind dad might not be the best fashion consultant. I'd show up for school in clothes with colors and patterns that clashed. I'd mix stripes and plaids. With my glasses, braces, and hair that looked like it had been through a blender, I was a walking billboard for fashion don'ts.

As I got older, the loss of my mother felt bigger. I knew I was missing something crucial that everyone else had and took for granted. My brother and I would play hooky the Friday before Mother's Day. We didn't want to sit in the classroom while kids made crafts and cards for their moms. Dad always planned something fun to keep our minds off such holidays. Still, it was hard to forget that everyone we knew was celebrating something we couldn't.

There were times when navigating girlhood without a mom felt impossible. Dad would constantly tell me that I could come to him with any problem and that I could tell him anything. But how do you ask your dad to take you bra shopping (especially since I was flat-chested)? How do you ask your dad to teach you how to shave your legs? (I opted to wear pants for years—even in 90-degree heat.) One day, I doubled over in such severe pain that I was convinced it had finally happened—I had cancer, just like Mom. I screamed and cried. "I think I'm dying." In a panic, Dad rushed me to the emergency room.

"What's wrong with her?" my dad breathlessly asked the nurse.

"Sir, she's fine," the nurse said, smiling kindly. "Your daughter just had her first period."

That moment could have gone down as the most mortifying event of my young teenaged years. But not quite. A few days later, a lady from our church casually stopped by the house with a box of tampons. She sat me down and proceeded to explain how to insert them. After she left, I told my dad no more church ladies substituting for my mom.

Besides, I had my female role models. They were Kelly and Pepper and Diana and Emma—my favorite characters in my favorite shows: *Charlie's Angels*, *Police Woman*, *Wonder Woman*, and *The Avengers*. I'd sit in the living room with my nose practically pressed up against the TV screen and be completely mesmerized by these strong, beautiful women. Best of all, they kicked ass.

I knew life was unfair, so I loved escaping into this world where everything worked out after a sixty-minute episode. These women always got the bad guy. They always solved the crime. They always made sure justice was served. As a girl without a mom to tell her how to dress and behave, I aspired to be these women. I wasn't sure exactly what I'd do, but I wanted to be just like them. Would I be a glamorous cop? Or a sexy private investigator? Or an undercover agent? Could I somehow possess superpowers? After all, my mom had told me that being a warrior was in my blood.

At school, I felt ugly, awkward, and uncomfortable. In my fantasies, I was a beautiful crime stopper. I'd memorize lines from the shows and act them out in my bedroom. I'd choreograph fight scenes. I'd pretend there were bad guys lurking around my house. I'd sneak into each room, my arms stretched out in front of me, squeezing my imaginary .38 Special just like Kelly from *Charlie's Angels*. "Freeze!" I'd yell into my closet or the bathroom or the kitchen. I'd karate chop and flip an enemy just like Emma Peel from *The Avengers*. I'd chase down a bank robber just like

YOU ARE A WARRIOR

Pepper from *Police Woman*. I'd zap my nemesis with my Bracelets of Submission just like my favorite of them all, Wonder Woman.

Then I'd go to school and be dorky, quiet Lisa, whom no one seemed to notice.

And then one day as I walked home from school, Richard ran up to me, crying. He had a big welt on his forehead.

"What happened?"

"Kevin stole my lunchbox," he sputtered out through sobs. Not only had Kevin stolen Richard's beloved Star Wars lunchbox, he'd whacked him in the head with it.

As I stared at Richard's reddening welt, I became furious. Richard was a shy boy who was having a tough time adjusting to life without Mom. A tiny, scrawny kid who looked so much younger than his eleven years, Richard was the perfect victim for Kevin, a big, burly, blond-haired kid who terrorized our middle school. He'd beat kids up and steal their money and lunch.

"Where is he?" I asked Richard.

He pointed to a corner of the playground.

I was blind with rage as I raced toward the playground. I spotted Kevin. He was hanging out with his gang, holding my brother's lunchbox and laughing. I ran up to him. He smiled at me. It was a smile that said, *Yeah, I've got your brother's lunchbox. What are you gonna do about it, you little dork loser?*

I clenched my fist and swung as hard as I could. I punched Kevin right in the face. As he was reeling from the shock, I grabbed Richard's lunchbox.

It seemed as if the entire playground came rushing toward me, including a teacher who had witnessed the whole event. I was given detention every day for two weeks. The school called my dad. That night, Dad lectured me.

"Lisa, violence never solves anything."

I nodded. But I was really thinking, *Well, I got my brother's lunchbox back—and no one's gonna pick on him again. So maybe a strong right hook does solve a few things.*

At school the next day, I was suddenly on the radar. I was Lisa, the girl who had taken down the bully. Nobody ever touched Richard again. Kevin and his gang looked away when I walked by. Yes, I was still a dork. But I was a dork with swagger. No one would mess with me. Or my little brother. Every kid in school saw me as a brave girl. More importantly, I did too.

Over the years, I've thought about that day. How could a mousy girl who was intimidated by bullies and steered clear of them become the tough girl who raced up to the bully and socked him in the face?

All those hours I'd spent playing superhero had been my personal bravery training camp. When my brother had come up to me crying, something had clicked within me. Richard was a victim, and he needed justice. I sprang into action, just like my TV heroes. Years later, when I'd give speeches about bravery, I'd explain how that moment when I'd confronted Kevin had taught me that if you practice bravery enough—even if you're just pretending in your bedroom—it becomes instinctual.

At the time I was thirteen and didn't understand this yet. What I did understand was that I was braver than I realized.

I thought about my mother. She *had* left me that final message.

Lisa, you are a Guerrero. You are a warrior.

3

Q-Tip's Revenge

There were close to four thousand kids at my high school in Huntington Beach. As a quiet girl who kept to herself, wrote in a journal, and read books alone during lunch, I felt invisible. It seemed as if all the girls at my school knew how to act, dress, wear makeup, and paint their nails. Without a mother to guide me about fashion, makeup, or social skills, I was clueless. And, at five foot eight, I towered over the girls and most of the boys in my freshman class. I became known as "Q-Tip" because I was tall and skinny with glasses, braces, no boobs, and a crazy mane of short, unruly hair. When I looked in the mirror, I saw a complete mess. I wished more than anything I could ask Mom for help.

I only had a couple of friends at school, but I wasn't super close to anyone. I didn't have much in common with them. It seemed as if their conversations revolved around hating their mothers. "My mom's such a bitch" was a common refrain. I'd silently simmer—until I couldn't stand it any longer.

"You're lucky you have a mom," I'd blurt out. The girls would look at each other, surprised by my uncharacteristic outburst.

Eventually, they'd sit somewhere else at lunch so they could commiserate over their horrible mothers without me sitting in judgment. It didn't make much of a difference to me. Whether alone or in a group, I felt an aching sense of loneliness. Looking back, I realize that these girls resented me for calling them out on what was a normal part of the mother–teenaged daughter dynamic. I wonder if I would have had similar complaints about my mom had she lived.

On weekends the kids from school would hang out at parties, the malls, the beach, and Disneyland. I'd spend weekends with my family at church events. My dad, brother, and I were like the Three Musketeers—we did everything together. In many ways, it felt like us against the world. I was never a wild child. I never drank, smoked, or stayed out late. I never rebelled. Whom would I rebel against anyway? My dad? I felt such deep sorrow for him after losing my mom that I didn't want to do anything to contribute to his sadness. My free time was spent with my family at the Salvation Army. I was in its choir, church plays, musicals, Bible studies, and Sunday school.

Known as Surf City because of its nearly ten-mile stretch of sandy beaches that are ideal for surfing (I never surfed—the waves terrified me. I'd sit on the beach and read or do homework), Huntington Beach is a city in Orange County, California, about thirty-five miles southwest of downtown Los Angeles. My family wasn't poor—we lived in a modest tract home. But most of the kids in school seemed rich to me, with their preppy designer clothes and handbags and shiny new BMWs and convertible Rabbits. While the girls from my class would meet at the upscale South Coast Plaza to shop, I'd peruse the Salvation Army's thrift shop for vintage dresses (shorts were out of the question—I still didn't know how to shave my painfully skinny legs).

My dad was a long-range planning consultant for the Salvation Army and conducted needs assessments and fundraising campaigns. As a social worker, he made an honest living, but we were far from rich. When I asked Dad for a car, he said I'd have to pay for it. I saved $1,000 from selling balloons at Disneyland's Tomorrowland as well as babysitting the neighborhood kids. When I got my license, I bought a used bright-orange Volkswagen Thing. It was a convertible with no upholstery—I'd hose off the interior when it became dirty.

Edison High School had its cliques:

The Soches—the popular, social kids,
The Jocks—the star athletes, and
The Loadies—the kids who would get drunk and/or high.

And me? I was an outsider. The weird kid with the weird car. I'd hide behind my books. I'd read or write in my journal at lunchtime and in between classes. When I tried out for cheerleading, I failed miserably. I wasn't quick enough. My timing was off. I was a few moves behind the rest of the girls. But even if I had gotten the choreography down, I wouldn't have made it anyway. The girls who were cheerleaders were beautiful and popular. And I was, well, Q-Tip. Instead, I joined the school's drill team.

Maybe because I felt so alone, I loved the word "team." I wasn't part of any social group, so in some ways, the drill team filled this void. We had to be perfectly synchronized. We had to dance the same way and kick at the same height and guide our formations perfectly. No one could stand out—and if someone did, it was because she was out of sync. It definitely wasn't a cool team to be on. We were pretty lame in our green velvet dresses and wiglets—hair toppers that matched our hair color—with really long feathers sticking out of them. I'm sure the cheerleaders and the other popular kids made fun of us. I didn't care—I loved every minute of it.

But I loved theater even more. Ever since my dad had enrolled me in theater therapy as a little kid to help cope with my mother's death, I'd been addicted to performing. I was able to channel my anger and sadness into a character. I'd leave Q-Tip behind and morph into someone else. I dreamed of one day becoming an actress. When I tried out for my high school's stage version of *Rebel Without a Cause*, I was cast as Judy Brown, the female lead made famous by Natalie Wood in the movie. I was ecstatic. I spent all my free time memorizing my lines.

A lot of high school has become a blur. But there's a moment I vividly remember. A makeup artist gently removed my oversized glasses and painted my face for dress rehearsal. She blew out my hair while styling it with a flat brush (brushing while blow-drying my hair had never occurred to me). When she finished, I looked in the mirror. I couldn't believe it. My mother was smiling back at me. My dad had always said I was so much like Mom. I thought he was trying to make me feel better about being so weird-looking.

When I walked onto the stage, the audience gasped. It was really an incredible moment. I'd always thought I couldn't become a professional actress because I was ugly. Suddenly I heard my classmates whispering to one another, "She's beautiful." I never imagined people would use that word to describe me.

After the play, I started wearing makeup and styling my hair. Boys who had ignored me started paying attention. When I drove into the parking lot in my Volkswagen Thing—a car kids had laughed at—the football players would gather around to ask me about it while their cheerleader girlfriends would pull them away. I never became popular, but I started to be accepted for being different and interesting.

And one day as I was eating lunch, a modeling agent who had been visiting for career day approached me.

"Have you ever thought about modeling?"

"Me? NO!"

I was sixteen when I signed with her local Orange County agency. All at once, the things I had hated about myself—my skinniness, my flat chest, my pterodactyl-like arms and legs, and my height, worked for modeling. I might have been Q-Tip, but I learned that the modeling world was filled with an assortment of Q-Tips. I started booking local print ads. Then I booked my first commercial. I was cast as the quintessential California girl riding shotgun next to her surfer boyfriend as we drove along a Malibu beach in a Ford Ranger. Next, I booked a commercial for Coco's Restaurant. I pedaled around on a bike while juggling a pie in one hand. When I modeled for Newport Blue Sportswear, the ad wound up on the bus stop directly across the street from my high school. The irony wasn't lost on me—the girl who had been invisible in high school was the first thing some kids saw when they got off the bus.

Maybe I could become an actress after all.

Instead of heading to a traditional four-year college, I attended Golden West College, a two-year community college near my home. In my spare time, I drove to Los Angeles and auditioned for acting roles. I used the money I made from modeling to pay for acting classes. I was accepted into the prestigious Richard Brander Acting Studio. At sixteen, I was the youngest in his master class. It was an added bonus that during one scene, I got to kiss the cute, talented guy I had a crush on. Unfortunately, after our performance, Kevin Costner never returned. He had been cast in a movie.

My only activity in college was cheerleading. Since I loved being part of a team, I auditioned for the squad and made it. It was easy, fun, and a great way to meet some of my classmates.

A few years earlier, a Golden West cheerleader had made the Los Angeles Rams cheerleading squad. Because this girl had accomplished what seemed an impossible goal, the Golden West squad made a tradition of heading to Anaheim each year to audition for a spot on one of the most prestigious professional teams in the country.

When my teammates explained this to me, I silently balked. I couldn't even make my high school cheerleading team. I'd be laughed off the field. Besides, we were just a junior college squad—our choreography was pretty basic, nowhere near professional cheerleader caliber.

"We'll all go. It'll be fun," someone said.

"We'll make it a party."

"What should we wear?"

"Danskins, headbands, and leg warmers, of course!"

Being a girl who lived in Orange County and a huge football fan, I'd been watching the Rams Cheerleaders, the first professional cheerleading team in Los Angeles, for a long time. Dressed in shiny blue-and-gold Lycra minidresses and waving enormous blue-and-gold pom-poms, they were gorgeous and glamorous with big hair and perfect bodies. I'd stare in amazement as they'd perform intricate choreography, kicking their endless legs over their heads. To me, they were goddesses and movie stars and not quite all human.

The moment we arrived at Rams Park, an old elementary school building in Anaheim that had been converted into offices and included a football practice field, I decided I'd made a big mistake. It was crammed with more than thirteen hundred girls auditioning for only seven rookie spots. (The returning girls had to audition again to round out the thirty-six positions—but they went directly to finals, and it was almost a given that they'd make it.) I'd been on dozens of acting auditions, but this was a cattle call—something I'd vowed never to do. I looked around the field—there were so many gorgeous women, and so many of them looked like professional dancers. They were stretching, practicing pirouettes and high kicks. They had blown-out hair and wore character shoes and leg warmers. I had my hair in a ponytail and wore my leotard with tennis shoes. Even though a lot had changed since my early teenaged years, I still felt shy and awkward. I looked like I'd gotten lost on my way to somewhere else. I thought they might kick me out before I even auditioned.

As I scanned the field, I saw them: the Edison High School cheerleaders from my old school. They were auditioning too. They looked over at me and laughed. My heart raced. I knew exactly what they were thinking: *There's that weird, lame girl who couldn't make our squad. And she thinks she can make the Rams?*

"This is crazy," I told my Golden West teammates. "I'm gonna go."

Some girls nodded in agreement. Others seemed to be on the fence. A few vehemently shook their heads.

"No! We came as a team. Let's see what happens."

"At the very least, we'll learn some great choreography."

"It'll be fun."

"Remember, one of us made it before. We can do it again!"

I was fortunate to be surrounded by positive women who encouraged the rest of us to achieve something for which we felt unqualified. I'm sure I wasn't the only girl who was intimidated by the gorgeous professional dancers pirouetting on the field. I'm sure I wasn't the only one who was afraid of being ridiculed. But instead of packing it in, we stayed—all because a few teammates explained how despite the outcome, we would benefit from the experience.

Since this audition, I've learned that if you look at challenges in this light, you will take more chances. We are too quick to judge opportunities as pass-fail. It's ingrained in us from the moment we audition for a sport or take a test or try something new.

If it hadn't been for these encouraging women, I would have walked off the field and missed a life-changing opportunity. How incredibly blessed I was to be part of a group of women who inspired me to seize an opportunity. Those people who motivate you infuse you with bravery.

As we waited to begin auditions, a hush fell over the place. I surveyed the field as a group of women walked toward the stage. They had big hair and dark tans and wore satin Rams jackets with amazing calf-high white leather boots.

They were the twenty-nine returning Rams Cheerleaders.

When they performed a routine for us, I was blown away. I'd never seen anything like it before—and television didn't do it justice. Their moves were fluid and flawless. They kicked and twirled and spun and waved their enormous gold-and-royal-blue pom-poms in perfect synchronicity. What was happening on that stage transcended cheerleading. It was a deep camaraderie unlike anything I'd ever witnessed. These women were working together to create something beautiful that was much bigger than each of them.

A shiver raced through me. What had started out as somewhat of a lark had turned into something I desperately wanted. I didn't quite understand it that day as I stood with the more than thirteen hundred wannabes, but this wasn't just about making the cheerleading squad. Because I'd grown up without girls or women in my life, I longed for a connection, a sisterhood. That's what these women had. And this was my chance to have it too.

We were lined up, put in groups, and taught a routine. Afterward, we had about twenty minutes to practice before we had to perform the dance. It was grueling. I had a hard time keeping up. So many of the girls had professional dance experience. I'd taken ballet and jazz as a kid, but nothing had prepared me for this type of intense choreography. When we were done, the judges read off the numbers of the girls who had made it to the next round. I was so shocked to hear my number that I had to check the tag on my leotard to make sure it was actually me.

During the audition, we were asked to perform a talent— we could sing or do gymnastics. I panicked. I looked over at the football field and saw a lone football in the middle of it. I thought, *What if I grabbed it and lobbed it fifty yards? Now, that's a talent!* Unfortunately, I wasn't brave enough. Instead, I sang a lame version of "Happy Birthday"—and somehow made it to the next round.

Each round became more complicated. The choreographer incorporated higher kicks. She taught us double pirouettes, which were nearly impossible to master in such a short amount of time. I didn't think I could do it, especially because with each round, the groups became smaller, the routines became more complicated, and the time to practice became shorter. After each round, I expected to be eliminated. Instead, I kept progressing to the next round. The crowd shrank. Girls cried as they grabbed their duffel bags and ran off the field. I saw some of the Edison cheerleaders leave. I couldn't believe I was still on the field. Had someone made a mistake?

When my number was announced after the last round, I was in shock. I'd made it to next week's finals.

Part of the audition process included an interview. During the week before the finals, I headed back to Rams Park. Inside was a panel of interviewers, including Mardy Medders, the Rams entertainment director, as well as the choreographer, manager, and some of the cheerleading captains.

I was dressed professionally in a skirt and blazer. I handed them my headshot and résumé. They asked me a bunch of typical interview questions. My future goals. My strengths.

"Why are you trying out?"

Why was I trying out? I didn't look like a cheerleader. I couldn't dance as well as a cheerleader.

Being a professional cheerleader had never been something I had dreamed of doing. I was supposed to move from Orange County to Los Angeles in a few months and become an actor. Suddenly, I really wanted to be a Rams Cheerleader. I imagined what it would be like to be part of this squad, to be on the sidelines of a game I loved. I thought of the little girl who dreamed of one day being a professional football player.

"Ever since I was a little kid, I've loved football. Since I moved to Huntington Beach, I've become a Rams fan," I said. "My dad and I would watch football together every weekend. We loved the Fearsome Foursome, especially Deacon Jones. He's my favorite defensive player of all time."

I told the panel how my dad would have me name every starting quarterback in the NFL at parties. I told them of the arguments my dad and I would have over whether Vince Ferragamo should have replaced Pat Haden as starting quarterback. I was Team Ferragamo. My dad was Team Haden. I told them that when I was a little girl, I didn't dream of being a cheerleader. I dreamed of being a quarterback.

The panelists sat there with their jaws hanging open. I don't think they'd expected anyone to know so much about the Rams. I might have been the biggest NFL fan they had ever interviewed. I couldn't double pirouette as well as the other girls, but I could name every starting quarterback in Rams history.

The air was charged with electricity during the finals at Anaheim Stadium. My dad came to cheer me on. So did Kal, my boyfriend. (I'd met him when my car broke down on Pacific Coast Highway and he left a beach volleyball game to help me.) There was a panel of ten judges—choreographers, agents, and celebrities. Cameramen, photographers, and reporters were running around, snapping photos and interviewing some of the wannabes.

During the first round of finals, I did a high kick—something I had practiced and stretched for all week. As my leg shot up in the air, a searing pain ran through me. I'd strained a hamstring. I smiled as hard as I could as I finished the routine. When it was over, I limped off the stage and collapsed. This type of injury could take weeks to heal. I thought, *That's it. This is where the dream ends.*

As I was sitting there, feeling sorry for myself, a bunch of the girls ran up to me and asked what had happened. Instead of silently gloating that my injury meant one less girl to compete against, these women taught me stretches to alleviate some of the pain.

"You can do this," they said. "Don't give up. Walk it off."

For a girl desperate for female support and friendship, I had a group of women inspiring me to continue. I became so focused on the prize that I couldn't focus on the pain. Trust me, it hadn't subsided. It was a hot knife slicing through my hamstring. But I kicked and spun. I forced myself to smile as wide as I could.

I made it through each round. And then it was time for the final cut.

My heart pounded. My leg throbbed. All the wannabes sat in the stands with their families and friends as we waited to hear the final results. I sat next to Kal and my dad. We were too nervous to speak.

It was all very dramatic. Mardy, the cheerleading director, gave us one of those predictable speeches where she said she'd never seen so many talented people in her life.

"I know you're all going to go on to have amazing careers in show business or whatever business you choose," she said. "If you don't hear your name called this year, take some dance classes and come back again next year."

As Mardy announced the names of girls who'd made the cut, I did the math: *Seven rookie spots are available. Now six. Five.*

My dad, Kal, and I held our breath.

Four.

There was screaming, shrieking, cheers, and applause after each name. I looked around the bleachers. There were only four spots left and so many girls still waiting in the stands. One of the Edison High School girls was there. We locked eyes. Maybe I was imagining it, but she seemed to be saying, *What the heck are you still doing here! You sucked in high school!*

Only four spots left. It was impossible to imagine that I'd make it. There were so many talented girls. I told myself I should be proud for getting this far. I told myself that it was okay if this was the end of the line.

Then I told myself, *Who are you kidding? Girl, you want this!*

I took a deep breath.

Three.

And then . . .

They said my name.

I can't begin to describe that moment. It was an out-of-body experience. I couldn't breathe. I couldn't move. Time froze. And then my dad jumped up and screamed louder than I'd ever heard him scream, "That's my daughter! That's my daughter!"

I jumped up and hugged him and Kal. I ran onto the field and was mobbed by a gaggle of shrieking cheerleaders. They wrapped me in a big group hug. Through the din, I could still hear my dad: "That's my daughter! That's my daughter!"

I was in complete shock. Just a few days ago, I'd been about to walk off the field because I thought being a Rams Cheerleader was a ridiculous goal. But because my squad had encouraged me, I'd stayed. And when I'd thought I'd injured myself out of the running, another group of women had pushed me to continue. So often women are portrayed by the media as being mean and backstabbing to each other, especially during competitions. But I've always encountered the opposite. When women lift one another up, they can overcome fear and pain. They can be more courageous than they ever imagined.

"You're an official Los Angeles Rams Cheerleading Entertainer," Mardy said to us after the final name was announced.

"Congratulations! And welcome to the Ram-ily."

4

Squad Goals

"What celebrities were there?"
"Was Hef in his silk robe?"
"Did you go in the grotto?"

When friends heard I'd become a regular guest at the Playboy Mansion for movie night through my modeling agency, they'd bombard me with all types of questions. But the truth was, I didn't mingle with the crowd of actors, directors, and producers. I was twenty-one. The other guests seemed ancient, even though most were probably in their thirties or forties.

And the grotto? Gross! To me it sounded like a petri dish of communicable diseases.

I went to movie night for one thing and one thing only: the free food.

An enormous buffet would be spread out on a big dining table. There would be steak, lobster, roast beef, and fried chicken. Sometimes the dinners would have themes, like Italian or Mexican or Asian. There was also a table filled with pies, cakes, and cookies. I love to eat, and it was all delicious.

I had a system: I'd hide in the dimly lit hallway. When the guests retreated into Hugh Hefner's screening room, I'd sneak out and head to the buffet, armed with a big bag. Then I'd pull out my Tupperware and load up on all the delicious food.

And guess what? I never watched a movie.

Actually, I'd be home before the film ended to avoid the pervy producers and middle-aged Hollywood bad boys who would stream out of the screening room looking for a hottie to hook up with. I was not that girl. Instead, I would speed off in my shitty Toyota Celica to the safe confines of the Brentwood apartment I shared with Lynn, my Rams cheerleader roommate.

This was my routine for months—until one night as I was filling up the Tupperware, a woman came out of the kitchen.

"Miss!" she said, shaking her head.

I wasn't sure what would happen next. Would security kick me out? Would I be banned from the most famous home in Los Angeles?

She smiled and handed me a bag already filled with containers of food.

"Next time, you look for me and I'll just give you the food."

And that was my wild time at the Playboy Mansion.

Being a professional cheerleader sounds exciting and glamorous—and it sometimes was. Crowds screamed our names. We signed autographs. We were escorted through velvet ropes and into the hottest clubs on Sunset Boulevard. We performed on *The Tonight Show* with Johnny Carson and on Bob Hope specials. We were "celebrities"—that is, celebrities without the financial perks that usually accompany celebrity.

"This is not your profession. This is your part-time hobby," Mardy told us after we made the team. But I quickly learned that there was nothing part-time about it. The team had three-hour practices twice a week and before each game. Because I needed additional instruction, I rehearsed every night in smaller groups with various girls who were also struggling. Additionally, the cheerleaders were expected to represent the Rams at promotional and nonprofit events a couple of times a week. We were compensated $25 a game plus about $75 for corporate events. And we were expected to do dozens of team and charity events for free.

Even though most of us had side gigs, it was hard to devote much time to them. That first year, I turned down a lot of modeling jobs—and a lucrative contract to model in Japan—because I couldn't juggle my college courses along with rehearsals and events.

Being a cheerleader was financially draining. When we represented the team, we had to have perfect hair, nails, tans, makeup, uniforms, and, of course, bodies. But we had to pay for it—the hairstylists, manicurists, tanning-booth sessions, dry cleaning, and gym memberships (which meant plenty of step and aerobics classes—this was the '80s). We also had to drive all over Los Angeles and Orange Country for promos. Often the money I earned from the event would just about cover the gas to get there and back.

Those were lean years. Money was tight. I struggled to keep my expenses to a minimum. I continued to shop at thrift stores and flea markets. I went on a lot of bad dates for the free dinner. (Don't judge—I was young and poor.) When a guy would ask me where I wanted to eat, I'd automatically say, "Versailles." It was an inexpensive Cuban restaurant with enormous portions. I'd order the same thing every date—the garlic roasted half chicken with rice and beans and plantains. Since I could only eat about one-third of it, I'd ask for a doggie bag. It was a win-win situation. Guys were happy I was a cheap date. I was happy to have dinner for two more nights.

Despite the money woes, I loved being a cheerleader. From the moment the team pulled me into that group hug, I'd found my tribe. There was a sentiment that ran through the squad—if you had what it took to make the team, you were welcomed into its embrace (incidentally, one of our nicknames was the Embraceable Ewes). Ever since I was a kid, I'd loved being part of a team. And the Rams Cheerleaders took the word "team" to another level. We did kick lines, roll-offs, and field routines as one connected unit. If one of us failed, we all failed.

I'd watch the other girls perform intricate choreography, and I'd wonder, *How the heck did I make this squad?* These women were incredible dancers with extensive training in ballet, hip-hop, jazz, and tap. I quickly understood that being a cheerleader was tantamount to being an elite athlete. The difference is that pro players aren't required to smile while wearing three-inch heels on the field.

Those first few weeks of rehearsal were brutal. Mastering the choreography seemed impossible. I struggled and bungled through the routines. For a long time, I believed that a drastic mistake had been made during my audition. Maybe they'd confused me with someone else. During every rehearsal, I expected Mardy to kick me out.

"You're coltish," Nancy Gregory, our choreographer, told me during our weeklong training camp at a rustic cabin campground in Lake Arrowhead. "You need to learn to rein in your arms and legs. They're all akimbo. You're going to have to practice more than the other girls to be as good as them, but I know you can do it."

Nancy, who was in her mid-thirties, was a world-renowned choreographer as well as a really kind woman. She showed me an endless amount of patience. Instead of telling me I wasn't talented, she'd explain why I was having trouble: "Because you're so tall and long-legged, you have a higher center of gravity than the other girls. You have to learn to bend your knees when you spin. Your limbs are so long that you have to release faster on your kicks and turns."

During football games, cheerleaders were arranged in four lines of eight—with the tallest in the middle and the shortest on the ends. During each quarter, the lines would rotate to different corners of the field. Since I was one of the tallest, if I was picked to be in one of the lines, I'd be in the center of it. The girls in the center had to perform flawlessly since their mistakes could throw off the other dancers. If I wanted to be in a line instead of an alternate or, worse, cut from the squad, I needed to drastically improve. I had my doubts, but Nancy believed in me. She saw a spark of something I didn't yet see. She kept pushing me to be better. The other girls pitched in by holding smaller rehearsals for me. My new friends were rooting for me to succeed.

Still, it was a really stressful time. Exhausted, I'd collapse into tears after rehearsals. Most of the girls picked up the choreography quickly. As soon as I felt comfortable with a routine, we'd already be on to the next one. I didn't have upper-body strength. Those pom-poms may look like cotton candy, but they were enormous, metallic, and heavy. Halfway through a rehearsal, my biceps would burn. By the end of rehearsal, I couldn't lift my arms.

"You all need to make improvements," Mardy told us. Dressed in an endless parade of brightly colored muumuus, she reminded me of a bleached-blonde version of Mama Cass. She'd walk around the room and stop in front of one of us. She'd smile as if she were about to bestow a compliment. Even her tone was syrupy. And then she'd open her mouth:

"Oh, I wish you were a little bit thinner."

"I wish you had a bit of muscle on those arms."

"I wish you had a more outgoing personality."

When she'd stop at me, I'd hold my breath. "I wish you were a better dancer. Oh, well, hopefully you'll improve one of these days." Then her eyes would graze my head. "And I also wish you had lighter hair. Put in some gold highlights. We have too many brunettes."

"Okay," I'd squeak out. I loved being part of the squad so much that if Mardy had told me to shave my head into a mohawk, I would have asked her to hand me an electric razor!

But Mardy could really break some of the girls' spirits, especially those who struggled with weight. Every rehearsal concluded with some girls weeping in the bathroom.

"If you're going to cry, maybe you shouldn't be on the team," she'd say.

Fortunately, I wasn't really on her radar for long. She knew I was working hard to become a better dancer. But Mardy had her favorites. I discovered that it was important to be on Mardy's good side—not only did she decide who performed, she determined who was sent on promotional events, where you could earn some extra cash. If you questioned her decisions, she would accuse you of having a bad attitude. If you had a bad attitude, she wouldn't cast you in promos that week.

At training camp, I discovered that cheering was just one part of my job description. We were also brand ambassadors. We were tasked with mingling with the fans at promos to heighten the public image of the team.

"You are now representing this iconic brand. Everywhere you go, you have to sit up straighter, hold your head up higher, smile brighter," Mardy said.

She explained that as "Ram-bassadors," we would be attending events at trade shows, store openings, bars, and golf courses. Sometimes it would be a group of girls, other times just two. This was 1984, so we'd carry a boom box and a cassette with some of our music. Then, after we performed a routine, we had to introduce ourselves to as many people as possible. Since I was a girl who'd grown up reading instead of socializing, the thought of interacting with strangers terrified me.

Mardy eyed me as if she knew what I was thinking.

"We are going to scare the shyness out of you. If you are a *Los Angeles Rams Cheerleader Entertainer*, you cannot be bashful. You have to go up to every single person in the place, shake hands, and encourage them to become season ticket holders."

They gave us suggestions on how to interact with the fans:

- Never tell them where you live. If they ask something personal, steer the conversation back to the Rams. Ask them who their favorite player is.

- If you're talking to a couple, always look the woman in the eye. You have to make sure she likes you and doesn't think you're flirting with her guy.

- Stay with the other girls. Walk in together and leave together.

- Whenever you are wearing your uniform, no drinking, smoking, or chewing gum.

- If a fan asks you for a photo, put your arm behind him and around his waist. That way, he has to put his hand on your shoulder and can't grab your butt. (We were told that drunk fans were known to do this. In retrospect, they should have suggested we leave immediately if fans got drunk—and not allow them to get close enough to take photos with us.)

For me, training camp was about much more than rehearsals and classes. It was a crash course on being a woman. I didn't realize how much I didn't know until I was thrown into a room with dozens of ladies. The things these cheerleaders considered common knowledge were foreign to me. As I listened to discussions on health, beauty, and fitness, I felt like I'd been winging the whole womanhood thing. For instance, nutrition. I had never given my eating habits much thought. I'd grown up on junk food—McDonald's, Burger King, and pizza. When I modeled, no one cared about what I ate as long as I was thin. But these girls told me about the healthy diets that helped them stay fit and energetic. Until that moment, it had never crossed my mind that the junk food I consumed was why I felt tired during rehearsals.

All of a sudden, I had thirty-five female role models. At times it was overwhelming and confusing. Imagine, thirty-five women advising you on diet, beauty, and exercise? But I couldn't have been happier to have these new "sisters" in my life.

Even though the seasoned performers were just a few years older, I felt much younger. Some would gently tease me because I was so innocent—I was still a virgin, and I didn't drink (when we'd go out at night, I became a designated driver). I really was very naive. I actually gasped the first time I saw a girl in G-string underwear. "What the heck is that?" I asked. The girls laughed; they thought I had to be joking. "Really? Lisa? You haven't seen thong underwear before? Don't you hate when your panty lines show?" I nodded. I didn't tell them that having panty lines was something I'd never even thought about.

At the end of training camp, we were assigned to our lines. I prepared myself for the worst. Mardy had drilled into me that I needed to be a much stronger dancer. I thought I'd be cut. At the very least, I'd be an alternate. I was shocked when I made a line.

Still, most dancers on the team were better than I was. As the preseason inched closer, I was terrified I'd screw up. The week before, I stayed up all night practicing. The night before, I couldn't sleep. I imagined all the different ways I could ruin a routine. Would I trip in my three-inch-heeled boots? Would I drop my enormous pom-poms? Would I forget the intricate choreography?

I was exhausted on game day. I wasn't sure how I'd get through an intense rehearsal and four hours of dancing in the heat without collapsing. I wasn't a big coffee drinker, but I made myself a big pot of joe. After a few cups, I was wired, jittery, and more nervous than ever. Plus, I had a new concern: What if I had to pee during the game?

The first home preseason game was on a sweltering August day. The Rams were playing the Green Bay Packers at Anaheim

Stadium (NFL cheerleaders don't travel—unless it's for the Super Bowl).

My hands were shaking as I dressed for the game. I put on two padded bras to fill out my uniform. I pulled on my flesh-colored tights and my flesh-colored fishnets over them (before the days of Spanx, we wore these to hold in our butt, tummy, and thighs). My hair was blown out, teased, and sprayed. (We'd joke that Mardy wanted our hair so big that you could see it from the top level of the stadium.) No one tells you this, but being a cheerleader is incredibly uncomfortable. We were strapped up and sucked in. Not a thing was jiggling—except our cleavage. Even my face felt weighed down by pounds of heavy makeup.

"Lots of energy, girls," Mardy said in the locker room. "Don't forget, chin up and smile so the people all the way up in the stands can see you. And keep those lines straight."

We burst out of the tunnel and into the stadium. We raised our pom-poms over our heads in a V and raced to the middle of the field as Earth, Wind & Fire's "Rock That" blared.

"And now your Los Angeles Rams Cheerleading Entertainers!" the announcer said.

Despite all the practice and all the stories, nothing can prepare you for that moment. It's nearly impossible to describe the noise. You think you've heard what a crowd sounds like when you're in the stands, but when you're in the middle of it, it's completely different. The roar of the crowd envelops you. It's almost like it's inside you, running through your nervous system like electricity. It was overwhelming—tens of thousands of people screaming and stomping and applauding and chanting. For us! My adrenaline went into overdrive.

I can't remember much about the game. I don't even remember if the Rams won or lost (I looked it up—they won).

But I remember the exhilaration I felt after I nailed each routine. I remember being utterly drained by the end of the game. We'd spent four hours dancing in the brutal heat, the sun baking us. Even my fingers were sore from clawing the pompoms' plastic handles for hours.

I'll never forget the first time I walked into the cheerleader parking lot. Hundreds of fans were waiting for us. They cheered and yelled. They called for me. They knew my name! I couldn't believe it.

"Lisa, can I have your autograph?"

Wow! I felt like a star.

That night, all the cheerleaders headed to the Red Onion, a Mexican restaurant and bar. We gobbled down burritos and tacos while guzzling margaritas and piña coladas (mine was a virgin). We could hear neighboring tables whisper, "Those are the Rams Cheerleaders."

After we finished eating, guess what we did?

We got up on the dance floor and danced until closing!

And just like that, I had a huge social life. I went from having just a few acquaintances to having this enormous group of women to go out with on weekends. Everywhere we went, doors opened for us. We never waited in lines at the Palladium or any of the other clubs on Sunset. "They're the Rams Cheerleaders," someone would say. We'd walk right in. I hated the taste of alcohol, except for a few sips of Baileys (I had a sweet tooth). So I drove and watched everyone else get silly. I didn't mind. It was fun. I'd found my squad.

These women were so supportive of each other. If I booked a modeling job, there would be an enormous amount of truly genuine happiness for me. If someone got engaged, we'd throw a party. Every event was a cause for some kind of celebration. If someone broke up with a guy, she'd have twenty shoulders to cry on. And if someone got sick, there would be twenty girls bringing over chicken soup.

After a few games, I stopped having anxiety about tripping or falling behind. And then one day, it hit me: I wasn't thinking about trying to keep up—I just was. The routines had become muscle memory. When we learned new routines, I picked them up just as fast as the other girls.

Mardy stopped telling me that I better improve . . . or else. Although nearly every practice, she'd stare at my hair: "You need to go lighter."

One day about three years into my cheerleading career, my dad looked at me funny.

"You do realize you're a blonde?"

I laughed. Then I checked my reflection. He was right. I was a blonde. Actually, I wasn't just blonde, I was bleached blonde! It had happened so gradually that I hadn't noticed.

I suppose I had had an identity crisis when I hit my twenties. Ever since I was a teenager, someone else had controlled my appearance. When I modeled, my agent or the client told me how I was supposed to look. Then Mardy would tell me to change something, and I would. No questions asked. I felt like a character in Mardy's personal theater troupe.

I was a stranger with big, bleached-blonde hair, acrylic nails, and a deep tan. Nothing about me was real. Nothing about my appearance reminded me of my mother, of a Guerrero.

We all blindly followed Mardy. But why?

My cheerleading spell had been broken. During my third year, I started questioning everything. Why did we work so hard for a multimillion-dollar organization (now it's valued at $4.8 billion) while being paid next to nothing? As a matter of fact, cheerleading had put many of us in debt! Why did such draconian rules about appearance and behavior apply to us but not the football players? Why would it be grounds for dismissal if a cheerleader dated a player, but a player could date a cheerleader? How did this even make sense?

The promos began to wear on me. When I started out, the attention from men felt like harmless flirtation. The men didn't aggressively hit on me the way they did the more voluptuous cheerleaders. However, when I became a blonde and filled out, men's attitudes toward me changed.

"Come sit on my lap, honey," they'd say. Every guy thought he was being hilariously original when he'd ask me to sign the team poster "Thanks for last night" or "You're a tiger." I'd smile and sign it, "Cheers! Lisa." But I could feel the anger simmering. I started considering an event successful if I got out before someone pinched my ass. These men believed they had some claim on me. This was a myth that the NFL was all too ready to perpetuate. (Try not to let the drunk guy grab your ass, but don't push him away either, I was told during training camp.)

When I was a rookie, I was thrilled to be on the squad. I worked hard and cheered harder. I didn't ask questions. As for the constant makeovers and the body-shaming of those who gained weight? I believed the organization's beauty standards represented how women were supposed to look. I realize that because I didn't have a mother to emulate, my role models were the women I had watched on television in the 1970s. I thought these women—with their voluptuous bodies—were the feminine ideal. I didn't understand that characters such as Wonder Woman, the Bionic Woman, and Charlie's Angels were created by men to appeal to men. The shows' producers, directors, writers, and casting agents were almost always male.

And the first time I saw a naked woman was when I surreptitiously thumbed through a *Playboy* magazine while my dad was getting his hair cut at the barber shop. So whether it was in magazines or on television shows, I spent my formative years viewing women through a man's eyes. I didn't have a mom to tell me that these standards were not only ridiculous but impossible to achieve.

As I became a more seasoned cheerleader, I started to question everything—why did I have to look a certain way? Why did I have to follow certain rules? I saw myself—and my fellow performers—for what we really were: cheap labor with hot bodies designed to play into male fantasies.

Since the 1970s, dancers have played a crucial role in transforming the NFL into the world's most lucrative sports and entertainment franchise. (The NFL's thirty-two franchises are worth a combined $80 billion, according to Forbes.) Cheerleaders have boosted the brand, built television viewership, and courted sponsors. But cheerleaders have never been even remotely compensated for their contributions. We were conditioned to believe that being a cheerleader was a great honor. We didn't dare question the pay, the rules, or the endless makeovers. I'm proud of this new generation of professional cheerleaders who are bravely speaking out about the ridiculous wages along with the rampant sexism, racism, and misogyny that have been perpetuated in cheerleading culture for nearly as long as women have waved pom-poms on the football field. Recently, the Dallas Cowboys agreed to pay $2.4 million to four former cheerleaders who accused a high-level executive of voyeurism. According to an ESPN report, Rich Dalrymple, the senior vice president of public relations and communications, was accused of "standing behind a partial wall in their locker room with his iPhone extended" as the cheerleaders changed their clothes. After a successful thirty-two-year career with the team, Dalrymple retired in 2022.

Unfortunately, anecdotes like these are hardly the exception. In a recent *New York Times'* exposé, five former members of the Washington Redskins (now known as the Washington Commanders) cheerleading squad said that in 2013, they were flown to Costa Rica, stripped of their passports, and required to pose topless before wealthy fans. During this trip, the cheer squad's director allegedly told nine of the thirty-six cheerleaders to act as personal escorts at a nightclub. While their participation didn't involve sex, many cheerleaders felt like the team was "pimping [them] out," according to the *New York Times* report. In 2020, the Washington Commanders reached a settlement with former cheerleaders who had appeared in lewd videos made without their knowledge during swimsuit calendar photo shoots in 2008 and 2010. The videos, which exposed the cheerleaders' partially nude bodies, were compiled from outtakes during those shoots and allegedly given to the team's owner, Daniel Snyder.

In 2014, when Lacy Thibodeaux-Fields, a former Raiderette, filed a lawsuit against the then Oakland Raiders alleging wage theft (her story was highlighted in the PBS documentary *A Woman's Work*), a rash of lawsuits brought by cheerleaders from other NFL squads followed. They all say that they were paid far below minimum wage, not compensated for required activities like practices and public appearances, and forced to spend thousands of dollars on uniforms and beauty routines. (Some of these suits have been settled out of court; others are ongoing.)

In 2018, six former cheerleaders filed a federal sex-discrimination suit against the Houston Texans, saying they were paid less than the state's minimum wage and relentlessly body-shamed by the squad coach, who called them "crack whores" and "jelly bellies."

It's important that cheerleaders are coming forward with these stories. I was lucky—my experiences pale in comparison to these women's complaints. Yes, I should have been compensated for my hard work and better protected at these events, considering that I was an important cog in a multibillion-dollar wheel. However, I loved cheerleading. I don't regret the lessons I learned. Having the "shyness scared out of me" helped me practice bravery nearly daily and greatly prepared me for a career on camera. I was trained as a dancer, but I was also trained to be assertive. I had to walk into unknown situations, introduce myself to strangers, and help market an NFL team. I bet I'm the only investigative journalist who owes a debt of gratitude to her professional cheerleading days. Sometimes courage can be gleaned from the most unlikely situations.

One day during my third season, Mardy was fired. There were rumors, but we never knew for sure what led to her termination. We let out a collective sigh. She was then hired to start a cheerleading team for the Los Angeles Clippers, an NBA team. She called each of us, telling us to join her new, better squad.

She actually convinced several girls that the Rams Cheerleaders would fail without her leadership. As more dancers talked about abandoning the Rams for the Clippers, I wondered if she was right. Then I snapped out of it. Mardy had been so domineering for so long that she was still controlling us.

I leaped into action. I called each cheerleader. I told them that we were the team, not Mardy—and we didn't need her to succeed. By the end of the day, I had convinced most of the girls to stay.

This was the first time I'd ever stood up to Mardy, or really anyone, since that elementary school bully. Shortly afterward, I was named a line captain. The shy girl who couldn't keep up with the other girls had become a leader. If you'd told me that a few years earlier, I would never have believed it.

During my fourth year, I was ready to move on. At one of my final games, I watched a CBS sports reporter as he jotted down notes, interviewed players, and did live shots. Even though I'd seen reporters at the games hundreds of times, I was suddenly intrigued.

"I'm going to do that," I blurted out to the cheerleader next to me.

She laughed. "Girls aren't sports reporters."

"Not yet."

In all my years on the sideline, I'd never seen a female reporter covering our games.

Would it be possible for me to swap my pom-poms for a microphone?

I loved so much about cheerleading, but my favorite part about it was the strong friendships. I still feel a kinship to the hundreds of women who are now Rams Cheerleaders alumnae.

A lot of people assume that when you get a group of women together, they're going to be catty or jealous. This is a myth because some men are afraid of what really happens when women join forces. We wield tremendous power.

After women left the Rams, many became successful in other endeavors. We always support each other. One of the women sells insurance, so we buy from her. Another woman is a Realtor—and that's whom we rely on if we're in the market to sell or buy a house. It's been more than thirty years since we put down our pom-poms, but we meet for dinner or events several times a year. We take trips and have reunions. I recently traveled to Hawaii with a group of Rams Cheerleaders alumnae. (That's where I was on Wednesday, June 30, 2021, when I learned that I had sold my proposal for this book to a major publisher—Hachette. My girlfriends screamed with joy and embraced me just as they had on that day in 1984 when we made the squad.)

When we were younger, we cheered for football players. Now we cheer for each other. I like that much better. Female empowerment is important to me. When women build each other up, they become an indomitable force. I love cheering these women on through their challenges and successes. It's much more rewarding than cheering for a bunch of guys on a football field.

And on July 23, 2022, when I was inducted into the inaugural class of the Pro Football Cheerleader Hall of Fame, my cheerleader friends cheered for me.

5

Pom-Poms and Binders

I have a confession.

I broke the cardinal rule of professional cheerleading—I dated a player.

But at six foot five with blue eyes and black hair, Hugh Millen was hard to resist. And when I heard he was considered one of the smartest guys in the NFL, I was smitten. Tall, dark, handsome, and smart—that's how I like 'em.

One day before my fourth season as a cheerleader, I was autographing our squad's posters at Rams Park when Hugh approached my table and smiled.

"Would you sign one for me?"

As I scribbled my name, he whispered, "And can I have your phone number?"

I had a secret crush on the backup quarterback from University of Washington. I looked around to make sure no one was watching. Then I slipped him a piece of paper with my number on it.

Our first date was at a beachfront restaurant far from any Rams hangouts. As we ate prime rib and chatted, I started falling for him. He wasn't arrogant like so many of the other players. He was a bookish nerd who became animated when he talked about science, especially physics. I found it endearing that the guy was making lots of money, yet he had picked me up in his old Pontiac Bonneville, the car he'd had since college. So many players flaunt their paychecks, but not Hugh. Some teammates would tease him about being cheap. Hugh didn't care what people thought.

After a few dates, I was in love. I told a couple of close friends on the squad about Hugh, but it was a secret. When I was named captain, I felt like a hypocrite for ignoring one of the most important items in our contract—no dating players. (Management wanted to hire women who were passionate about cheerleading, not the players—many of whom were married.)

When the season ended, I quit the squad so I could date Hugh guilt-free. Hugh and I had it all planned out. It had been a rough two years for Hugh—he'd been on injured reserve with a fractured ankle during the 1986 season. The next year, he had missed fifteen games due to a back injury. He had recovered and was ready to compete for the next season's starting quarterback position. Meanwhile, I'd focus on my acting and modeling. Everything was moving along even better than I had planned. But, well, you know what they say about plans. One day, Hugh was cut by the Rams and placed on the "waiver wire," which meant another team could claim him. He was picked up by the Atlanta Falcons.

The Atlanta Falcons? Oh, boy. They'd just finished their 1987 season with the worst record in the league. Besides, Los Angeles was where I had to be if I wanted to seriously pursue my acting dreams. Hugh was incredibly disappointed. Then, after a few days of moping, he changed his outlook. He thought playing for the Falcons might be a good career move.

"I'll have a much better chance of being their starting quarterback," he said. "But I want you to come with me."

My career was heating up. I was meeting with casting directors. Pilot season was a few months away. I had visions of landing roles on TV shows. Could I really sacrifice my dreams so Hugh could pursue his?

Yup. I was in love. (Insert eye-roll emoji here.)

I got on my computer and researched the city and surrounding suburbs. I learned that a few TV shows and commercials were shot in Atlanta. I found names of local casting agents. This was all great, but I wanted to be more than a football player's girlfriend. I wanted a career. Freelance gigs modeling and acting in a smaller market such as Atlanta weren't going to satisfy my desire to throw myself full-time into something I loved. Could I possibly find work with the Falcons organization?

I discovered that they didn't have professional cheerleaders.

Well, they'd had a squad a few years earlier. But some of the women had had a reputation for hard partying and public drunkenness. The squad had disbanded, and no one wanted to bring it back. During the last few years, the local college cheerleaders had performed at the games. They were a co-ed squad that did collegiate-style routines and stunts to the nearly empty stadium. If you were a sports fan in Atlanta, you were most likely rooting for the Braves, the city's winning baseball team.

I started formulating a plan: What the Falcons desperately needed was a squad of professional-style dancers to reinvigorate the game-day experience. Besides boosting morale at Fulton

County Stadium, the cheerleaders would serve as brand ambassadors, very much in the same vein as my Rams squad.

I spent weeks developing an ironclad pitch designed to show the Falcons management how important a cheerleading squad could be for their brand—and how important it was that I be in charge of it. By the time I was finished, I had a thirty-page proposal. It covered every aspect necessary to create a professional squad—auditions, choreography, uniforms, community outreach, training camps, and sponsorships. The plan also addressed the fears management most likely had of history repeating itself—I'd hire a diverse group of women who would be smart, educated, and career-minded. These women would be more than hot girls who could dance. They'd be articulate spokespersons for the team. I'd secure paid promotions for them so they'd be able to make decent money. I didn't want the girls to struggle like I'd had to.

I called management and requested a meeting. They agreed.

As I walked through the hallway of the Falcons corporate office in Suwanee, Georgia, to my appointment with Tommy Nobis, the general manager, and Carol Breeding, the director of community relations, I knew this wouldn't be an easy sell. They'd had a bad experience with the last pro-style squad. Would they be able to take a cheerleader like me seriously?

I reminded myself that I was no longer a cheerleader—I was a businesswoman. I was carrying binders—not pom-poms. I was prepared to answer any questions that came my way. Actually, I may have been overprepared. I knew there was nothing they could ask that I couldn't answer.

When I look back at those seconds before my interview, I realize they were a pivotal moment in my career. Because I took myself seriously, I knew that management would. With each step, my confidence increased. When I walked into the meeting and handed out my binders, Carol's and Tommy's eyes widened. I don't think they had expected a former cheerleader—or anyone—to have done so much research for a position. I'd definitely caught them off guard. I felt emboldened.

"You need me," I said. "The Falcons aren't a good football team. They play in a lousy stadium. Attendance is terrible. There's a real lack of energy around the team. You have to create a reason for people to be enthusiastic about the Falcons. I can do this. I can fire up the crowd for you."

I outlined my plan. I told them about sponsorship deals and paid promotional appearances. I spoke about the importance of hiring accomplished women who'd double as community ambassadors to promote the team all around the city. Before the meeting ended, I'd won them over. I was thrilled to find out a few days later that I was hired.

I've used the lessons I gleaned that day for every job interview. Since my career has gone through several transformations, I often have little of the traditional experience the position calls for. However, I'm always overprepared. I'll know as much—maybe even more—about the company, network, or organization as my interviewers. I didn't realize it then, but I'd already done this years before. When I auditioned for the Rams, I wasn't nearly as good a dancer as my competition, but I knew more about football than the people who were interviewing me.

When I step into a meeting, I'm acutely aware of what skill set I'll bring to fill a void they might not realize existed. "You need to hire me," I'll say. Then I'll explain why. They'll be shocked by my boldness. By the end of the meeting, they'll agree: They do need me! Being overprepared for an interview, a meeting, or a conference is like possessing a superpower. When there's no question you can't answer, you don't have any reason to be afraid. You can have the audacity to be bold . . . to be brave.

I was ready for the move to Atlanta. I just had one more thing to handle.

"If I move, I want to be your fiancée, not your live-in girl-friend," I told Hugh.

A few days later, we were engaged. Hugh proposed with a two-carat diamond ring. So much for the rumors that the guy was cheap. I'd never seen a rock so big and sparkly. When we had it appraised for insurance purposes, I was agog. The ring was valued at $30,000. For a girl who shopped at thrift stores and drove crappy cars, I couldn't believe I was wearing something on my finger that cost more than anything I had ever owned.

In Atlanta, I threw myself into my work. I wanted to create a team that represented the diversity of the city. I hung up flyers in dance studios and colleges. I spoke about the squad on the radio and local television shows. Success! Hundreds of women turned out to audition for my new squad. When I finally assembled the team—some of whom had no cheerleading experience—I became consumed with turning them into professional-style dancers. I borrowed some elements from the Rams. But I wanted my squad to be different from them too. Instead of Rockettes-style kick lines, I fused hip-hop, funk, and street dance. Instead of high heels, the squad wore tennis shoes. Some of the women were gymnasts, so those dancers would perform roundoff back handsprings—moves that were impossible in high-heeled boots. Between the terrible conditions on the field and this new style of dance, I believed tennis shoes were the way to go. I also retained some of the male cheerleaders from the former college squad so we could incorporate stunts into my choreography.

MC Hammer, a huge Falcons fan, would watch the girls from the sideline. "They're amazing. I love them," he yelled over to me after a game. The girls were thrilled when he included them in his video *Too Legit to Quit*.

I incorporated the best parts about being a Rams cheerleader—the camaraderie, the intensive training, the innovative choreography. I was a tough and demanding director, but I wouldn't insult or demean anyone to get results. I was sensitive to the girls who fell behind because I had been that girl. It blew my mind that the dancer who had struggled through choreography was now in charge of choreography.

"You work too hard," Hugh would say. "You're hardly ever home."

By the second year, I was promoted to entertainment director. At twenty-six, I was the youngest entertainment director in the NFL. I was also the first female entertainment director the Falcons had ever had. I was in charge of all entertainment during the game—the pregame, halftime, and postgame shows, The national anthem and all of the music clips heard throughout the game. Jerry Glanville, the new Falcons head coach, presented me with a game ball after the first preseason game. Game balls are traditionally given to the game's MVPs. "Your squad is fantastic," he said. I may be the only entertainment director ever to receive one.

Being an entertainment director had never been my calling, but I loved my job. It filled that part of me that yearned for a sisterhood. This time, instead of being mentored, I was the mentor. "I'm always here for you," I'd tell my squad. They'd often take me up on this. The girls would call me up at all hours of the day or night to ask for advice on jobs, friends, boys, breakups. If a cheerleader was struggling through choreography, I'd hold extra practices for her. I'd drop everything to be there for whoever needed me.

Hugh would roll his eyes and sigh whenever the phone rang.

"Where are you going this time?" he'd ask as I'd grab my purse and head to the door after a phone call.

"Waffle House to cry it out. One of the girls broke up with her boyfriend."

"Why? This isn't your job."

How could I explain to him what an amazing honor it was for me to be in this position? I felt like a mother to these young ladies who were only a few years younger than I. They needed me, but I needed them too. However, being so available to these thirty-six women definitely took a toll on my relationship with Hugh. He felt that I put the squad before him—and, well, I guess I did. I was also starting to feel frustrated with our relationship. We'd been in Atlanta for two years and had yet to set a wedding date.

"Do you still want to get married?" I asked him.

"Let's plan it once the season ends."

After the season ended, I set a date for us to meet with a wedding planner in Newport Beach, near my hometown. My dad came with me, along with my new stepmom, Pam. Two decades after my mom died, my dad had finally found a second love. The three of us waited . . . and waited . . . and waited. Hugh never showed up.

He'd gotten cold feet.

"I'm done," I told him.

He pleaded with me to reconsider. "I want to marry you. I just want to be a starting quarterback before I do. Once I'm the starter, I'll have some security. Then we'll get married. I promise. Just wait a little longer."

I was thriving in my career, plus I'd scored some commercial and acting gigs (I had a guest-starring role in an episode of the TV show *In the Heat of the Night*, which was filmed in Atlanta), but Hugh was extremely disappointed with his. Since he'd arrived in Atlanta, the team had been plagued by devastating losses, including the tragic deaths of three teammates in the span of a year. During his second year, the Falcons closed the season with a seven-game losing streak. Morale on the field—and in the stadium—was so horrible that the last game drew only 7,792 fans—a franchise record low.

When Hugh asked me to wait, I understood. He needed a few breaks.

And then he got one. After his third season, he was traded as a free agent to the New England Patriots in a one-year deal worth over half a million dollars. He was thrilled. It seemed like a great opportunity.

"Come to Boston with me," he said.

Did I really want to move? I loved everything about Atlanta—the city, the people, the diversity. Most of all, I loved my job, the girls, my bosses.

Did I want to follow this guy around—again?

He looked at me with those big blue eyes.

"Let's plan our wedding," he said. "This is going to be a great new adventure."

He seemed sincere. I loved my job, but I loved Hugh more. We found a beautiful condo in Quincy's Marina Bay overlooking Boston Harbor. I was ready for this next exciting chapter.

And guess what? The Patriots didn't have a cheerleading squad. Actually, their story was nearly identical to the Falcons'. The team was horrible—it had finished the 1990 season with a record of 1–15, the worst in franchise history. Their field was considered one of the worst to play on. Morale was at an all-time low. Boston sports fans preferred to root for the Red Sox or the Celtics. And the fans who did show up at Foxboro Stadium were legendary for being drunk and unruly. The highlight of game day wasn't in the stands but in the parking lot, where fans would tailgate for hours, sometimes missing the game entirely. Many would be drunk before kickoff. Fights would often break out in the stands, in the parking lots afterward, and even on the nearby roads. There were stories of fans peeing off the upper terrace of the dilapidated stadium. This was not a place for family-friendly entertainment. It was so bad that in 1981, the Foxboro selectmen forbade night games. Because of this, the team was banned from hosting *Monday Night Football* from 1981 to 1995.

Armed with my binders, I met with Victor Kiam, the team owner, and explained how I could solve some of their problems. I was hired on the spot. It was probably the quickest interview I've ever had.

During the first two years, I worked for two different owners and was given complete autonomy. I created a great squad, but the conditions for the women were pretty horrendous. The sound system was abysmal—sometimes it was hard to hear the music, especially over the loud, drunk fans who'd scream at the team, the cheerleaders, the referees, and each other. Sometimes the girls would cheer to empty stands. They danced on what was considered the worst field in the league. Nevertheless, they cheered—in rain, ice, slush, mud, and snow—even if no one was watching them.

I was having big doubts about my relationship with Hugh. During his fourth game of his first season with the Patriots, he was named starting quarterback. When the season ended, he signed a $1 million contract for the next year—becoming the first million-dollar quarterback the franchise had ever had (this was a few years before Tom Brady and Drew Bledsoe). But even though his reality exceeded his dreams, we hadn't set a wedding date.

"Just a little longer," he'd say. "My career's finally starting to take off."

Despite his unprecedented salary, Hugh's second season didn't go as he had hoped. The Patriots' offensive line proved to be weak, which resulted in Hugh getting sacked multiple times per game. His shoulders took the brunt of these beatings and were constantly separating. During halftime, doctors would shoot him with cortisone, pop his shoulder back into place, and bandage him up. Then, during the second half, he'd be crushed again. It was a vicious cycle. This was not at all how he had envisioned his professional football career. He was in peril of losing his starting position, something he'd fought so hard for. He was depressed and in constant pain. The team sucked.

And then a rumor started swirling through the clubhouse. I heard Hugh was hooking up with one of my cheerleaders.

It seemed like everyone in the organization was gossiping about us. I had to remain professional and pretend it didn't bother me. There were days when I struggled not to cry at work. I'd hold it in until I was in my car. At home, I'd get into it with Hugh.

"I can't believe you'd cheat on me with one of my girls!"

"It's not true," he said.

"How could you?"

"Trust me, I didn't. I wouldn't. I love you. Let's stop fighting over stupid rumors."

I took off my engagement ring. "How can I believe anything you say? I'm done."

He thought about this for a few minutes.

"How about we go out to dinner and set a wedding date? We'll start over. I'll even propose to you again with a new ring."

I wanted to believe him so badly. I really loved the guy. I agreed. A few days later, during a romantic dinner, he slipped a bigger, shinier ring onto my finger. He said he wanted to spend the rest of his life with me. He told me he loved me.

"Will you marry me?"

I said yes—again. A few days later, I heard the rumors— again. We fought—again. Then we broke up—again.

This time I was done—for good.

I was heartbroken and angry. I'd spent seven years with Hugh. I'd followed him around for the last five. For what? And now what? Should I stay with the Patriots? I loved my job, but was it really my calling? Maybe not, but I was kicking ass. In a few years, I could work toward an executive position at the NFL's corporate headquarters in New York City. Was that what I really wanted? Although I managed to do some acting and modeling on the side, I'd really put those aspirations on the back burner. Was this breakup a sign that I should head back to Los Angeles and give it a real shot? After all, I was still in my twenties!

I moved into a small one-bedroom apartment in Boston's historic Charlestown Navy Yard district. I decided to regroup there while I searched for a house or condo to buy. Hugh had told me to keep the engagement ring, and so I figured I would sell it and use the $30,000 for a down payment. I asked a jeweler I knew if he'd be interested in buying the ring.

He called me a few hours later.

"Lisa," he sighed, "I really hate to tell you this, but that ring . . ."

"Yes?"

" . . . It's cubic zirconium."

"No, it can't be. We had it . . ."

It was a punch in the gut as it dawned on me what he'd done. Talk about duplicitous! He'd switched my diamond with cubic zirconium when he'd asked for the ring back and proposed to me for the second time. I was sick and disgusted. I'd wasted so many years with this guy. (When I decided to write this book, I reached out to Hugh for his side of this story. He said that before we got back together, I had asked for a new ring because the two-carat ring represented a broken relationship. He said he decided to secretly buy me a two-and-a-half-carat cubic zirconium ring because he wasn't sure we'd make it to the altar. He said if we went through with the wedding, he planned to replace the cubic zirconium with a real diamond. In retrospect, Hugh did me a huge favor. We were young and immature. He eventually went on to marry the right woman for him and moved back to his home state of Washington to start a family. And his wife received an actual diamond.)

* * *

No one was certain what the future held for the Patriots. Rumors had been circulating for the past year that the team might even move out of Boston to the latest owner's hometown of St. Louis. Some had heard that this owner even had a new name picked out: the St. Louis Stallions.

Then, surprisingly, the team was sold.

And once again, I had to interview for my job.

Robert Kraft, the new owner, seemed like a nice old guy. He'd been a loyal Patriots fan and a season ticket holder since the 1970s. He met with me for a few minutes in what seemed like just a formality.

"Glad to have you back onboard," he said, smiling and shaking my hand. It appeared that nothing would change. Since the team had undergone a quick succession of owners—he was the third in three years—I secretly wondered how long this new guy would last.

A few days later, Robert Kraft's assistant called me.

"Mr. Kraft is going to have his son oversee the entertainment of the team. His name is Jonathan Kraft."

I'd always reported directly to the owner. This time, I'd report to the owner's son, who was about my age and had never worked for an NFL team. I wasn't too concerned. I figured it was just a title to give him something to do. Since I'd arrived two years earlier, no one had questioned my decisions on uniforms, choreography, or music. I assumed things would remain the same.

I was wrong.

Jonathan wanted to judge the cheerleader auditions. He wanted to invite his friends to watch rehearsals with him. He wanted to change the uniforms so they looked more like what the Dallas Cowboys Cheerleaders wore. He wanted the cheerleaders to pose in bikinis instead of in their official uniforms for the calendar. I was adamantly opposed to doing a bikini calendar. I had a gut instinct that this could lead to trouble. I must have been prescient because since then, several cheerleading squads have said that bikini calendar shoots led to instances of being spied on and preyed upon by owners or sponsors.

No. No. No. No.

I chalked Jonathan's requests up to the fact that he was young, inexperienced, and extremely privileged. He had been placed in a position of power, and he seemed like a kid in a candy store. I felt that these women needed me as their advocate to shield them from his seeming misogyny. After all, I understood what it was like to be a cheerleader who had to perform in uncomfortable clothes and high-heeled boots. I wanted something better for my squad.

I calmly explained that our cheerleaders played in freezing weather and couldn't wear skimpier uniforms. I said that high heels wouldn't be practical while dancing in snow, ice, and mud. I told him the girls would feel uncomfortable having an audience of dudebro friends of the owner's son at the rehearsals. And auditions were judged by people with some kind of credentials in the entertainment world.

Jonathan and I butted heads on everything—and the season hadn't even started. This was the first time in my life that I was living by myself. My problems at work felt magnified since I was alone. I'd call my dad to complain.

"Maybe it's time to come home," he'd say.

Maybe I'd eventually come home, but not until the season ended. I had a signed contract to fulfill. Even though I was only a few years older than the women, I felt like I had thirty-six daughters. If I left the organization, my replacement might consent to Jonathan's demands.

I want to see the playlist.

Jonathan left me this message a few days before the first home preseason game. In my years as entertainment director, I'd never had to turn in a music list for approval. I loved my playlists. I'd always feature a crowd-pleasing blend of music— rock, Motown, country, and pop. I couldn't imagine he'd find any reason to complain about my music selection. Maybe he'd want to add a favorite song or two. Fine.

But I was worried. Each interaction with Jonathan seemed more hostile than the last.

So when I handed Jonathan the list, I braced myself. He studied it for a few minutes. He looked up at me.

Then he asked me to remove all the Black music.

I thought I'd heard him wrong.

"What?" It took a few seconds for the words to sink in. If he had slapped me across the face, I would have been less shocked.

"No Black music?" I asked as if I somehow still hadn't heard him correctly. "That's racist," I blurted out.

He explained to me that in New England, fans preferred classic rock. But I wasn't buying it. To me, his request smacked of racism. Besides, there was classic rock on my playlist.

I shook my head in confusion. "But most of the players are Black. And everyone in the stands dances to Michael Jackson and Prince."

He dismissed me, telling me to come back the next day with a new list of songs.

That night, I sat on my couch, staring at the list. Michael Jackson. MC Hammer. Aretha Franklin. Prince. Take them off? Because they were Black? I was sick about it. This was a clearly racist demand and made no sense to me. I knew if I didn't go along with his request, I'd be fired. But if I did go along with it, could I live with myself?

I called my most trusted adviser—my dad.

"I guess you have a lot of thinking to do," he said. "You have to decide if these are the type of people you want to work with. Is this what you really want to do with your life?"

I hung up the phone. Then I looked around my apartment. It was sparsely furnished with a couch, a coffee table, and not much else. I hadn't had the time or energy to decorate the place. It was a reminder that since Hugh and I had broken up, I hadn't completely committed to being in Boston.

I walked toward my window, looked out at the harbor, and cried. If I fought Jonathan on his request, my career with the NFL would be done. For the past decade, cheerleading had been my life. It was what I knew. Could I throw it all away? I'd invested so much in this career. Would it end so terribly?

That night, I really missed my mother. I flashed on that day with her at Pier 1. I'd been proud of Mom because she wouldn't allow that horrible woman to silence her. Wasn't that exactly what Jonathan was doing by editing my list? Silencing the Black artists? I imagined that Mom would have been outraged by this request. As I thought about Mom, I realized that I was the same age she had been that day in Pier 1. I heard her voice reminding me that I was a Guerrero, a warrior.

I woke up after barely sleeping. But I wasn't upset anymore. I felt oddly calm as I prepared to head to the office. When I got there, I walked right into Jonathan's office and put my playlist on his desk. The same playlist as the day before.

He studied it for a few minutes. Then he looked at me. I stared right back. We locked eyes for a few seconds. Neither of us spoke.

As I turned on my heel, I knew this would be the last time I'd be in this office or this building. My NFL career was over.

Days later, the phone rang. It was the general manager.

"You're fired."

I took a deep breath. "Okay. But you owe me my salary. We have a contract."

It turned out they didn't agree.

Part of me wanted to get out of Boston and put this horrible experience in the rearview mirror. But I couldn't let them get away with this. I'd completed all my obligations—running auditions; selecting and training the cheerleaders; choreographing the routines; designing the uniforms; shooting, marketing and distributing the posters and calendars; and securing sponsorships for the rest of the season. I was owed my final payment of $25,000. (I was twenty-nine. This was a lot of money three decades ago—at least to me.) I picked up the Yellow Pages and began cold calling lawyers.

Each call was a version of this:

"You want to sue Robert Kraft?"

"Yes."

"*The* Robert Kraft of the Patriots?"

"That's him."

Click!

The consensus was that I had to be crazy to even think about going up against Boston royalty. This was Robert Kraft, who'd kept the beloved Patriots in Boston. Maybe I *was* crazy.

The odds seemed greatly stacked against me. But I kept calling. Hours later, I finally found an attorney way out in the suburbs. As an added bonus, Fred Golder specialized in employment law.

"You definitely have a case," he said. "You can sue the Krafts for wrongful termination. They're in breach of contract. But just know that they're a powerful family, and they're going to try to humiliate you. Are you sure you want to do this?"

"Yes."

Fred was right. When we filed the lawsuit, the press labeled me a disgruntled employee who'd been fired for incompetence. They said I was filing the lawsuit for publicity because I was a struggling actress. Funny thing was, I turned down every interview request, including one from Larry King on CNN. I didn't want publicity. I just wanted the money they owed me.

It was a difficult and humiliating time. There were moments when I thought it would be easier to quietly head back to Los Angeles and start over. No one would have to know I'd been fired.

But could I live with that decision? I'd been asked by my boss to do something that I felt was wrong. If I allowed the Krafts to get away with their behavior, they'd keep doing it, knowing that there would never be any consequences for their actions.

I wasn't going to roll over for them. They owed me the balance of what I should be paid. I'd stood up for my cheerleaders when Jonathan had wanted to oversexualize them. This time, I had to stand up for myself.

My body was shaking when I entered Norfolk County Superior Courthouse for the civil arbitration hearing (which is like a trial but without a jury or spectators). When I glanced around the courtroom, I saw that Robert Kraft and his son had assembled a group of high-powered attorneys. And me? I had Fred—and my rolling cart.

But that cart was pretty impressive. It was filled with everything I'd ever done as an entertainment director. I even had cassettes with irate voice messages that Jonathan Kraft had left on my answering machine.

Robert Kraft may have had a bunch of lawyers, but I had my notebooks, folders, cassettes, and binders.

As I spoke to the judge, I referred to my documents. Since the Krafts were claiming that I'd been terminated because I wasn't good at my job, I had my ammunition ready, including a handwritten and signed card that Robert Kraft had given me just weeks before I'd been fired, saying I was doing a great job and that he was proud to have me as his cheerleader director.

When it was Robert Kraft's turn to speak, he blurted out, "She's nothing but a terrorist."

Me, a terrorist? Even the judge's eyes widened.

I had rattled Robert Kraft.

Fred and I looked at each other in shock as the judge retreated to his chambers. He took some of my files with him, including that card from Robert Kraft. Later, my lawyer would tell me this was the most damning piece of evidence.

The judge ruled in my favor. Robert Kraft owed me the rest of the money from my contract. I had won. The Patriots had to cut me a check!

This experience taught me a lesson: You can be great at your job, but if your bosses don't have the same values and beliefs as you do, the job isn't worth it. Our society has created this myth that if you work hard and are good at what you do, you will be rewarded. But I worked my ass off for years, sacrificing nights and weekends. And guess what? It didn't matter.

Women put up with so much garbage in their careers. We're told to work hard, be enthusiastic, and smile; don't be confrontational; don't be demanding. But when you see red flags at work, it's important to speak up. Don't be afraid of being "that bitch" who makes waves. Even if you have a "dream job," if you're putting up with bad behavior, the job will become a nightmare. Voice your objections as soon as possible. Don't let them pile up. Once you become too invested, it will be harder to leave. If you speak up at the first hint of trouble, you'll know where you stand before you waste too much time with a company. Maybe the boss will change. Or maybe you'll realize it's time to find another job.

It has been ingrained in us that we should never burn bridges. But if you've been mistreated, sometimes you have to burn that bridge. Head to human resources. Submit a complaint. File a lawsuit if it comes to that. Don't stay in a bad situation. There will be other bridges. I've burned a lot of them during my career, but I've always found a better path.

A few years after my court date, I returned to Boston and attended a Patriots game. As I suspected, the women were in skimpier uniforms and high-heeled white boots. I noticed some fans holding the cheerleader calendar. As I looked closer, I saw that the women were clad in bikinis. And the music?

Every single Black artist that had been part of my playlist was gone.

When I won the suit, I didn't know how big this victory was. I had no idea, and still don't, whether anyone had ever successfully sued Robert Kraft. I had no idea that within the next few years, Robert Kraft would become famous for creating one of the NFL's greatest franchises. I had no idea that under Robert Kraft's ownership, the Patriots would wind up qualifying for ten Super Bowls and winning six of them. I also had no idea that years later, Robert Kraft would be humiliated in two major incidents: Spygate (the team was disciplined by the league for cheating by videotaping the New York Jets' defensive coaches' signals) and a massage-parlor scandal (he was accused of soliciting sex, which he later denied).

All I knew was that I had enough money to put a down payment on a little Spanish-style house in the Hollywood Hills.

And I was ready to go home.

6

Becoming Lisa Guerrero

"**Y**ou should come back home to Los Angeles and sign with me. You'll be a star in sportscasting." Was this a prank call?

The more Ken Lindner spoke, the more I realized he was the real deal. Ken—or Kenny, as he came to be known—was a big-time broadcasting agent who represented hundreds of news anchors, sportscasters, and reporters around the country as well as some of America's most successful hosts and broadcasters.

"There's no one like you on TV. I saw your work on *Sports Gals*. You could have a huge career."

Sports Gals? Years later, I still have no idea how a Los Angeles–based agent had seen this weekly New England cable show. *Sports Gals* had been the brainchild of Eddie Andelman, a Boston radio legend. One day, I heard Eddie trashing Hugh on his radio show. Being the dutiful girlfriend, I called the station to defend him. What should have been a few-minutes call-in segment morphed into a two-hour conversation about the Celtics, Bruins, and Patriots. Eddie was floored by my sports knowledge. On a whim, he invited me to WEEI to cohost an episode of his radio show. We were inundated with callers trying to challenge me. No one believed a woman could know so much about sports. They thought I was being coached by someone.

After the show ended, Eddie shook his head and smiled. "I've never seen someone who looks like you who know sports like you do." He told me that he had a production deal at Sports Channel New England, a local cable station. Soon *Sports Gals* was born, the first sports talk show hosted solely by women. Two other female sports journalists—Barbara Borin-Franzosa, a TV sports anchor, and Janet Prensky, a radio sports show host—and I shot eight episodes. We talked about the latest news and controversies in football, basketball, and baseball. We interviewed players, coaches, and managers live in the studio. I loved every minute of it. But I didn't think anyone outside New England had watched it. And I definitely didn't think it would change my life.

When I returned to Los Angeles to begin this new phase of my life, I reflected on the last decade. It had been a sometimes fulfilling, sometimes exasperating ride. But throughout the journey, I'd given someone else the wheel. I'd moved for Hugh and chosen a career because it was in proximity to him. I was good at it, I enjoyed it, but it wasn't my dream job. I'd spent the last six years trying to force my career into a calling. But the things I truly liked about my job—the sisterhood and the camaraderie—had nothing to do with the career and everything to do with my need for strong female relationships. I'd always known that being an entertainment director wasn't my destiny.

I decided to pick up where I'd left off before I'd moved all those years ago. I'd figure out exactly who I was and what I should be doing.

The first order of business? The salon.

"I want all the blonde out. I want it dark—my natural color."

The stylist's eyes popped. This was definitely an unusual request. When she was finished, I looked into the mirror. It was as if my mother had returned to me. I was twenty-nine—the same age she was when she died. We looked so much alike.

More than two decades had passed since Dad had woken me up that awful Valentine's Day morning. "Your mother's in heaven with God." Despite all those years, I felt her absence through so many big and small moments. Would she have picked out a prom dress with me? Styled my hair for *Rebel Without a Cause*? Screamed "That's my daughter" alongside Dad when I made the cheerleading squad? Cried with me when Hugh and I broke up? Begged me to come back home?

I wanted to pay tribute to her. Over the years, I had considered taking her last name. I believed changing my name to Guerrero would connect me to my mother and the heritage she'd proudly reminded me we shared: *Lisa, remember you're Latina too.*

I'd stop myself from taking it beyond a thought. I didn't want to hurt my dad—the best father a girl could ever have.

But one day when I was at my dad's house, I blurted it out.

"I've been thinking of taking Mom's last name to honor her."

My dad looked at me, his eyes filling with tears. He didn't speak for a few moments. I was afraid he was upset.

"I think it's a great idea. Your mom would be so proud of you. I'm so proud of you. You have my blessing."

Kenny said I could have a career as a sportscaster. But I wasn't sure if I wanted to completely abandon my acting goals. Both sounded like dream jobs—so why limit myself? I decided to pursue each with equal gusto and see what happened. I'd be a "sportscactress." If I was more successful with one endeavor, then that was what I was meant to do. I shot two different headshots and wrote two different résumés. I signed with a theatrical agent and didn't tell her I was pursuing broadcasting. And I didn't mention to Kenny that I was also auditioning for acting roles. To keep this double life a secret, I used the name Lisa Guerrero for sports gigs. Since I was already registered as Lisa Coles with the Screen Actors Guild, I'd keep that name for acting auditions.

This double life was confusing but exhilarating. And it was certainly unconventional. Whenever I mentioned what I was doing, I was told I couldn't possibly juggle acting and broadcasting. No one could point to any specific reason why not, just that it had never been done before. But why did I have to fit into some box? I liked blazing my own trail.

* * *

"This job sucks!" I yelled to Kenny as I stood in the middle of a fake Wild West town somewhere outside Los Angeles. It was a blisteringly hot day, and I was covered in dust and dripping with sweat. Clad in a ridiculous twenty-pound dress with a hoop skirt and corset, I had called Kenny on one of those mid-1990s oversized portable phones just as I'd stepped in a mound of steaming horse shit. It felt like a sign—this job was crap. When Kenny said he'd make me a broadcasting sensation, I had visions of reporting on professional sports. Instead, I was K. C. Clark, a "journalist" for the *Broken Neck Gazette*, reporting on cattle roping, barroom brawls, and gunfights.

Wild West Showdown was a Western-themed game show produced by the American Gladiators team. It pitted cowboys against outlaws for cash prizes. Dressed like a character from *Little House on the Prairie*, I'd interview the contestants after the various competitions as the show's cohost, described as a "plucky but pretty newspaper reporter."

"What went wrong?" I'd ask a soaking-wet cowboy who'd attempted to cross a stream on a bunch of logs. Then I'd pull a twig pencil from behind my ear and pretend to jot down answers in my notepad.

I don't know what I had expected from my first foray into sports reporting. I didn't have any credentials—except for one line on my résumé, *Sports Gals*. I didn't have a degree in journalism. I didn't even have a college degree (I'd taken some classes at the local community college but not enough for an associate's degree). But I had visions of something a little more twentieth century than chasing after cowboys shooting paintball guns and "robbing" stagecoaches.

"You told me I'd be a sports reporter," I said to Kenny, hitching up my prairie skirt as I paced back and forth along a dusty desert road.

"Lisa, think of this as experience. You need more stuff on your résumé. Besides, no one's ever going to see this show. So don't worry about it. Besides, it's good money."

Kenny was good at calming me down. I wiped the poop off my boots and went back to interviewing cowboys and outlaws. When the show aired, thankfully, no one did watch. It's almost as if it never happened. You can barely find anything about it on the Internet. Although I've been told it was big in Japan.

"Give it some time, Lisa. You have to have patience," Kenny said.

Little did I know that this was just the beginning of the call and response I'd have with Kenny throughout my broadcasting career. I'd beg him to get me out of a job, and he'd tell me to stick it out, that it would be a good button on my résumé.

"Have patience," he'd say over and over. "Better things will come."

* * *

Building a résumé was not as easy as I'd thought it would be. As an actor, I had small parts in big productions that taught me valuable lessons along the way. The following were some of my favorite gigs.

Because *Batman Returns* was one of the most expensive features ever made, auditions were grueling. I auditioned about ten times for a very small role called "Blonde Volunteer." There was callback after callback. Finally, I met with Tim Burton, the director, who cast me. I was ecstatic. *Batman Returns* was part of one of the most successful movie franchises of all time—and I'd have a cameo in it.

When I arrived at the Warner Studios lot, I was shown to my trailer. I couldn't believe how big it was. There were floral arrangements and a big fruit basket waiting for me. If this was what I got for my small role, I couldn't imagine what was in the trailers for the stars—Michael Keaton, Michelle Pfeiffer, and Danny DeVito.

Tim Burton is a perfectionist; he's known for shooting many takes before being satisfied. So my scene kept getting bumped as the scenes before mine took longer and longer to film. Every day,

I would get a new, enormous fruit basket in my trailer. Then I'd head into the makeup trailer to get made up in case they got to my scene. Danny DeVito was always there, chatting it up. He'd spend hours getting into his silicone prosthesis to become the Penguin. When I first walked in, he asked who I was and what role I was playing. He couldn't have been nicer. When it was finally my day to shoot, Danny called me over to his makeup chair.

"Lisa, this is your day," he said excitedly. "Savor the moment. Make sure you order something special for lunch. You should ask for the prime rib."

He really pumped me up for the scene. Then he said, "I hope you're okay with this, but I'm going to be spitting black stuff out of my mouth. It probably will get on you."

Of course I was okay, I told him. I was up for anything— I was in *Batman Returns*!

In the scene, Danny plays the Penguin's alter ego, Mr. Cobblepot, a candidate for Gotham City mayor. He descends a sublime spiral staircase. I'm at the bottom, eagerly waiting for him.

"Mr. Cobblepot, you are the coolest role model a young person could have," I say.

He leers at me as he sticks a campaign pin on my chest.

"And you are the hottest young person a role model could have," he retorts.

We did a bunch of takes from different angles. Finally, Tim Burton said, "That's a wrap."

"Stop," Danny yelled as the actors and extras were dispersing. Everyone turned to face him. It sounded urgent.

Danny pointed toward me. "I want everyone to acknowledge Lisa. She's been here all week, and she did a great job. This is her last day on the set."

The cast and crew applauded. I don't remember much about my time on the set, but I'll always remember that moment. Danny made it really special for me, even though I only had one line. He had also encouraged me before my scene, which had pushed me to do my best. Imagine if the guy had been stand-offish or rude? I would have been professional and done a good job. But I'm certain Danny helped me nail the scene.

I took a friend to the premiere. When the movie ended, I waited to see my name in the credits. Instead of "Blonde Volunteer," it read "Volunteer Bimbo." I was crushed. If I'd known that they would change the name of my character to that, I wouldn't have auditioned for it. I've never forgiven Tim Burton for that. Fruit baskets be damned!

* * *

Frasier was such a critically acclaimed show (it won thirty-seven Emmys—more than any other comedy series) that I had to audition several times for a guest-starring role on the season cliffhanger. I was thrilled when I landed it. *Frasier* had been my favorite show.

The plot involved Frasier getting dumped by a woman at the airport. While he's drowning his sorrows at an airport bar, I walk up to him and ask him for directions to my flight to Acapulco. He pretends he's on the same flight. We exchange pleasantries on the way to the gate, and he follows me onto the plane. The show ends for the season. Could this be the start of a great romance? And a regular role for me?

The week I spent on the set was such fun. The cast was friendly and welcoming. Kelsey Grammer would play the piano while we'd stand around him and sing songs from *Cabaret*. John

Mahoney, the actor who starred as Frasier's dad, was a big sports fan. He and I would talk college football during breaks.

A few weeks later, Lorraine Berglund, my manager, received a call. The producers and cast loved me and wanted me back for the first episode of the next season. I would be a guest star and play Frasier's love interest.

"This is going to be your big break," Lorraine said. With her British accent, it sounded even more official. I couldn't believe it—this was my favorite show; I loved the cast; and I was going to be Frasier's love interest. I believed Lorraine was right. This was the big break I'd been waiting for.

Two weeks before shooting, the producers called Lorraine.

"We're so sorry about this, but Sela Ward wants to be on the show. We're going to cast her as Frasier's love interest instead of Lisa. But Lisa's still going to be in that episode."

My part was reduced to one scene. I'm on the plane with Frasier when I realize he stalked me. I panic and ask to change seats. That's it. I'm gone. Frasier goes to Acapulco and has an affair with Sela Ward.

Well, that's show biz.

Years after my disappointment on *Frasier*, I had a very different experience on *The George Lopez Show*. The casting director reached out to ask if I'd like to appear on the hit ABC show, guest starring as George Lopez's long-lost adopted sister, Linda Lorenzo. (She doesn't realize she's adopted and thinks she's Italian instead of Mexican. After seeing what a marvelous life she's leading, George doesn't have the heart to break it to her.) I jumped at the chance to play the part. I was a huge George Lopez fan, plus I knew how important the show was to millions of Latinos who didn't see themselves or their families represented on prime-time television. It remains one of the best experiences of my acting career.

* * *

I was riding in an elevator when I realized the man next to me was staring. Actually, it was more than staring—he was drilling holes in my face. When the elevator stopped, I jumped off as fast as I could to get away from the creeper. But he was right behind me.

"I'm sorry to stare at you," he said. "But I work for Mattel, the toy company. You look just like Teresa."

He explained that Teresa was the recently introduced Latina Barbie. She looked like Barbie, but her features were a bit different. She had a square jaw, wider cheekbones, rounder brown eyes, and brown hair. He handed me his card.

"I want you to meet our marketing team because we hire actors to portray our characters."

I thought about this. "Does it pay?"

"It's Mattel." He laughed. "It pays *very* well."

As a little girl, I loved everything Barbie. I'm convinced the reason I wanted to live in Malibu was because for Christmas one year, I received the Malibu Barbie Dreamhouse. I also had the Camper, Corvette, furniture, clothes, accessories, and dolls. (I had a Ken doll too, but my Barbie was into the more rugged G.I. Joe.) I knew how Barbie dressed, so when I walked into the meeting, I wore a pink minidress. There were three Mattel executives in the room. They stared at me, their mouths hanging open. No one spoke. It was really weird.

"It's her!" someone finally said. The others nodded.

"Can I see?" I asked.

They pointed toward the doll. I walked to the table Teresa was standing on.

I was a bit stunned—I looked exactly like that doll!

"I know. It's you," one of them said.

I got the job.

There were a bunch of women hired who represented different Barbies—blonde Barbie, Black Barbie, Barbie's little sister, Skipper. (The teenager cast as Skipper was cute as a button and absolutely hilarious. She shared that she wanted to be an actress, like me. She lived in Arizona, but I had a feeling she was special. I invited her and her mom to stay with me in Los Angeles and introduced her to Lorraine, my manager, who signed her on the spot. Busy Philipps immediately shot to fame on *Freaks and Geeks* and *Dawson's Creek*. She went on to host her own talk show on E!.) We had to memorize multiple pages of scripts that we'd recite for buyers at toy fairs, conventions, and sales meetings. We had to know all about Mattel's marketing plan, sales projections, and Barbie inventory. In some ways, this was much like being a Rams brand ambassador except that I got to wear Bob Mackie gowns and make much better money. The Arizona Pre–Toy Fair ran for two weeks; Toy Fair New York was three weeks long. I was paid $500 a day.

Being Barbie was more than being cute; you had to have poise and be articulate, likable, and knowledgeable about the iconic brand. If you didn't know your information, you could cost the company serious money. There were teams of people whose sole job was to create real-life Barbie worlds—the homes, clothes, furnishings, and accessories. Buyers from all across the globe descended on the toy fairs to check out the latest in all things Barbie and to place orders to sell the products in their stores.

This gig was really fun and provided me with some great opportunities. I dressed in a cute fringe dress with a guitar as Country Rose Barbie and stood on the stage at Nashville's Grand Ole Opry. I felt a little like Patsy Cline as I waved to the audience. For a children's charity event, Beverly Hills' Rodeo Drive was shut down and transformed into a Barbie fantasy land with twenty thousand square feet of "Barbie pink" carpet. When the Barbies arrived, the place erupted into hysteria. Hundreds of little girls were screaming at us. I imagined that this was what it must feel like to be a rock star (or *Monday Night Football*'s John Madden—more on that later).

If you're a Barbie collector, you know what a big deal Holiday Barbies are for die-hard fans. Every year, Barbie would wear a different holiday gown created by a famous designer. It would instantly become a collectable. When Holiday Barbie was a brunette, I represented her at sales meetings and charity events, such as the Salvation Army and Toys for Tots. I wore an ornate burgundy velvet jacket with a white fur collar and cuffs and a gold lamé hoop skirt. My look was topped with a big faux-fur hat. I truly felt like a princess in that outfit.

A few days before Christmas, someone from Mattel called me. Casey Kasem, the legendary radio DJ, wanted to hire Holiday Barbie to surprise his daughter, Liberty, at his house on Christmas Eve.

"You're not obligated to go. But he'll send a limo and pay you $1,500 for twenty minutes."

That was a crazy amount of money. Plus I thought it would be really cool to meet Casey Kasem. I'd grown up listening to his *American Top 40*. He was the voice of my adolescence. I couldn't believe I was going to meet him and see his mansion. Being a Barbie was really awesome.

The limo drove through Casey's gate and down a long driveway. When we arrived at the entrance to his sprawling Beverly Hills estate, Casey and his wife were waiting outside for me. They gave me big hugs and thanked me for giving up part of my Christmas Eve. They escorted me into an enormous foyer.

"Liberty, someone's here to see you," Casey called.

As I waited for Liberty, I wondered if she'd be as excited about meeting me as her dad imagined she would be. Being such a rich kid, maybe she was used to this kind of thing. Maybe it would be no big deal for her.

But Liberty's eyes nearly burst out of their sockets when she saw me. She screamed as she raced toward me. She collapsed into my arms and squeezed me tight.

"You're my favorite doll ever," she said as she clung to me. "I can't believe you're here!"

She was ridiculously cute. It didn't matter that she was a really rich kid—she was a regular little girl who loved Barbies and was so excited that I was in her house. She was around the age—maybe seven or eight—that she was old enough to play with Barbies but still young enough to believe that I was a real-life Barbie. I played with her for a while. When it was time to go, Casey walked me to my waiting limo and handed me a check.

"Thank you so much. You were so wonderful with my daughter," he said. "This meant so much to us."

That was a Christmas Eve I'll never forget. It was an important reminder that you can't judge anybody by who you think they'll be before you meet them. Liberty was a sweet little girl who loved dolls. And Casey Kasem was a regular dad trying to make his baby girl happy. In some ways, the Kasems were just a normal family.

Well, almost.

After the limo pulled away, I opened the envelope with my check inside. It was for $5,000! I couldn't believe it. I had been at the house for twenty minutes! Merry Christmas to me!

* * *

I love everything about auditions—learning the lines and playing characters. I even love being judged for my performance. To me, casting directors and producers are an engaged and enthusiastic audience.

But there's always an exception to the rule, especially when the guy casting you opens the front door in a silk kimono.

I was asked to audition for the female lead in Steven Seagal's movie *Fire Down Below*. But when I was told that the audition was being held at Steven Seagal's Beverly Hills mansion instead of an office, my instincts went on high alert.

"Absolutely not."

"That's how he works. He has a production office at home where he holds auditions," an assistant at the casting office told us.

I thought about it. Maybe it would be okay—but I'd take Lorraine, my manager, with me, just in case.

When we arrived at his home, Steven opened the door wearing a silk kimono. His eyes lit up when he saw me. Then he noticed Lorraine. She was standing behind me. I introduced us.

He rolled his eyes as if I were a small child and he was exasperated with me. "What? You can't come here without your manager babysitting?"

"Darling, here I am," Lorraine bellowed out in her proper British accent. "Shall we get started?"

We were ushered into a formal living room that was Asian themed. In the middle of the room was an oversized ornate chair on a platform. Lorraine and I looked at each other, thinking, *Can you believe this guy? This chair? The kimono?* It was all bizarre. He asked me to read the scene a few different ways and directed me while sitting on his throne.

"You're amazing," he said when we were done. "I loved your performance. You're perfect for the role. Great job."

Even though the experience had been completely strange, we left believing I'd been cast.

"He loved you," Lorraine said.

"It went really well," I agreed. "But what was the deal with the throne?"

A few hours later, Lorraine received a call from the casting office. "He loved her. He wants to offer her the lead. Just one small thing . . ."

"Yes?"

"He wants her to come back tonight for a private rehearsal."

A private rehearsal? On his casting throne? No, thank you!

Lorraine relayed the message to the casting office. They called a few days later. "You don't have the lead because you refused to go back for the private rehearsal, but we would like to offer you a smaller role."

My instinct was *Take your small role and shove it*. But it was a one-day shoot, and I was an actor who needed credits on my résumé. It would be good for my reel. Plus, the scene wasn't even with him. I said yes.

I should have gone with my instinct—it always knows best. In my experiences with relationships, work, and life, I've learned that I should always listen to that quiet inner voice. Sometimes there will be louder voices—voices screaming about money, success, and national exposure (much more on that later). It's important to tune those voices out and really listen to your gut instincts—your gut doesn't react to money or fame; it is always telling you what's best for you.

When I first spotted Steven on the set, he was with some other male cast and crew members. They were giggling and leering at me as if someone had just told a lewd joke. I was the only woman in the vicinity, so I knew it was directed at me. Then Steven walked up to me and asked me to go to his dressing room. I turned bright red. I was thirty-one years old, but I felt like a child.

I said no. He gave me a dismissive look and walked away. I believe my role was completely cut out of the film because I declined his offers three times. I don't know for certain because I've never seen the movie.

The worst part of this situation was that there was no one to complain to. Steven was the star and the producer. He was the boss, and he called all the shots. He was completely in charge. He could do whatever he wanted with no consequences.

Years later, my experience became a viral story during the #MeToo movement, as I was the first woman to recount my troubling experience with him. Soon afterward, Portia de Rossi, Jenny McCarthy, and Julianna Margulies shared similar inappropriate encounters. Two young actresses said they had been raped by Steven Seagal—one during a private audition.

After my *Inside Edition* piece aired, an actress messaged me that she had been asked to come in for a "chemistry test" for *Under Siege 2*. The audition was at Steven Seagal's hotel room. She said that he answered the door in just a robe and later assaulted her. I read her email and cried. I remembered how lost and alone I'd felt on that set because I had nowhere to complain. I'm happy that these stories are being told and that these powerful men are being held accountable for their bad behavior.

* * *

When it came to 1990s TV, no one was bigger than Aaron Spelling, the creator of *Beverly Hills 90210* and *Melrose Place*. When I was asked to audition for a part in his new daytime soap opera, *Sunset Beach*, I knew this was a huge opportunity. Aaron Spelling launched careers. It was the first time he'd ever done daytime TV. It was going to be sexy and campy and oh-so-over-the-top.

When you audition for a contract role, you have to jump through a lot of hoops. My character was Maria, a "rape victim" (it was the late '90s—today she'd be described as a rape survivor). I had an initial audition with a casting director and a few callbacks. Then I was brought in to do a screen test.

Maria was dealing with the aftermath of a sexual assault. The script described her as upset and vulnerable. The scene called for her to sob as she talked about her assault.

I thought, why did she have to be played as a victim? If I'd been raped, I'd be furious. I'd want revenge. I wanted Maria to be filled with outrage. She wouldn't cry. She wouldn't collapse into a man's arms. That was how I played the scene in each of my early auditions.

As I was in hair and makeup waiting for my screen test, I watched the three or four girls auditioning before me on the monitors. They were beautiful women who were crying and emoting through the scene. I wondered if I'd made a mistake. But I knew I couldn't change my interpretation at the last minute. I had to trust my instincts.

I was doing the scene with Timothy Adams, a gorgeous blond model-turned-actor who'd already been cast as series regular Casey Mitchum. His character was described as a Sunset Beach lifeguard who has a knack for rescuing damsels in distress. We introduced ourselves and shook hands.

"You ready to go?" he asked.

I nodded and headed toward the door where I would make my entrance.

"Action!" the director yelled.

I waited a few beats. Then I burst through the door in a fury. Tim's jaw dropped, and he forgot his part. His face went completely blank.

"Cut," the director said.

Tim was mortified. "I'm really sorry. I just didn't expect that at all."

I did the scene again, the same way. This time, Tim was prepared. I thought I did a great job. But I also knew it wasn't what they were looking for.

I called Lorraine from the car and told her what had happened.

"He forgot his lines? I've never heard that happen before. No one forgets their lines when they're auditioning someone else," she said.

When I didn't get the part, neither of us was surprised.

"We loved her. We thought she was great," they said.

Yeah, yeah. They always say that.

But as in any good soap opera, maybe there would be a plot twist.

* * *

KCBS-TV wanted to hire a weekend sports guy with extensive sports broadcasting experience. That was what the job description called for—they definitely weren't looking for me. But somehow Kenny finagled an interview with the general manager and the news director. I showed up to the meeting with a skinny résumé in one hand and a skinny caramel macchiato in the other.

But I had done my research—I was prepared for any reservation they might have. My attitude was—they needed me; they just didn't realize it yet.

"You really should hire me," I told them. "There are no other female sportscasters on the field or in the locker rooms in LA. Where are the women covering sports on TV? And I'm Latina. The Hispanic market is huge and growing here in Los Angeles, but where are they on television?"

In order to be further convinced, they gave me an assignment before they made a decision.

"Interview Eric Karros."

Eric Karros was a star first baseman for the Dodgers. He'd recently had knee surgery and was rehabbing with the San Bernardino Stampede, a minor league team.

Sounded like a simple assignment.

The problem? He wouldn't speak to the press. At all. Nobody had been able to score an interview with this multimillion-dollar player ever since he'd been with the Stampede.

The news director assigned Les Rose, a cameraman, to cover the story with me. Les was already respected in the industry. In a few years, he'd win several national photojournalism awards, including five Emmys. He'd work as a field producer and photojournalist for *CBS Evening News*, *CBS Sunday Morning*, *48 Hours*, and *60 Minutes*.

We hopped into the news van and headed out for the one-hour ride to San Bernardino. As Les talked to me about the assignment, he spoke in what sounded like a foreign language. What the hell were stand-ups and IFBs? I had a choice—do I nod and pretend I understood? Or be honest and risk not being taken seriously?

"Les, I don't know anything. I've never done this before."

Les nodded. "Well, then, we have a lot to cover."

He gave me a one-hour crash course in reporting while dodging the traffic on the I-10.

I learned that a stand-up is when a reporter literally stands up in front of the camera and delivers part of the report directly into the lens. An IFB is an abbreviation for an interruptible foldback, a monitoring system for one-way communication from the director or assistant director to the on-air reporter.

We discussed how we'd report the story. Eric Karros had just signed a contract for twenty million dollars. As we talked, we realized that his contract was more money than the combined worth of the Stampede's stadium and all of its minor league players. Yet Karros's entire career with the Dodgers hinged on him successfully rehabbing with the Stampede.

When we arrived, we hit the field running. I interviewed teammates, coaches, even the mascot. We filmed the team's lunch—peanut-butter-and-jelly sandwiches made with generic discount white bread just short of its sell-by date (I checked the tag)—and compared it to the elaborate gourmet spreads the Dodgers feasted on.

From the corner of my eye, I saw Eric watching us.

"How are you going to do this?" Les asked.

I approached the Stampede's media coordinator. "Can I talk to him?"

"No."

"Just for a minute?"

"No!"

"A few seconds? I really need to interview him for this story."

"No!"

I inched closer and closer to Eric. He looked at me. His entourage looked at me.

I tiptoed a little closer.

I thought about the situation. If I didn't talk to him, my career would be over before it began. If I did approach him for an interview, the worst he could do was say no. So what? I could live with rejection, but I knew I couldn't live with a *what if?*

I took a deep breath and walked up to him.

"Listen, my name's Lisa Guerrero. I have an opportunity to get a contract with Channel 2. They've given me this assignment.

Whether or not I get it depends on whether or not you give me an interview."

"So are you saying you won't get a job because of me?"

"Yup."

He studied me for a few seconds.

"Well, I don't want to be responsible for you not getting the gig," he said. "I guess we better do this interview."

I learned so much that day, and it didn't have to do with baseball or contracts or IFBs or stand-ups. I realized that sometimes it takes bravery to be honest. I told Les I didn't know anything. I told Eric I needed him. It's hard to admit vulnerability, but when you do, more often than not, people will respect you for your honesty and want to help you. Sometimes the hardest—and bravest—words to say are "I don't know." But they can be the most satisfying. When you admit you don't know, you open yourself up to learning and growing.

* * *

There are some dates in your life that you never forget. One of them for me is April 22, 1998. I was eating lunch with my acting class at Gladstone's in Malibu. We were chatting about auditions we'd been on and roles we'd landed or almost landed. Then my phone rang. I saw that it was Kenny. I walked to the parking lot to take the call.

"CBS-2 loved your Karros interview. You're hired," he said.

"What?"

"Lisa, you're going to be their weekend sports guy."

I would be the first woman to earn a contract at that network affiliate in Los Angeles. I floated back to my table and excitedly told my acting class. As we were toasting my good news, my phone rang again. I headed back to the parking lot. This time it was Lorraine, my manager.

"Lisa, you're not going to believe this. Aaron Spelling saw your *Sunset Beach* audition and loved your spunk. He said you reminded him of Rita Hayworth in *Gilda*, his favorite film of all time."

"That's my favorite film too!" In fact, I had a poster of Rita Hayworth from *Gilda* matted and framed on my living room. She too was a Latina—and I admired her beauty and tenacity.

"Lisa, they're writing a role for you," Lorraine said breathlessly.

"What? I thought . . ."

"You're going to be introduced in this huge summertime promotion. You're playing Francesca. She's a home wrecker, a jewel thief, a blackmailer. She's awful. She's terrific—a real disrupter. Lisa, this is the one! This is the one!"

To say I was stunned is an understatement. My sportscasting and acting dreams had come true—on the same day while standing in a parking lot.

I loved acting. I loved reporting. But I couldn't do both.

Or could I?

7

Split Personality

I was on a first date at an Italian restaurant in West Holly-wood when a couple approached the table.

"I hate to bother you, but we have a bet," the man said. "My wife thinks you're on some soap opera. I told her she's wrong—you're Lisa Guerrero from Channel 2 Sports."

I smiled wide. "You're both right!"

"What?" He shook his head incredulously.

"I *am* Lisa Guerrero from sports, and I *am* Francesca from the soap."

The couple looked at each other and then at me as if they didn't quite understand what I'd said. How could a woman who talked sports play a villainous vamp on a soap? It didn't make sense to them.

It didn't make sense to anyone, including my agents and manager, who told me it was impossible to do both. I loved proving my doubters wrong, even though there were times I wasn't sure I could juggle the two gigs. After much negotiating, the lawyers hammered out an agreement where I could work as a lead on NBC's *Sunset Beach* on Monday through Friday from

6 a.m. to 6 p.m. and be a sports reporter and fill-in anchor for
CBS on the weekends and two nights a week.

How did I do it? I hardly saw my family, let alone friends.
I had no social life—unless a social life can consist of scarfing
down free Dodger Dogs in the press box during the seventh
inning with my cameraman while being serenaded by Nancy Bea
Hefley, the stadium organist. Oh, that date I'd been on when the
couple approached me? It had been a rare night out. The dude
seemed nice, but I had no time for a second rendezvous. And
that about summed up my love life in the late '90s. I'd go on a
first date, but I couldn't commit to a second. Well, until I met
Melrose Place heartthrob Grant Show, but that's for a bit later in
this chapter.

How did I keep track of my crazy double life? I had one of
those fat leather-bound organizers and planned out every single
moment. A few years ago, I discovered those old organizers. As
I thumbed through them, I realized it was even worse than I
recalled. I thought I had a Type A personality, but I was more
like Type A-plus-plus. Each space was crammed with notes—on
the edges, in the corners, spilling off the pages. I scheduled
everything, including stops for gas as well as the best, fastest
drive-through restaurants.

I ate absolute crap (the Doritos in the vending machine at
the station were my go-to snack and occasionally my dinner). I'd
plan my routes to and from games based on fast-food options.
There were two El Pollo Locos near CBS (I'd jotted down in my
notes that one was a few minutes quicker) and a Roscoe's House
of Chicken 'N Waffles across the street (that was for when I had
time to sit down for a few minutes). Unfortunately, the only

choice on my way to the Forum was a McDonald's, so I'd drive a few blocks out of the way to Wendy's. God forbid I was hungry while covering the Angels—the best option on the route home was a Taco Bell.

When I'd walk in the door, Chappy—my black-and-white rescue cat (named for Charlie Chaplin because of his side-to-side strut)—would be waiting for me. He'd curl up on my lap while I memorized lines for the next day's *Sunset Beach* shoot. I'd pass out around 11. Then, my bedside alarm would shrill at 5 a.m. I'd hit it and doze off. And since I had already prepared myself for that reaction, my coffee-maker alarm in the kitchen would go off five minutes later. This time I'd have to get up. I was always exhausted—thank God for Visine and under-eye concealer. They were the most crucial components of my beauty regimen.

I loved my 1920s Hollywood Hills home that overlooked the lights of Universal Studios. But I was rarely there except to sleep. I had named the one-thousand-square-foot place Casita Encantada (little enchanted house) because it reminded me of a Spanish-style dollhouse topped with a perfect tiny turret. My bedroom had the original floral stained-glass windows. The galley kitchen with its lacquered wood cabinets looked like something a shipbuilder had designed. After I'd wake, I'd head to the pantry for my breakfast—coffee with an obnoxious amount of vanilla creamer and a Snickers bar.

Did I ever cook? Of course not! I didn't want to burn my hats.

I'd decided my kitchen would be more efficient as a combined closet–makeup room–cat condo. In lieu of a table, I had a cheetah-print three-story tree house–scratching post. But it really didn't matter that I had nowhere to sit for a meal, I couldn't cook in the oven because that was where I stored my hats. Instead of pots and pans, my kitchen drawers held sweaters and shirts. As for the kitchen counters? That was where I kept my jewelry and accessories. I didn't have a knife set, but I had a great collection of earrings.

Actually, the only things I used in the kitchen were the coffee maker (I existed on caffeine) and the microwave. My idea of cooking was microwaving Lean Cuisines. If I was feeling particularly ambitious, I'd make a tuna sandwich. That's if I had all the ingredients. My refrigerator was usually empty except for a bottle of chardonnay, coffee creamer, and an assortment of condiments.

I'm not complaining. I loved my life. I loved my house. I loved being alone (Chappy was great company). I even loved my junk food. For years I had kicked, scratched, sacrificed, and scraped by. Finally, I'd been given a wonderful opportunity to earn a living doing the two things I had dreamed of doing.

I was possibly America's first "sportscactress."

Francesca Vargas: International Jewel Thief. Blackmailer. Homewrecker.

When I joined the cast of *Sunset Beach*, I knew my time on the set would be short-lived. My character, Francesca, was a disrupter whose mission was to destroy as many lives as possible. Her fate was sealed: Someone would kill her. The question was, who? Everyone had a motive. My storyline was a rip-off of the hugely successful "Who Shot J. R.?" cliffhanger on *Dallas*, the nighttime soap opera that ran from 1978 to 1991. More than ninety million people tuned in to find out who shot J. R. Ewing. As it got closer to my demise, NBC ran a big promotion: "Who Shot Francesca? Everyone's a Suspect on Sunset." I made the cover of *Soap Opera Weekly*.

If you play a contract lead role on a soap, then you're in certain story lines. Sometimes it's a front-burner story line; other times, it's a back-burner. It goes in cycles, and nobody works all day every day. Schedules tend to ebb and flow. Most soap-opera leads work about three days a week. But because every main character had to have a motive to kill me, I was in more story lines than was typical. I'd have hair and makeup at 6 a.m. Then I'd have rehearsals followed by wardrobe and a blocking rehearsal, where the director would guide us through the scene. There would be a break for lunch; afterward we'd come back and shoot.

Not only was I in so many scenes, but I had to drive the action in those scenes. Being Francesca was exhausting. It's energy-zapping to play a character who is so relentlessly evil. Here are just a few of my sins:

1. I blackmailed Gabby, the good girl who was dating the sheriff but had had an affair with his brother . . . the priest.

2. I seduced Cole, my ex-lover and former partner in jewel thievery, who was married with a newborn baby.

3. I stole the "Rosario Jewels," causing myself and others to prematurely age by fifty years (I hastily returned those accursed gems!).

4. As I was dying, I purposefully accused the wrong person of my attempted murder, just to screw with them.

5. After I died, I was sent to hell (really!) and came back to regularly haunt my Sunset Beach enemies.

Playing Francesca on this campy soap was a hoot. Who doesn't want to be the bad girl? Especially when that bad girl was an international jewel thief with exquisite taste in clothes. Being on an Aaron Spelling show meant that no expense was spared when it came to our wardrobe budget. Francesca always looked fantastic. She wore beautifully tailored suits, silk skirts, and designer shoes—that is, when she wasn't vamping it up in lingerie, leather catsuits, or a single tiny towel that was practically a washcloth.

When I was done shooting a scene in an outfit I loved, I'd "borrow" it for my reporting gig. I'm sure the wardrobe department saw me on the news and got a good laugh. I swear, I returned the items within the next day or two (except for the rhinestone tiara I wore as a beauty contestant in the Jerry Springer dream sequence. Every girl needs a crown).

And those steamy love scenes with *Sunset Beach* heartthrob Eddie Cibrian? A lot of the time, kissing scenes are faked. But I went all in. Can you blame me? He was the hottest guy I'd ever seen in my life! Those kisses were as real as it got.

So was the slap I thought would get me fired.

When Francesca is introduced in the show, she's on a cruise with Phillip, her husband, a horribly abusive man. One of my first scenes that week on set involved Francesca slapping Phillip, who was played by Michael Sabatino, a veteran soap star. There are techniques for faking a slap, but I hadn't mastered the art.

"You can just slap me," Michael said during rehearsal.

We practiced a few times, and it was fine. But when it was time to shoot the scene, I was nervous and amped up. I slapped Michael so hard you could actually hear the echo of the slap reverberating through the enormous soundstage. My hand was ringing.

"oowww," Michael shouted as he rubbed his face. That was when I noticed a beet-red spot on his cheek. I'm sure he was thinking, *Why did they hire this psycho?*

Everyone on the set gasped. I heard castmates whispering.

"Oh, my God!"

"She really hit him hard!"

I thought I'd be fired. But I wasn't. In fact, Francesca spent a lot of time slapping people. Since then, I've mastered the fake slap. Thankfully, Phillip was killed off after our cruise ship capsized. I never had to slap him again, for which I am sure he is eternally grateful.

"That's a wrap," the director would yell at the end of my day of threatening, stealing, extorting, and homewrecking. The actors would head home or go out for drinks. Not me. Instead, I'd drive to cover a game at Dodger Stadium, the Great Western Forum, or the Coliseum.

Bubble Gum and Jockstraps

I'll never forget the first time I stepped into a men's locker room. The first thing I noticed was the smell—sweat, stinky feet, mildewed towels. The second thing I noticed was that there was no safe place to look.

I was in the Dodgers locker room, and I didn't know what to do with my eyes. Butt-naked men were spilling out of the showers to my left. Guys in various stages of undress were all around me. The only place for my eyes to focus was the floor or the ceiling. When I looked down, I saw a soiled jockstrap. I looked up—a wad of chewing gum the size of a baseball dangled precariously above my perfectly coiffed head.

Besides the naked guys, there was also a pack of seasoned male reporters. They were more interested in watching me navigate the boys' club—in my candy-apple-red suit (from Nordstrom Rack, not *Sunset Beach*) and kick-ass four-inch stilettos—than in getting scoops for their newspapers and magazines. My assignment for CBS-2's *Sports Central* was to grab some postgame interviews and feed the best sound bites to the studio from our satellite truck in the parking lot. Then I'd head out to the deserted field to do a live shot before "throwing it" to my interviews.

When I was first given the assignment, I imagined it unfolding something like this: I'd walk into the locker room, and a few (fully dressed) Dodgers would approach me.

Hi, Lisa. Did you enjoy the game? Are there any questions you'd like to ask me?

It hadn't occurred to me until that moment that no one would want to talk to me. The Dodgers had lost big. I'd have to find someone willing to give me an interview. I had twenty minutes to get the sound bites I needed.

Gary Sheffield, the all-star outfielder who'd gone hitless that day, was the logical choice. I only wished his locker wasn't so close to the showers. Not only would it be hard to avoid the naked players, but the steam would frizz my hair. (For the record, in over a decade as a sportscaster, one of the major reasons to get out of the locker room as fast as possible was less about male nudity and more about humidity.)

I tapped my cameraman's elbow and mouthed, "Sheffield." Frank shot me a look that I realized in retrospect meant *Don't do it. He's an asshole.* But in the moment I took it to mean *That's a great idea. I'm sure he'll be more than helpful.* I probably should have known this was a bad idea considering there were no other reporters around Shef's locker.

"Mr. Sheffield, can I ask you a couple of questions about . . ."

"No!"

He turned and walked away. I blushed furiously while staring at the empty locker. Behind me, a bunch of guys snickered. I didn't know if it was coming from the players or the reporters. It was probably both.

I had eighteen minutes until my live shot. I turned and saw Raúl Mondesí, another all-star. Best of all, he was fully dressed.

"Mr. Mondesí, do you have a minute?"

Raúl turned and looked at me as if I was from another planet. After checking me out from head to toe, he spoke in Spanish, smiled, and walked away. I had no idea what he'd said.

I started to panic. My heart raced. I had only about fifteen minutes left. My eyes quickly scanned the locker room, trying to avoid the naked men.

Suddenly someone tapped me on the shoulder.

I turned. It was second baseman Eric Young.

"Having trouble?" he asked, grinning.

I bristled as I thought about my encounter with Eric earlier that day. During the seventh inning, I'd been taking notes from the photographers' pit next to the Dodgers' dugout when a batboy gestured to me and then lobbed a baseball at my head. Because I have catlike reflexes and an aversion to getting smacked in the face, I caught it. I was about to hurl it back when I noticed something written on it.

Hi, can I get your number? E. Y.

I looked over. Eric Young was standing with a dozen players waiting for my response.

"Dream on," I said. I tossed the ball to a kid above me in the stands, who was probably confused about why the Dodgers star would want his digits.

And here I was, standing next to Eric Young, maybe my only hope for a sound bite. It was awkward, but I did need a quote. Desperately.

"Looking for an interview?" he asked.

"Looking for a number?" I said, smirking. Then I asked him about the game.

His interview became my first in the locker room. When we finished, he introduced me to some of his teammates who answered my questions. I wound up making my live shot with ninety seconds to spare. E. Y. and I became pals. It occurred to me a while later that he probably wasn't hitting on me. More likely, he was putting me through some kind of initiation.

I also befriended another Eric—Eric Karros. Remember him? He loved to tell people that I owed my career to him. "If I didn't give her an interview, she wouldn't be here," he'd joke. I could always count on him for a sound bite.

In the years to come, I'd be put through many tests as one of the only women covering sports. Some of them didn't have so pleasant an outcome. But that night, when I drove off the lot at Chavez Ravine, I smiled and thought, *I love my job.* I also thought, *I have to memorize twenty pages of dialogue before I can go to sleep tonight.*

Lights . . . Camera . . . Silence?

I was about two weeks into my gig with CBS when I was assigned an interview with Tony La Russa, the manager of the St. Louis Cardinals, the team the Dodgers were playing that day. As I walked through the visiting-team locker room toward the team manager's office in the back, a few guys whistled at me. I continued on, staring straight ahead and remaining expressionless. More guys whistled. Then there were catcalls followed by horrible animal grunts and groans.

With each step further into what seemed like an endless locker room, the noise became louder and more frenzied. My heart hammered, and I froze. A flush rushed across my ears, face, throat, and chest.

Rodney Hunt, my cameraman that day, was right behind me. He stopped short when I did. I felt as if I'd been punched in the gut and couldn't catch my breath. I felt naked, embarrassed, humiliated.

And then Rodney hoisted his camera onto his shoulder. He flipped on the light and started *spraying*—shooting—the room from side to side. As soon as the players realized they were being filmed, the noise stopped.

A few seconds ticked by. There was complete silence.

Rodney boomed, "That's the power of the media, Lisa. Don't ever forget that you're in control."

Rodney flipped off the light and dropped the camera. We walked toward La Russa's office. The only sound was my heels clicking against the floor.

Sadly, Rodney died of complications from COVID-19 in 2021. But the lesson he taught me has stayed with me whenever

I'm reporting a story. I was a rookie, still figuring out my way around the newsroom and locker rooms. Rodney showed me that because I was a journalist, I also possessed power in the locker room—and it was my workplace too. When you shine the light on wrongdoing, the bad guys scatter like cockroaches—sometimes even literally.

After that moment in the locker room, I was no longer afraid to interview anyone. I realized I wielded this power, a superpower, really. I felt a bit more fearless after that day.

I started having fun with my stories. When UCLA basketball players were plagued with injuries, I brought out the board game Operation and played it on camera to illustrate an injury a player had sustained. Broken femur? I'd pull it out of the board game with the tweezer.

When there was a rumor that Dennis Rodman might join the Lakers, I said to my producers, "Let's give him a Hollywood welcome." Rodman was such a huge personality that Tinsel Town seemed like the next logical place for him to be. After all, he'd dated Madonna. He had even married himself in a much-publicized white wedding dress. I did a piece on some of the places he might frequent—lingerie stores and hair salons. I went to tattoo parlors and posed the question: "If you could give Dennis Rodman a tattoo, what would it be?"

Since we spent so much time talking to players, coaches, and team owners, I created a segment called "Fan Cam" for *Sports Central* where I'd interview fans at sports bars. I didn't take into account how absolutely inebriated the fans would be. As I interviewed these drunkards, they'd grab me, pinch me, attempt to kiss me—live on camera. I'd laugh it off and defuse the situation with humor. "I hope your mother is watching," I'd say, smiling. Viewers loved the segment. Everyone thought I was a good sport. The attitude was *Let's watch Lisa get pinched on TV. Let's watch Lisa give some drunk dude the business. Let's watch Lisa try hard not to lose her cool.*

Let's not watch Lisa lose it off camera.

Because that was what I did. By the time I reached the parking lot, I'd feel the tears coming. I'd jump into my car and have a good cry. What I thought would be a great opportunity to give fans a voice turned into a segment I loathed. I was pinched so much and so hard that I'd have bruises on my butt. CBS eventually insisted that the sports bars provide security for me. When I interviewed fans at the Rose Bowl, I stood on a platform that had a fence built around it so fans couldn't grab me.

This taught me another lesson—drunk people don't care how bad they look on camera. (Although I bet their bosses, wives, and moms sure did!)

When Francesca Met Jake

Because of my busy schedule, I hardly ever watched television. But I'd make an exception for my two favorite shows, *Sex and the City* and *Melrose Place*. Since *Sex and the City*'s Carrie Bradshaw was a reporter of sorts, I could relate and felt I was the sports version of her—minus the endless amount of free time to socialize with my girlfriends, given that all of my time was devoted to working. I watched *Melrose Place* for one reason and one reason only—Grant Show.

Grant played Jake Hanson, the gorgeous yet sensitive resident of *Melrose Place*. I, along with most red-blooded women in America, had a crush on him.

Aaron Spelling Productions was hosting a party for its shows when I first saw Grant Show in person. I looked at him, and we locked eyes from across the room. I know it sounds corny, but I felt the chemistry between us. He strolled over.

"Nice jacket," he said.

We had on nearly identical black leather biker jackets. Actually, we were dressed alike in black jeans and boots.

I think I giggled and was a bit speechless. It was Grant Show! He was very charming and soft-spoken. Before the night was over, he asked me out on a date. A few nights later, we went to dinner at an Italian restaurant. Soon we were exclusively dating. He had just bought a big Spanish-style house in the Hollywood Hills, not far from me. He was renovating it himself. I'd hang out there while he'd walk around shirtless with this big tool belt around his waist. I'd think, *It's Jake come to life!*

He knew better than to come to my place for dinner (he'd seen my kitchen and was appalled when he opened the oven and discovered my hats). But he was a good cook. He'd make me these delicious steamed artichokes with a dipping sauce. I had no idea how to cook anything, so I was amazed by his culinary skills. I was overwhelmed by this gorgeous, kind man who made meals for me. Funny thing, he knew nothing about sports, although he golfed and tried to persuade me to take it up (he even bought me a set of clubs). He took me to his golf course and paid for me to take lessons with his golf pro. But I found it brutally boring.

After six months of dating, Grant was offered the male lead in *Wit*, a drama on Broadway starring Judith Light, the actress from *Who's the Boss?* He flew me to New York for his opening night. He was brilliant in the role of a doctor treating a cancer-stricken patient. He asked me to live in New York with him.

I'd learned my lesson about moving cross-country for a guy. I told him I needed to stay in Los Angeles and follow my dreams. Years later, Grant met my then husband at a celebrity golf tournament. He congratulated Scott for marrying "the one that got away."

The Reporter Who Made the Worm Squirm

I was sleeping in on a rare day off when my producer from *Sports Central* called.

"Get to Planet Hollywood. Dennis Rodman's holding a press conference."

With my head still buried under the covers, I mumbled, "Okay. I'll be there." I tumbled out of bed. I'd been up until 3 a.m. memorizing lines for *Sunset Beach*. I was scheduled to shoot five scenes the following day. This was going to be the first day off I'd had in months (not that I was counting).

But I was excited. Not only would this be my first press conference, but the Rodman story was huge. Rumors had been swirling for weeks that "the Worm" would sign with the Lakers. The media had been all atwitter at the prospect of covering one of the most outrageous and colorful NBA players ever—just in time for the opening of the brand-new, tricked-out $375 million Staples Center, where the team would play.

As I grabbed my go-to breakfast, a Snickers bar, I decided I'd bring my script to the press conference and find a quiet park somewhere nearby to study my pages when it ended. Then I would venture into a grocery store and get some actual food for dinner. I'd go to bed at a decent hour—after all, I had to be in the makeup chair for a 6:30 a.m. call time.

I washed down my candy bar with coffee. I turned on my computer and researched Rodman. His résumé was outstanding: a two-time all-star, he had won five NBA Championships with the Detroit Pistons and the Chicago Bulls. He had been twice named the NBA defensive player of the year and was a seven-time rebounding champ.

Rodman had just been released by Chicago and had made it clear that Los Angeles was where he wanted to be. Known for tattoos and ever-changing hair color, Rodman seemed like a perfect fit for Hollywood.

After I finished my research, I threw my dirty coffee cup in the sink and headed to my bedroom to find an outfit for the presser. I threw open the closet door and smiled. Fortunately, I had Francesca's hot-pink suit. I thought it would be perfect. As I dressed, I listened to sports radio in my bathroom while watching ESPN's *SportsCenter* on the TV in my bedroom. It was all about Rodman. They announced that they would be covering the press conference live.

The atmosphere at Planet Hollywood was electric. Media was grouped in clusters around the room sipping coffee and chewing on pastries (pro tip: nothing gets the press on your side like free food). Interestingly, no one from the Lakers was there. That didn't make sense. Also, if Rodman was going to announce that he was signing with the team, the presser should have been held at the Lakers offices.

I looked around the room. Of the thirty or forty people there, only two were women. As I edged my way toward the coffee dispenser, I felt eyes on me. A few men snickered. Within seconds, my cheeks were as hot pink as my suit. I poured a cup of coffee.

"Who invited Barbie?" (If they only knew!)

"She's probably with one of those entertainment news shows."

"I bet she's one of Rodman's chicks."

I turned toward the group. "No, I'm here for the free Danish."

I walked away and found a seat near the front of the rows of chairs facing the riser. As I jotted down some notes, I glanced at my watch. My producer wanted me to do a live shot in front of Planet Hollywood for the noon broadcast immediately after the presser. But it was 11:15, and Rodman was nowhere in sight.

I could hear the comments around me.

"Of course he'll sign."

"Phil Jackson loves the guy."

"Are there any donuts left?"

As the minutes ticked away, I was becoming more and more annoyed. I'd miss my live shot. This was supposed to have happened already. I had every minute of my day off planned. I had thirty-seven pages of dialogue to memorize. I had loads of laundry and a sink full of dirty coffee cups from the previous week.

Rodman was already a half hour late. Reporters were calling producers and editors, explaining the delay. The back of the room was lined with cameras. In the center of the room was the crowd from ESPN, ready to take the feed live once Rodman arrived. We were all concerned about meeting deadlines. And the free food was gone. I reapplied my lip gloss. I waited and simmered.

As if in slow motion, the two side doors to the left swung open, and Rodman, clad in a black suede shirt, black sunglasses, and a multicolored velvet beret, strode into the room. Next to him was his wife, Carmen Electra, in a barely-there strapless, skin-tight white dress. He was flanked by a couple of slick-looking men in suits (his agents) and a tall woman holding a wooden box (Debra, his sister, with his collection of championship rings).

The collective mouths of the media hung open.

This is gonna be good. I flipped my notepad open. That was when the scent hit me. As Rodman and his entourage piled onto the podium, I smelled booze, stale cigarettes, and weed.

Were they hung over? Or still high?

As Rodman and Carmen Electra snuggled at the podium, he started rambling about the sex they'd had. Carmen "really pleased me last night, if you know what I mean," he said. Carmen smiled and added, "Dennis is an amazing lover." Then they argued about who did what to whom in bed. It was a foul-mouthed, incoherent word salad better suited for the pages of *Penthouse* than a press conference.

"I don't really have an announcement to make," Rodman said, laughing. "I just wanted to see if you'd all show up."

What? Was he serious? The writers and broadcasters around me shifted and murmured. We looked at each other. *Was this a joke?*

He was wasting our time. On purpose. We'd been punk'd.

I thought about my day. I had so much to do—and I'd had it all figured out until this press conference popped up. I'd agreed to go to it on my precious rare day off because I loved being a reporter, and I loved covering the Lakers.

And Rodman had called this presser as some lame gag?

My anger grew from the pit of my stomach up through my chest until it settled like a dark, throbbing ache in the back of my head. I was pulsating with fury. How dare this asshole waste my precious time?

"I haven't decided if I'll sign yet. But if I do, I don't want to be a, y'know, distraction."

Blood pounded in my ears as I tried to wrap my head around his outrageous statement.

"If I become a distraction, then I'll leave the team," he added.

Since he wasn't on the team, his statement made zero sense. I thought about the time I'd wasted—thirty minutes on makeup, forty minutes on hair, twenty-five minutes to drive into Hollywood, and then an hour sitting here. All for what? So this egomaniac could have an audience for this crass rant about NOTHING!

I couldn't contain my anger any longer. I jumped out of my chair.

"Excuse me, but aren't you already a distraction to the team?"

I could feel the entire room stare at me, but I didn't care. There was absolute silence for several seconds. Then I plowed on: "You've caused this whole media circus yourself by prolonging your signing."

Dennis looked at me, stunned.

"Don't you think that's incredibly selfish for someone who claims to be a team player?" I added.

The room went still. I couldn't believe I was standing up in front of a live national TV audience and confronting Dennis

Rodman! My knees were shaking, and my heart was pounding. In all my years as a sports fan, I'd never seen a reporter admonish a star athlete like that. From the corner of my eye, I spotted Jim Hill, the sports anchor for my station. (He was the sports reporter whose presence on the football field when I was cheerleading had inspired me to consider this career.) His mouth was hanging open. Would I be fired?

"Are you kidding me, honey?" Rodman growled. "You're calling me selfish? I've been a team player, honey. I've been a team player for thirteen years. . . . All of a sudden, I do something like this and I'm selfish?"

And then this six-foot-seven giant burst into tears.

"I'm never going to win. No matter what I do for this league, for the game of basketball, I'm never going to win." He opened a piece of paper and pointed to some letters. "I've got ten charities here that I'm going to give $10,000 to. You tell me if that's selfish." (I found out later that he was holding up a takeout menu.)

"That's okay. That's okay," Debra, his sister, said, trying to console him. "He's worked so hard, and these people cut him up."

A man stood up. It was Bill Plaschke, a sports columnist for the *Los Angeles Times*. "She just said what we were all thinking. You are selfish. You've kept the Lakers waiting for two and a half weeks."

The rest of the media murmured in support. Rodman continued to glare at me.

"You will never understand me . . . ever," Rodman said, still crying. Carmen, his soon-to-be ex-wife, looked on in confusion. Then he stormed off the stage. The entourage, hot on his heels, glared at me in contempt as the door slammed behind them.

After a second or two of silence, chaos erupted.

The men flew out of their seats and peppered me with questions.

"Who are you?"

"What was that?"

"Who do you work with?"

"That was a setup, right? You guys planned it."

"Are you an actress?"

"Well, yes," I stammered. "But not today. Today I'm a sports reporter for Channel 2. Tomorrow I'm an actress."

That confused the group even more.

"So you and Dennis scripted that?"

"No," I said. "I'm a reporter just like you." (Except for the bad toupees.)

Bill Plaschke, whose column I read religiously, came up to me. "Great question. Are you a new reporter here?"

I nodded.

"Welcome to the club."

I was speechless. It was like being blessed by the pope, if the pope lived in LA, inhabited press boxes, and second-guessed the Dodgers lineup.

Then he interviewed me for his column.

Within the next ten minutes, reporters from ESPN and local sports radio interviewed me. Everyone wanted to know who was that girl in the pink blazer who had made Dennis Rodman cry. I cut off one interview. "Wait, I've got to get outside and do my live shot!"

When I did my report, the anchors in studio brought up the story of the press conference and threw it to me, saying, "Lisa, what exactly happened there today?"

I explained how Rodman had been late and disrespectful to the media. "He mentioned a lot of inappropriate sexual content that I can't repeat on the air during the day."

The anchors laughed. After I finished my report, my grizzled cameraman gave me a high five and grinned.

"Awesome job! Now, *that* is what a journalist does!"

The funny thing is, I didn't think of myself as a journalist in that moment with Rodman. I was a busy, exhausted, and pissed-off woman with a script to memorize.

Two days later, Rodman finally signed with the Lakers.

Who Killed Francesca?

Sports Illustrated sent John Walters, a reporter, to shadow me as I worked at CBS and on *Sunset Beach.*

Sports Illustrated is the Bible. To be featured in the magazine with two photos was an enormous deal. It was as if I'd just become a member of an exclusive club, and one of its perks was instant credibility. For as long as I could remember, I'd had a subscription and would read it cover to cover, usually the same day it arrived.

The article about me was called "Split Personality: *Reporter Lisa Guerrero isn't a villainous vamp, but she plays one on TV.*"

Well, not for much longer. After nearly a year on the show, Francesca was about to be killed. (She'd been so wildly popular with viewers that NBC had kept extending my contract from three months to six months to nine months and then a year.)

Francesca popped out of a birthday cake wearing a catsuit, even though she'd been mortally wounded by a bullet. Of course she didn't die immediately. She lingered in a coma for a while, even dreaming that she was a beauty contestant on *The Jerry Springer Show*. She briefly woke from the coma to accuse the wrong person of murder, just for the hell of it. Finally, Francesca died. She went to hell in a slinky red dress surrounded by flames.

With Francesca dead, the ratings plummeted. (Francesca had helped propel the soap to the fifteenth position in daytime syndication in the United States.) The producers talked to my agent about bringing me back as Francesca's "eviler twin." But before that could happen, the show was canceled. (Ironically, *Sunset Beach* went on to be an international success—and hit number one in prime time in the UK. It was so popular in Great Britain that each episode ran three times during the week. Francesca also became a cult favorite with gay audiences all over the world—for which I'm extremely grateful.)

But thank God Francesca didn't have a sibling and was really, truly dead. My sports broadcasting career was about to go next level.

As I prepared for Francesca's demise, I made a career decision: I would focus on broadcasting. There were thousands of wannabe actresses in Los Angeles, but I was one of the few female sportscasters on television—and the first woman to earn a contract covering sports at CBS in Los Angeles.

At ESPN, a group of women, including Linda Cohn, Suzy Kolber, and Robin Roberts (who in 2005 would cohost *Good Morning America*), were making a name for themselves in this predominantly male landscape. In 1989, Hannah Storm became the first female sports anchor at CNN. (She went on to cover the Olympics, the NBA, and the NFL for NBC and was the first woman to anchor the pregame coverage of Major League Baseball games.) But these were the few exceptions to the rule.

It was a boys' club. If a woman wanted to gain entry, she had to fit in rather than stand out. There was a consensus in the business that for a woman to be credible, she had to take her cues from her male colleagues on how to report sports. Women were told to dress in suits, cut their hair short, and wear just a hint of makeup.

I felt that women could bring a much-needed change to sports coverage. So many of the *male* sports reporters treated these athletes like heroes. They avoided the tough questions. "Outstanding game. How did you do it?" seemed to be the recurring theme of all too many interviews. I thought about the Dennis Rodman press conference. Dressed in my hot-pink outfit, I was considered a joke. "Barbie doll," the guys had laughed. Yet I was the only reporter in a sea of men who'd had the guts to call out Rodman. My *male* colleagues had remained silent. They had been so shocked by my boldness that it became the news story. But why? Shouldn't all reporters call out players for behaving badly?

I didn't feel that I had to become part of any boys' club to succeed in the business. I wanted to do it differently—I wanted to be glamorous, sexy, bold, and at times irreverent. I wanted to pave my own way.

I could become a pioneer for other women who wanted to pursue sports broadcasting. I could be that person a girl could point to if she was ever told, "Girls don't do that." I liked that my Hispanic last name was on the chyron—a daily reminder to other Latinas that this goal was attainable.

8

Life in the Man Cave

fter the Rodman presser, I was recognized everywhere as the reporter who had made the Worm cry. Strangers would high-five me. "Good for you!" "Way to go!" "You sure are brave."

Truth be told, I was a bit ambivalent about the whole thing. I appreciated the props—from strangers and the media—but each high five seemed like a small celebration of this man's breakdown. He had looked absolutely destroyed on the stage. I wouldn't have guessed that underneath the bravado, the histrionics, and all that facial hardware was a really vulnerable guy. (Years later, I was a guest alongside Rodman on the *D. L. Hughley Show*, a late-night talk show. Rodman said he didn't remember any of it.)

Soon after the press conference, I was offered a better-paying job with more responsibilities at the competition—KTTV Fox-11, the local Fox station. I became the correspondent and fill-in anchor for *Fox Extra Innings* and *Fox Overtime*. I was eventually named the first female anchor of the *Southern California Sports Report* on Fox Sports Net.

I was in the locker room after the Lakers won the NBA championship—their first win in twelve years. I clinched exclusive interviews with sports luminaries like Gary Sheffield (the Dodgers outfielder who wouldn't talk to me my first day in the locker room), Kobe Bryant, and Wayne Gretzky, to name a few. When Shaquille O'Neal announced that he was boycotting the media, I relentlessly pursued him, stationing myself by his locker, befriending his flacks, and procuring unedited versions of his favorite show, Fox's *You Gotta See This!* When he agreed to a sit-down with me—the first interview he'd given in months—it was picked up by news outlets across the country. I even scored another nice mention in *Sports Illustrated.* I was gaining credibility and visibility. I even survived being boycotted by the Dodgers. As the Dodgers beat reporter, I covered a game where they lost big late in the season. I said on camera that the team seemed to be "phoning it in."

The next time I walked into the locker room, Chad Kreuter, the Dodgers catcher, confronted me. "You're done. No one will talk to you anymore."

"Why?"

"You're supposed to support the team."

Was that what the team thought? I was in their locker room, at their batting practices, at all their games. But I was a reporter, not a supporter.

"I'm not your cheerleader."

"We thought you were a fan," he said.

I looked at Chad. Then I looked at the rest of the team, who nodded in agreement.

"I've been a fan of the Dodgers long before you got here, and I'll be a fan long after you're gone."

The players grudgingly nodded. They appreciated anyone who could take their shit and dish it back. And that ended their boycott before it really began. But it made me realize what a precarious position I was in as one of the few reporters who also was expected to be opinionated on camera. I had to make sure I was fair—and not accuse an entire team of apathy, even if it made a better sound bite.

And I was right—Chad was gone the next year.

But that wasn't the end of my interface with him. Years later, I received a surprising phone call from Kenny, my agent. I was asked to play myself in *Moneyball*, a movie starring Brad Pitt as Billy Beane, the manager of the Oakland A's.

The producers, including Brad, had seen archival footage of me giving the business to a bunch of Oakland A's baseball players and liked my tough reporting tactics. When I asked about the script (cowritten by Aaron Sorkin), I was told to improvise my lines.

Playing myself was a fun experience. During filming, I said to an extra cast member who was also playing a reporter, "Get out of my shot!" Bennett Miller, the director, yelled, "Cut!" He said he didn't understand why I'd done that. I explained to him that as a female reporter, I had to elbow and hip-check other journalists to force them out of my one-on-one interviews so that they couldn't steal my sound bites. A few minutes later, as I grilled the players for the scene, Bennett yelled, "Cut!" again. "Would you really ask these tough questions?" Before I could answer, a voice boomed from the corner of the soundstage: "Yup. And I was the target of it."

Out came Chad, a consultant on the film. We had a good laugh. My part remained in the film. It's one of the best experiences I've had as an actor and a reporter.

Lisa G: Tomb Raider

As I was in the midst of covering baseball, football, and basketball, Kenny called me with a completely different assignment.

"You're not going to believe this. But would you like to go to Egypt with Hugh Downs?"

Hugh Downs? One of the most respected broadcast news journalists ever?

Ahhhh . . . yeah!

Off I went to the Bahariya Oasis, deep in the Western Desert of Egypt, as the correspondent for a two-hour network special, *Live from Egypt: Opening the Tombs of the Golden Mummies*. My travel companions were Hugh Downs and the actor Bill Pullman, who was also an amateur Egyptologist.

It was the opportunity of a lifetime—and to this day, I consider it one of the greatest reporting assignments ever. The discovery of a labyrinth of underground tombs—believed to cover four square miles and be more than two thousand years old—was the most spectacular Egyptian archaeological find since Tutankhamun's tomb. Never before had so many mummies been uncovered at a single site. Dr. Zahi Hawass, the noted archaeologist and Egyptologist who led the excavation, believed there were close to ten thousand mummies buried there. I couldn't believe I had been chosen for the assignment. And to be working alongside Hugh Downs was exciting, intimidating, and surreal.

I met Hugh and his wife, Ruth, at a crew dinner in Cairo. He talked about my work—and I was blown away that this news legend had researched me and knew who I was.

Hugh Downs was the definition of professional. Even though it was a sweltering 100-plus degrees, he dressed impeccably in collared shirts and slacks. I traveled with Hugh, Ruth, a Bedouin guide, and Nola Roller, our wardrobe stylist, on a three-hour trek from Cairo to the Bahariya Oasis. As we drove through the White Desert, we passed sandy mesas and natural springs. Then we came upon what looked like a mound of shimmering diamonds. Our guide told us this was Crystal Mountain. We got out of the car to take a closer look.

As our guide explained that the diamonds were actually calcite crystal, he suddenly pulled up his robe, squatted, and took care of business. The mature me reminded me that this was a cultural difference. However, the twelve-year-old inner me was screaming, "He's pooping. I can't believe he's pooping!"

Of course, the twelve-year-old me could barely hear what the mature me was trying to say. As I struggled not to giggle, I eyed Hugh. I wasn't the only one. It seemed that the group was taking its cues from the veteran newsman. For a split second, I thought I saw his eyes widen. But that was it. He maintained his composure and kept asking questions. To me, that is the definition of the consummate professional.

When we arrived at the excavation site, vapors were swirling through the air. We were told they were gases escaping from the just-unsealed tombs. Still, it felt supernatural, as if the mummies' spirits were haunting us. Throughout our travels, locals would tell us that we should stay away from the discovery. There were rumors of unexplained deaths at other excavation sites.

"Don't breathe the air. Don't touch anything. Don't cast your eyes upon the skulls," they'd say, adding that we'd suffer the consequences of entering such a sacred place. "You will die within a week."

I have to admit, part of me was a bit terrified. But I understood that this was a rare experience, and I had to take advantage of all of it—even if it meant giving live reports from the middle of a tomb that had just been opened. As I walked into the cemetery, I was surrounded by rows and rows of mummies. I smiled for the camera but thought about the villagers' warnings. I was the first person to touch pieces of pottery in more than two thousand years. Would I somehow be punished for this?

During the final segment of the special, Hugh asked me to share the anchor desk with him to do a wrap-up. Then he asked for my impression live on camera. I hadn't expected the question, but I discussed how this glimpse into an ancient civilization served as a reminder that although thousands of years and continents apart, we aren't as different as we think.

Hugh nodded. "That's right, Lisa."

When we finished, he patted my hand.

"That was wonderful. Did you ever think about doing real news?"

I was flattered. Hugh Downs had seen how hard I worked and thought I had the chops to be a news reporter.

"I love sports," I said. "There are very few women doing what I'm doing. I think I could be a trailblazer."

Hugh sighed. Then he smiled. "Lisa, you're very likable, and you're a natural storyteller. Don't settle for sports. Reach higher."

Sometimes I wonder how different my life would have been if I'd said, "Okay, Hugh. I'd love to give it a try." He saw a spark of something in me. Why didn't I take this venerated newsman's assessment more seriously and explore another option? I've learned that part of being brave is opening yourself up to every opportunity. I was so focused on sports that I didn't allow myself to consider anything else. Who knows? Maybe I missed the chance of a lifetime. Or maybe the opportunity wouldn't have been right. But I should have given it a chance before dismissing it. That way, I'd never wonder, *What if?*

Hugh Downs had told me to reach higher. *What if* I had listened to him? *What if* I had seen where that road would have taken me?

What if I hadn't returned from the best trip ever and signed on for the worst job ever?

The Worst Job Ever (Really)

"This job sucks!"

I was standing in the bitter cold in the middle of nowhere dressed in leggings and a tank top while covered in some stranger's blood, snot, and sweat. Seconds earlier, I'd raced out of an arena after dodging flying beer bottles and pushing away creepers groping at me.

Then I picked up the phone to call the guy I always call when I hate my job.

"Kenny, how can they call this sports reporting?" I asked. "Because this is not a sport! It's two drunk knuckleheads trying to beat the shit out of each other. They have no business being in the ring."

"Lisa . . ."

"I've got some cretin's blood on me! It's nauseating. This is the worst job ever."

Yes, I'd said these exact words to Kenny before. This time, it wasn't an exaggeration. Being a ringside reporter for *Toughman*, an FX show that pitted two amateur boxers against each other in the ring for three rounds, was the absolute worst assignment I'd ever had. And to top it off, just a few hours before this mayhem, my rental car had skidded on an icy road during a blizzard and slammed into another car. Fortunately, the other driver and I were fine. The rental car—not so much.

"You're getting national exposure," Kenny said. "The ratings are enormous. Besides, you have a contract."

"I don't care. Get me out of it!"

Toughman had seemed like a decent gig. The show had been on for a few years and was extremely popular. I liked boxing. When I watched some of the *Toughman* reels, it didn't look so bad. But the tapes edited out the booze the boxers swilled before stepping into the ring. They edited out the brawls and knife fights that broke out in the crowd. They edited out the beer bottles hurled at the fighters—and ringside reporters.

I saw a polished, finished product hosted by Lawrence Taylor, the former New York Giants linebacker, and Matt Vasgersian, a sportscaster. If they were there, how bad could it be?

I found out—too late—that they actually weren't there. They commented on the fights from the comfort of a studio months after the bouts were recorded.

It was just another ringside reporter and me. Every week, Sean O'Grady, a former boxer—who did not have to wear a leotard—and I would travel to a different arena in some small town or city to interview these "fighters." The show called the boxers "amateurs," but these dudes didn't fit the definition of an amateur in the boxing world. Many of them had never even donned a pair of gloves. They signed up hoping to win a few hundred dollars in cash.

Then they'd pummel each other nearly to death. Between each round, I'd jump into the ring and try hard not to vomit. Their blood, sweat, and mucus poured onto me as I stuck a microphone in their face and forced a smile. The director would constantly demand that I get as close as possible to each boxer. I was literally under their armpits as their bodily fluids dripped all over me.

"This show is a disaster waiting to happen," I told Kenny. "Somebody's going to get killed, either a boxer, a spectator, or me."

The network wouldn't release me from my contract. But I got a doctor's note saying that the boxers' bodily fluids could result in my contracting HIV. Fox reluctantly released me. In 2005, a contestant died in a hospital hours after a competition—and *Toughman* was eventually canceled.

Tank Tops, Leggings, and Sports Geeks

After that debacle of a show, I was hired for a few sports pilots that didn't get picked up. Then I got a gig as cohost on *Sports Geniuses*, a sports trivia game. This show was perfect for me because I knew so many random sports factoids. I'd be on the street or in a restaurant or on an elevator, and I'd hear, "Lisa, name the starting lineup for the Los Angeles Lakers in 1984." "Lisa, who won the American League Cy Young Award in 1967?" I'd almost always know the answer (thanks, Dad). My friends and I would win free drinks at sports bars when guys would try to stump me (they never did).

I thought I beat out the competition because of my impressive sports knowledge. But when I headed to wardrobe that first day, I realized that my brain had nothing to do with it. My outfits again were tank tops and leggings. Meanwhile, Matt Vasgersian, my cohost (who was also the play-by-play analyst for *Toughman*), wore suits and ties.

I picked up the phone.

"Kenny, what the hell? I look like a Zumba instructor!"

"This is great exposure," he said.

"Oh, I'm exposed, all right. I thought I was hired because I know sports! I auditioned in a pantsuit. This is ridiculous."

"Lisa, you beat out a hundred women for this job," Kenny said. "Don't throw it away because you don't like the wardrobe."

He was right that dozens of women had auditioned. The show could replace me even faster than I could leave the building. So I backed down and sucked it up. Then I sucked it in so I could wriggle into those tights.

Back in 1992, when I'd first entered the broadcasting biz, a TV executive had told me to cut my hair short, wear conservative suits, lose the lip gloss, and stop smiling.

"You need to appear credible," he said, as if somehow credibility meant looking like a bank vice president.

What did "credible" even look like?

I believed I didn't have to lose my femininity to be taken seriously. "I'm going to wear what I want to wear," I said. "If I feel like wearing a dress, I'm going to wear it. If I feel like wearing a suit, I will. But you're not going to tell me how to dress."

But eight years later, I didn't fight back. Looking back, I realize my confidence had been eroded by a never-ending cycle of producers and executives weighing in on what my image should be in order to drive ratings. I believed I had to compromise in a way that I hadn't when I'd been a local reporter. I often wonder how different my career would have been if I had demanded a wardrobe change. What if I had threatened to walk if I didn't get to wear what I thought was appropriate? What if I'd confronted the executives and said, "How can I be taken seriously in this outfit when my *male* cohost is dressed professionally?"

But I thought if I balked, they'd just hire someone else.

Maybe they would have. Or maybe they would have agreed to my terms because I was too valuable to lose. At the time, I didn't see it that way. I didn't understand my value. I didn't realize that by acquiescing, I was setting the tone for the rest of my career at Fox Sports Net.

Damn my cowardice. I missed a huge opportunity to bravely demand the respect I deserved. But I didn't have the confidence to realize this back then. I was so afraid of losing something I desperately wanted that I didn't realize I had lost a bit of myself.

My job duties changed too. I had auditioned to be a cohost but ended up being the token hot girl. I displayed prizes and bantered with the contestants.

My skimpy outfits were a constant reminder of the compromises I'd made. I certainly wasn't a prude. I simply wanted to wear dresses that were comfortable and flattering—not leotards. Every time I'd step into wardrobe, my anger would start to simmer. My silent fury carried into my performance on the show. I was known as the smart-ass sports chick in a leotard who gave everyone a hard time. The contestants had no idea that underneath this tough girl facade was a woman who felt like a coward.

Best Damn/Worst Damn

Rumors had been swirling around for a while that Fox Sports Net was creating a groundbreaking show that would be billed as its answer to ESPN's *SportsCenter*. The brainchild of David Hill, president of FSN, *The Best Damn Sports Show Period* would feature a cast of superstar athletes, A-list celebrity guests, and a live studio audience. We heard that the network was pumping a fortune into it. On the Fox Studios lot in Century City, construction had begun on a multimillion-dollar set. Every day, there would be new intel about the show:

"The set looks like a man cave."

"Chris Rose was named the host."

"I heard they're auditioning comedians."

We learned that Tom Arnold had been hired to serve as the voice of the fans.

"They're going to cast a woman as a cohost."

Wait, what?

We'd hear the names of various female sports reporters and anchors from around the country who were being brought in to audition. No one had been hired, and the show was set to debut in a couple of weeks.

For one of the lame sports shows I was cohosting, I was dressed as a sexy feline in a tight leather catsuit for the Halloween episode. When we wrapped, I got a message that David Hill wanted to meet with me.

Hill had technically been my boss since I had started working at FSN a few years earlier, but I had never met him. I imagined this was about *Best Damn*, and I was thrilled. I wanted to make a great first impression, so I rushed to my dressing room to change into a suit. A production assistant stopped me in the hallway.

"David Hill wants to see you right now."

"I know. I'm just going to change."

The production assistant shook his head.

"He said to come up *right now*."

So I headed to David Hill's office dressed as a sexy cat. We laughed about it. He said he admired my moxie as a reporter and enjoyed my work as an anchor on *Southern California Sports Report*.

"You have a great balance of reporting on sports, news, and scores. And you're able to mix it up with your male cohosts." He said he thought I'd be perfect for *Best Damn*.

For years, that was how I'd recall my meeting with David Hill—a funny anecdote where I showed up to an interview with my boss in a leather catsuit.

He was a nice guy! The meeting went really well!

But that anecdote isn't completely accurate. I entered his office feeling extremely underdressed. While he sat behind his desk in a suit, I stood in front of him, dressed in a tight catsuit. My ears burned—always a telltale sign that I'm embarrassed and uncomfortable. He asked me questions, but I felt that he wasn't really listening to my answers. When I left his office, I was creeped out. I felt that I was being considered for the job not simply because I had the talent but because David had noticed me in a catsuit.

The gig would entail anchoring the sports updates during the show as well as debating the latest sports controversies with the male panel of mostly athletes for what was called the A block, the opening twenty minutes of the show.

There were rumors about a few women who were close to being hired. I watched some of the auditions. They were all beautiful, but they were laughing and agreeing with the guys, not having a real debate. I thought, *I'm going to go out there and have fun. But I'm not going to be afraid to disagree.* Even though the hosts were superstar athletes, I had something they didn't—a reporter's perspective. I would push back and ask tough questions, not just suck up to a bunch of millionaires, no matter how famous they were or how many championship rings they wore. Once again, I would be overprepared. They wouldn't expect it. This had always been my secret superpower. Still, I was nervous because this was the opportunity of a lifetime. I really wanted this job—maybe too much.

"They loved you," Kenny said a few hours after my audition.

I was named the update anchor and the first woman to cohost *The Best Damn Sports Show Period.* For the first twenty minutes, I'd debate the latest sports controversies with my cohosts. Then I'd head to my cubicle on the third-floor newsroom, where I'd shoot three-minute live sports updates against a green screen every twelve minutes for five hours. It was a really intense part of the job. Runners (young interns) would race up to me every few minutes with shot sheets—the highlights from all the games that day. I'd barely have time to review them before we'd go live. Then I'd narrate the action unscripted while watching a video of the highlights for the first time. I'd try to mix humor, sarcasm, and pop-culture references into my reports. I liked to show clips of strikeouts or bloopers along with home runs and touchdowns. I was on the air for about one hundred minutes of live TV a day, making me one of the most visible reporters in sports—male or female. Since I had to report on all the games, Benjie Kaze, my producer, and I were always the last to leave, sometimes after midnight.

In some ways, the show was truly groundbreaking. I was the lone female voice on the biggest dudefest ever. I debated sports controversies with athletes. But my take on issues was often very different from theirs. Unlike my colleagues, I wasn't a former pro athlete who'd earned millions of dollars. I was the daughter of a social worker and an immigrant. Looking back, I realize that my position on various controversies signaled the beginning of my social awakening. While the issues we discussed were rooted in sports, they often transcended sports.

For instance, there was an impending players' strike in Major League Baseball. The guys on the show—Tom Arnold, a comedian; John Salley, an NBA star; John Kruk, a Philadelphia Phillies first baseman; and Michael Irvin, a Dallas Cowboys wide receiver—were all for the strike, arguing that the players should be making more money.

"Rookies only make $200,000 a year," John Kruk bitched. The rest of the panel shook their heads as if this was a ridiculously low amount of money.

And I was thinking, *What? Are you kidding me? That's a lot of money! It's about twice what I'm making!*

These guys were superstar millionaires. They sounded clueless about the lives of regular folks, including me.

I thought about all the hours I'd spent at Dodgers Stadium as a beat reporter. I'd show up earlier than the other journalists because I liked to catch the batting practices of the home and visiting teams. Oftentimes, that was when I'd get some of my best stories. Tommy Lasorda, the former Dodgers manager, saw me there so often that he'd invite me to his Dodgers suite for pasta to "fatten me up."

As I watched the players get in their swings, the stadium workers—hot-dog and beer vendors, ushers, security staff, and cleaning crew—would trickle in. Many of the workers were Latino, and when they discovered my last name was Guerrero, I became one of them. But it wasn't our ethnicity that truly bound us. It was our love of baseball, especially the Dodgers. These are the guys I thought about when I heard that the players might go on strike.

"There are four sides to the issue," I said. "There are the players, the owners, the fans, and the people who work at the stadium, like Ruben Gutiérrez, who's been working at the stadium for thirty-three years. In 1994, he couldn't pay his utility bill because of a strike. That's who I care about more than the players. The owners won't miss a meal. The players won't miss a meal. But the people who work at the stadium might not be able to pay their gas bill."

This was one of my favorite moments on the show. It struck a chord with the audience, who burst into applause. (Years later, Ruben's widow told me that he had watched the show that night, and my comments had meant a lot to him.) Michael Irvin changed his opinion on the issue. "She's right," he said. And Tom Arnold? Well, he dug in his heels. "Boohoo, poor stadium workers."

I left the set proud of speaking out on behalf of these part-time and minimum-wage employees.

Then I heard, "LISA GUERRERO, PLEASE COME TO THE CONTROL ROOM!"

George Greenberg, the show's executive producer, was always calling me into his office or the control room for one reason or another.

"Stop being so argumentative," he said.

"But I'm debating my position. Isn't that what I'm supposed to do?"

"You need to be less combative."

What? The guys were constantly arguing with each other. Why was I being singled out for doing so?

"Can you at least smile more?" He paused. "And Lisa, my wife has a few suggestions on how you should do your makeup."

Are you kidding me?

There was so much I loved about *Best Damn*—the debates, the anchoring gig, the camaraderie on the set with the guys, who became like brothers—but every moment was rife with negotiations. Smile more. Argue less. Show more leg. The executives wanted me to be sexy and wear clothes that showed lots of skin. Every day, I'd take a few deep breaths before heading to wardrobe, wondering, *What getup will they have me in today?* I wasn't a star who could demand certain outfits. I like looking feminine, but I didn't want to overdo it. Most importantly, I wanted to be taken seriously as a journalist. After a while, I became proficient at negotiating my look. If I was in a blouse showing cleavage, I'd nix the miniskirt in favor of a longer skirt. If they wanted me to wear a short skirt, I'd ask for a more modest top. Every now and again, I'd sneak on a pair of slacks. The executives hated that. My legs—the very same legs that had once embarrassed me—were now a commodity. When the execs realized they had been obscured by a coffee table during the first few shows, they moved me to the right side of the set, where the camera could shoot my legs unobstructed.

Years after I left, I discovered that the sexism and misogyny that I experienced while at Fox Sports were standard operating procedure throughout the Fox organization. In 2016, Gretchen Carlson, a former Fox News journalist, filed a sexual harassment lawsuit against Roger Ailes, the chairman and CEO of Fox News, which led to an internal investigation of the network and a wave of sexual harassment claims against Ailes. In total, more than twenty women accused Ailes of misconduct, including Megyn Kelly, then a rising star at the network. The investigation resulted in the ouster of Ailes along with Fox News star Bill O'Reilly and Fox Sports President Jamie Horowitz.

A few years ago, when I watched *Bombshell*, a film based on the sexual misconduct charges against Ailes, I got chills. It was like glimpsing at moments from my Fox career. Ailes demanded that the desks and tables be glass so the audience could see the women's legs. Plus, female employees were encouraged to wear skirts instead of pants. When Ailes asked a young female hire to spin and hike up her dress to show off her legs, I felt as if I were reliving my interview with David Hill. By the time the movie ended, I was in tears.

The sports department has always been referred to as the toy department of the newsroom. At *Best Damn*, the women were the toys. The show's writers—primarily white, straight men—would create skits specifically so they could hire hot lingerie and bikini models; the more the better. There were sketches that called for well-endowed women to bounce around in skimpy outfits. In one bit, Tom Arnold played a doctor in a lab coat while a barely dressed woman sat on his lap and giggled. When the skits ended, some of the male cast and crew would descend upon these women. There were rumors of hookups and affairs.

The nameless women. That was how I thought of these voluptuous, scantily dressed women who breezed on and off the set. No one bothered to know anything about them, not even their names. To the cast and crew, they were interchangeable bodies sitting on a lap or jumping around the set or serving the guys Tecate or Coors. Sometimes when I'd catch a skit, I'd feel sick. These women were being marginalized and sexualized. They giggled through dumb frat-boy jokes that poked fun at them.

I understood these women all too well. They were models and actors—just as I'd been. They were hired to play a part on a popular show, believing this might be the big break that would catapult them to stardom. Some of the guys knew these women were hungry for exposure, and they dangled their power over them.

I felt a kinship with these women. Yes, the staff knew my name, but I was a woman being told to dress sexy, show leg, smile more, and argue less. I wanted to be taken seriously as a newswoman, but was it even possible in a climate where women were hired for their "hotness"?

I was conflicted. I had a foot in this misogynistic boys' club, but I wasn't a member (nor did I want to be). When I debated an issue with the guys, I felt like we were colleagues. We discussed and bantered and teased each other. But when I saw those nameless women running around the set, I wondered how these men truly saw me.

Years after I left, I discovered that a female executive at Fox had complained about sexually aggressive behavior by David

Hill. The woman, Paula Radin, had been a vice president for special events at Fox Broadcasting Company for seven years. She'd accepted a settlement in exchange for not filing a lawsuit. This had occurred in 1998—two years before I was called into David's office for my interview and eighteen years before Roger Ailes would be ousted from Fox.

A year after the settlement, Hill was promoted to chairman of Fox Sports Media Group. He had a successful twenty-four-year run with Fox, leaving in 2015 to open Hilly Inc., a Fox-backed production company. He also coproduced the 2016 Academy Awards. Paula Radin left Fox after she filed her complaint and became a freelance event producer.

This wasn't an isolated incident. I had heard that *Best Damn* was plagued by sexual harassment accusations and lawsuits. The female accusers represented every type of employee—executives, hair and makeup artists, wardrobe, and production. Rumors abounded that some of the lawsuits were settled out of court, while others were buried. One of the lawsuits described *Best Damn*'s atmosphere as an "environment of unrestrained sexual harassment."

Yup. That about sums it up.

I felt like I was alone on my own island. I was friendly with the guys, but I kept to myself. I'd occasionally sit outside with Tom Arnold while he smoked a cigar. But I wasn't included in their parties or nights out. My only friend was Benjie, my producer. He had an office near the newsroom, a few floors away from the man cave. He knew what was going on, but he was removed from it. When I wasn't at my update desk with Benjie, I stayed in my dressing room.

I was there preparing for a show when I heard a commotion down the hall.

"Oh, my God," a woman shrieked. "I can't believe he did that!"

One of the guys had apparently unzipped his pants and exposed himself to a female employee in what he thought of as a joke. She was pretty shaken up. I heard later that she reported the incident and sued Fox Sports Net.

None of this type of behavior happened in front of me. But the rumors were rampant. I began to feel increasingly uncomfortable. Most of the time, the women were encouraged to shrug it off. After all, we were just visitors to the man cave and expected to adapt to their caveman ways. If a woman did complain, the network settled quietly and the woman disappeared. And the harassers? Well, they were given extended contracts or promoted.

The Best Damn Sports Show Period was one of those shows people either loved or hated. After its July 2001 debut, it started to steadily build an audience. After a few months, it had established a cult following. Its popularity attracted superstar athlete guests like Sammy Sosa, Terrell Owens, and Shaquille O'Neal along with A-list celebrities such as Arnold Schwarzenegger, Ben Affleck, and Adam Sandler. A fan favorite of the show was a segment called "The Cage," where guests performed athletic challenges with the hosts. For instance, when Lance Armstrong was a guest, the hosts competed against him in a tricycle race.

By November, the show expanded from sixty to ninety minutes. In December, it jumped to two hours. By the summer of 2002, the show had launched a huge advertising and promotional blitz. We appeared on billboards and in radio and television ads.

Even harsh critics were praising the show's winning combination of sports, entertainment, and irreverent humor.

Best Damn's success and extended time slot provided me with the perfect opportunity to pitch my idea: serious, long-format sit-down interviews with sports superstars that would offer a glimpse into the person beyond their athletic achievement. I wanted to be the Barbara Walters of sports journalism.

I proposed my idea to George, the show's executive producer.

"Who are you going to get?" he asked.

I had thought about this. Why not shoot for the moon? I'd get one of the greatest and most controversial baseball players who had ever lived—and who rarely spoke to the press: Barry Bonds of the San Francisco Giants. He'd just broken the record for the most home runs in a season—seventy-three.

If I could get him, the others would follow.

I called everyone in Barry's camp—his agent, manager, and publicist and their assistants. When they didn't call me back, I called again and again until they did. I sent tapes of my work. After getting approval from Scott Boras, Barry's high-profile agent, my next task was to get the thumbs-up from his publicist, Rachel Vizcarra, who agreed to meet with me for lunch. As two of the few women in sports, we hit it off.

"I like you, but Barry makes his own decisions," she said. "Tell him he has my okay."

There were certain unspoken rules in baseball. One of them was that nobody approached Barry Bonds during batting practice. He was intense, and he loathed the media. The media was intimidated by him and stayed away. They'd watch his every move, but they wouldn't dare approach him.

But I finally had the blessing of his entire staff. They told me he knew I was coming.

A few minutes after Barry stepped out of the dugout, I marched over to him.

I could hear the rest of the media gasping behind me. "Oh, my God, what the hell is she doing?"

I introduced myself.

He nodded at me. "I don't do media."

"I know. But this isn't going to be your typical interview. I want to know what makes you tick. I want to know about your childhood and what you were like as a little boy. I don't want the latest controversy. I want to know about you. I even want to know why you hate the media."

He shook his head a few times. I prepared for his rejection, and then he surprised me.

"Okay, I'll do it."

Barry Bonds and Boogers

Barry Bonds's hatred for the media was palpable when I met with him in a conference room at Pac Bell Park, the Giants stadium (now called Oracle Park). I could feel the tension, and I could sense that he was questioning why he had agreed to the sit-down. His demeanor was making me nervous. There is nothing worse than conducting an interview with someone who clearly doesn't want to be there. I had to defuse the tension or I'd blow it.

"You have twenty minutes," Rachel said.

I thought, *How can I get this guy to loosen up even a little bit? How can I get his guard down?*

As a journalist, I've learned that humor is often a great way to cut the tension. If you can get your subject to laugh, you've established a rapport before the interview begins.

Then I thought, *Boogers.*

"Let's do a booger check," I said.

"A what?"

"Put your head back."

He laughed. "Nobody has ever checked me for boogers before."

"Well, that's why I'm a good journalist," I quipped.

He laughed hard. "Okay." He put his head back. "So, am I clean?"

"Yup!" I put my head back. "Am I?"

He laughed again. I relaxed—and got the most incredible interview of my life. This led to several more exclusives with him.

I was the first journalist to ask Barry on camera if he used steroids to enhance his performance (he denied it). He did admit to using creatine, a controversial substance used to bulk up, which was picked up by hundreds of news outlets. But what I loved most about our interviews were that they captured the guy off the field. At times, he seemed like any other dad bragging about his three kids. He also divulged that his animosity toward the media stemmed from his childhood. As a little boy learning to read, he felt like his dad, Bobby Bonds, also a major league ballplayer, was portrayed as a villain by the press. When he spoke of his parents' alcoholism, he was close to tears.

After the twenty minutes were up during that first interview, Rachel told me to wrap it up. But Barry smiled. "That's okay. I'll do more." We talked for another hour.

When the interview aired on *Best Damn*, I could tell the guys were blown away. John Salley turned to the camera.

"Lisa Guerrero's going to win an Emmy for that."

After the Bonds interview, other athletes agreed to be interviewed by me. I did sit-downs with stars like Alex Rodriguez, Randy Johnson, Curt Schilling, Kobe Bryant, Mia Hamm, and Nomar Garciaparra.

"I want to have my own show," I told George. "I want a spinoff where I can do in-depth sit-down interviews with star athletes."

This time, he didn't *okay, honey* me. He said it sounded like a great idea. I felt that I was a lot closer to making my Barbara Walters of sports dream a reality.

So what is Guerrero, a sports reporter or a sex symbol?

A *Los Angeles Times* sports media columnist posed this question after he discovered a photo of me braless in an orange shirt tied at my belly on the Fox website.

The article quoted Christine Brennan, a sports columnist and media critic. She said I wasn't a role model for women. Instead, I was performing a "disservice to [myself] and future generations of women coming up who want to be serious sports journalists."

"It plays to the oldest stereotype, that women can't be appealing with their brain, only with their body," she said.

Was this a fair criticism? Maybe. But the article was based on a photo of me in a shirt I never would have worn on FSN—in fact, it was from an old modeling shoot. I didn't understand—and still don't—why a woman has to be labeled either credible or funny, sexy or smart. Couldn't a woman be all of those things at once?

The article didn't mention my achievements as a sports reporter, my sit-down interviews, or the fact that because of my success, dozens of women were being hired at Fox Sports and at my previous stations. But they sure did mention—in lurid detail—the fact that I was braless in that modeling photo.

Super Bowl Pass

One of the perks of *Best Damn*'s success during the second year was that the entire cast would host the show from the Super Bowl at New Orleans' Superdome. We would be there the week before the game, providing me with plenty of time to line up a bunch of interviews.

A few days before we were set to leave, one of the executives summoned me to his office for a meeting. I assumed it was to go over the list of athletes I wanted to interview. Instead, he mentioned that we'd be staying at the same hotel and we'd have a lot of time to get to know each other better.

"You can stay in my room with me," he said. Was he joking? I felt my ears burn—a sure sign that I was turning bright red. I shook my head.

"That's not happening," I said, backing out of his office.

The next day, a production assistant told me I wouldn't be attending the Super Bowl.

"What? I've already been credentialed!"

"I was told you weren't going."

"Why?"

"I have no idea."

I called Kenny and told him what was going on. He made some phone calls and got back to me.

"They told me they're going in a different direction for the Super Bowl," he said. "They said it would be better if you did the live updates from the newsroom back here in LA."

But I knew exactly what had happened. I had been called into the executive's office a few days before we were supposed to leave so he could gauge my reaction to his proposition. If I seemed amenable, great. If I wasn't into it, he could switch me out before it was too late. And that was just what he did. Another woman replaced me. No matter what I accomplished, no matter what big names I got for the show, I felt like one of those nameless women with interchangeable bodies. I decided to shake it off and focus on the prize: my own show. Then I wouldn't have to put up with any of this anymore.

The Big Roast

My contract was set to expire at the end of the second season. Kenny was in the midst of negotiating a new one for me, but the network wouldn't include my spinoff show or specials in the deal. The executives kept telling me it would happen, but they wouldn't commit on paper.

And then John Kruk, one of the hosts, announced that he was leaving. He wanted to pursue other opportunities. As a send-off, the producers decided to hold a televised roast.

"Everyone's going to take a turn at the podium. Then we'll bring in some professional comedians to really roast him."

I was apprehensive. I'd seen some roasts—they got pretty nasty. I'd never roasted anyone before. It definitely wasn't my kind of thing.

"Don't worry. The writers will come up with something for you. You'll give him some shit, like you usually do. Nothing mean-spirited. It will be really short. Maybe two paragraphs."

The man cave was set up like a comedy club. The *Best Damn* boys and I sat on a dais. The audience—filled with big-name athletes—sat at round tables. Each of the *Best Damn* hosts stood in front of a podium and razzed John. When we finished, the comedians took over the stage.

I was glad to be done with my portion of the roast and ready to relax in my chair onstage. But as the first comedian started his routine, I realized that the roast was no longer just about John; it was about all of us.

The first comedian said some stuff about John, Tom, John Salley, and D'Marco Farr. Then he turned toward me.

"Lisa, who did you fuck to get this job?"

The crowd laughed. I was absolutely stunned. I felt dizzy. I couldn't catch my breath. My heart throbbed. The comedian continued, but I don't know what else he said. That line echoed in my head—along with the guffaws. I sat on the dais with the bright lights blasting my face and cameras pointing at me to gauge my reaction. I took some deep breaths and struggled not to lose it. I didn't want to cry in front of my colleagues and the audience of athletes.

But that wasn't the end of it. Comedian after comedian stood behind the podium ribbing John and the *Best Damn* guys. But they saved their most brutal attacks for me.

"Let's talk about that Barry Bonds interview," a comedian said as I braced myself for another assault. "Lisa, we know how you got that exclusive—you were on your knees!"

And then there was a barrage of jokes about my breasts.

Each comedian's repertoire was the same: I gave blow jobs for interviews, slept my way to the job, and had big tits.

As the lights blazed down on me, I struggled to rein in my emotion. But my eyesight went blurry as tears poured down my face. I quickly wiped them away. The cameras captured all of this. I thought about all the athletes in the audience whom I had interviewed because I'd earned their respect. Some of them looked at me with absolute pity.

There were other comments, but those are the ones I remember nearly verbatim. I replayed them over and over for years afterward. I also remember the laughter those comments received. Most of the audience roared. So did my colleagues.

I had spent the last couple of years working hard to earn the respect of my cohosts, bosses, the media, and the athletes I interviewed. The roast felt like a punch in the gut. As I sat on the stage, I was in shock. Confused. Furious. I felt assaulted. It was a massacre of the credibility I had worked so hard to earn.

I thought about the nameless women—I had pitied them because they had been the butt of so many jokes on set. But this seemed much worse than anything they'd endured. This was personal—as if the comedians had a vendetta against me because I was a woman who believed I belonged on that stage, because I was a woman who believed I had opinions that mattered.

There was a break in the middle of the roast. To this day, I have no idea if it had been scheduled or if it was because my face was wrecked. I quickly ran off the dais and headed to the control room, where George Greenberg and Eric Weinberger, another producer, were watching the show and hysterically laughing. They looked up at me.

"What's wrong?" George asked, grinning.

"What's wrong?" I repeated, shocked. I could barely speak through sobs. My face was a mess of tears, makeup, and snot.

"Are you listening to what they're saying about me?"

They stared at me but didn't speak.

"You cannot air this!" I continued. "I want this cut out. This is demeaning. This is outrageous. I can't believe they're talking about me like this. How can you allow them to call me a whore on our own show?"

They shook their heads and smiled as if I were a small child having a temper tantrum over something really silly.

"Lisa, it's all in fun. Don't worry. Everyone knows they're just joking."

"It's not funny. They're shredding my credibility!"

"Lisa, we'll deal with it later. It's no big deal. You have to get back onstage."

"I will not go back up there."

"You have to," one of them said. "We'll tell them no more jokes about you."

The makeup people repaired the damage, and I went back onstage. It was only for a few more minutes, but it felt like hours and hours. I couldn't wait to get off the stage. But at least there were no more comments about me.

Afterward, I went to human resources to file a complaint. Then I called the guy I always call when I'm furious at work.

My mother, Lucy Guerrero, was a Chilean immigrant who married my father, Walter Coles, when he was earning his master's degree in social service administration from The University of Chicago. Here they were as newlyweds in 1963.

After my mother died in 1972, my father raised my little brother, Richard, and me. Here we were in 1977 in San Diego. I was thirteen years old with glasses, braces, and hair I chopped myself.

"Q-Tip" as a freshman at Edison High School in Huntington Beach, California. I was still cutting my own hair, dressing badly, and dealing with a perpetually split bottom lip thanks to my braces.

I finally got my act together later in high school. Here I was on graduation day in 1982. The next time I stepped foot on campus was thirty-nine years later when I was inducted into the Edison High School Hall of Fame in 2021.

I slowly morphed into a blonde while cheering for the Los Angeles Rams from 1984–1987, becoming a captain my final season. During this era the Rams played at Anaheim Stadium in Orange County, California.

Photo courtesy of Jon SooHoo

After cheering for the Rams, I became the Director of the Atlanta Falcons Cheerleaders and then the New England Patriots Cheerleaders. Here I was with my squad in Atlanta before a game at Fulton County Stadium in 1989.

In the '90s I returned home to LA to pursue my dream of becoming a sports broadcaster. My first big break was at CBS2 on Sports Central. In this photo, I'm covering UCLA football at the Rose Bowl, shooting a postgame report.

After a couple years at CBS2, I jumped over to Fox 11—which quickly led to promotions from local, to regional, to national networks—and then I landed at Fox Sports Net in 2001.

While at Fox Sports Net, I covered the Dodgers, Lakers, Clippers, Kings, Chargers, UCLA, and USC. One of my favorite memories is interviewing Kobe Bryant, which I did multiple times, including this postgame interview in 2001, shortly before his team won another NBA Championship.

Christmas with the *Best Damn* boys in Season 2 of the show: Tom Arnold, John Salley, Chris Rose, D'Marco Farr, and John Kruk. I'm wearing yet another short skirt, which the producers preferred me in.

Interviewing New York Jets head coach Herman Edwards before the *Monday Night Football* regular season opener in 2003. This may have been the last time I had a natural smile on my face. After the game I made a flub that would haunt me the rest of the season. © *American Broadcasting Companies, Inc. All Rights Reserved.*

Later in 2003 the stress on my face became evident. I was criticized mercilessly for seemingly everything I did. After the game pictured here, a sports columnist wrote about how my silver hoop earrings were "distracting and unprofessional." Really?? © *American Broadcasting Companies, Inc. All Rights Reserved.*

One of the great joys in my career was getting to play myself in the Academy Award–nominated film *Moneyball* in 2011. I was told that director Bennett Miller, Brad Pitt, and the producers saw old video archives of me as a tough-talking reporter and wanted me to recreate that vibe in the film. Here I was shooting the locker-room scene.

Yes, *Melrose Place*'s Grant Show was as cute and charming as fans of his hit series would have dreamed him to be. We dated in 1999 while I was starring on another Aaron Spelling show, *Sunset Beach*, on NBC.

In 2004 following a tumultuous season on *Monday Night Football*, I married Scott Erickson, a World Series champion who had appeared in *People* magazine's "Most Beautiful" issue. We divorced a few years ago but remain friends.

One of my favorite assignments was as a correspondent on the Fox Network special *Live from Egypt: Opening the Tombs of the Golden Mummies* in 2000. Here I was with actor Bill Pullman on location near Cairo, Egypt.

When I was a sportscaster, I dreamed of becoming "the Barbara Walters of sports." Years later I was invited to be a guest cohost on *The View* and met (and got to spar with) the legend herself.

I especially loved working with Joy Behar and Whoopi Goldberg, who couldn't believe how brave I was to "chase bad guys" on *Inside Edition*. I said being brave on TV empowers others to be brave too.

Here I was at the *Inside Edition* newsroom in New York City with Deborah Norville. She's hosted the program since 1995, and it's always a pleasure to see her on my trips to the Big Apple.

In 2013 we shot an *Inside Edition* investigation into Rita Crundwell, a former Treasurer of Dixon, Illinois, who admitted to embezzling over $53 million from the city. Here I was asking her some tough questions on the way into court along with my cameraman, Filip Kapsa, and producer, Larry Posner.

On location in the Midwest for *Inside Edition* in 2018.

Hitting the red carpet in style for the 2022 Daytime Emmys! *Inside Edition* has been nominated for Outstanding Entertainment News Program for five out of the last six years in a row.

Shooting a stand-up in California for *Inside Edition* with an assist from producer, Larry Posner, on reflector duty.

Years ago, I began learning to create mosaic art using recycled materials along with various types of stained glass, ceramic, and found objects. Here I was with "Aztec Flame," a fireplace surround I built for my old Malibu Spanish-style beach house in 2009.

I spend a lot of time hosting and speaking at fundraisers and nonprofit events around the country. A few years ago I was a presenter at the Prism Awards, which honors the creative community for accurate portrayals of substance abuse and mental health.

My "Being Brave" keynote speech resonates with audiences around the world. Here I was in 2019 sharing my message with Town Clock CDC in support of survivors of domestic abuse.

This time, Kenny didn't talk about national exposure or ratings. He didn't tell me to be patient.

"I don't want to renew my contract," I told him.

He agreed. "There'll be other opportunities for you. I promise."

In many ways, the show had been a rewarding experience. I realized I could hold my own and had what it took to battle it out with my sports heroes over topics like draft picks, contract negotiations, or players' strikes. But the roast was yet another reminder that despite my hard work, I would never be given my own show.

I was done. I left *Best Damn* at the height of its popularity.

Years later, Tom Arnold called to apologize for not sticking up for me that day.

"You put up with so much. I'm sorry you went through it," he said. "I should have been there for you."

I told him he didn't need to apologize. He'd always been kind to me. Besides, what could he have done? I needed to take a stand—and I did. It was a tough decision. But it was a brave decision. I had gained the confidence to realize my value. I was courageous enough to know better things were on their way.

Best Damn ended its run seven years later, in 2009. It never garnered the ratings David Hill had dreamed of after those first successful couple of years. It would have been fascinating to see some of the issues we could have debated during the last few years, especially in light of the #MeToo movement. Would the show have tackled topics like sexism in sports? Players accused of domestic violence? NFL cheerleader lawsuits? Convicted sex offender Dr. Larry Nassar and the hundreds of female gymnasts he assaulted? Misogyny, racism, and anti-LGBTQ bullying in the NFL?

Probably not.

This was one man cave that has been buried in TV history along with the Neanderthals who ran the damn joint.

Good riddance.

9

Meeting Mr. Right

y friends and I had a name for my dating pattern. We called it my "three-date curse with the guys in nice shirts."

The first date would begin with my confession: "I'm a workaholic. I don't cook. I will never do your laundry or clean your house. I don't want to get married. I don't want kids. Ever."

Some guys left skid marks getting out of there so fast. But if a dude got through that rant before salad was served, things went well. They thought I walked on water because I can talk sports for hours and am not vegan, gluten-free, vegetarian, or a special-needs eater. I order off the menu and love steak and potatoes. By the second date, I'd be the dude's dream girl. Most likely this date would take place at some sporting event. I'd drink beers and eat hot dogs and talk more sports. Oftentimes, he'd say something like "I want you to meet my parents." Hell, he might even mention marriage.

And the third date? It has an auspicious beginning. The guy can't believe we're still talking sports. He thinks we have so much in common because, well, sports. But then, it happens.

Somewhere in the middle of that date, he'll ask me something about my job, and it will dawn on him that part of what I do involves spending a lot of time in locker rooms with naked millionaires.

Then the conversation goes something like this:

"You really don't want to be a sports reporter forever, right?"

"Wrong."

"But if we get serious, you'd quit, right?"

"Why is that?"

"Because my girlfriend isn't gonna be in a locker room with naked athletes!"

And there will be no fourth date.

After years of the three-date curse, I'd given up on relationships. I figured I wasn't going to meet anyone who would be okay with those locker-room interviews or my insane hours. And as for kids? Everyone—my family and friends—thought I'd change my mind when I met the right guy. But I knew I wouldn't. Even as a little girl, I had no desire to play with baby dolls.

I was thirty-eight. I had my family, friends, and work. My life was busy and fulfilling. But I'd be lying if I didn't admit that there were times I longed for romance and companionship. I'd just have to meet someone who was superconfident in their career so they wouldn't feel threatened by mine. The last decade had taught me that that was a nearly impossible task.

One of my proudest accomplishments during *Best Damn* was my Barry Bonds interview. When it wrapped, I was exhausted but exhilarated. I looked over at my producer, Benjie, and I knew we were thinking the same thing: This was our Emmy moment.

And then Rachel Vizcarra, Barry's publicist, opened her mouth. I figured she was about to heap some praise on me.

"Barry, don't you think Lisa and Scott Erickson would make a great couple?" she said.

Barry thought for a moment. "Yeah, they'd be really good together."

What?

I had just conducted the greatest interview of my career! And they were pimping me out to some baseball player? I was a bit offended. And very, very not interested. I'd never met Scott, but I'd reported on him during *Best Damn*. He was a superstar pitcher for the Baltimore Orioles. A few years earlier, he'd played for the Minnesota Twins and had thrown the first ever no-hitter at the Metrodome. And he had won a World Series.

All this meant one thing: This guy must have an enormous ego.

Rachel scrolled through photos on her cell.

"Scott was named one of *People* magazine's '50 Most Beautiful.' After the story ran, modeling agencies wanted him to sign with them. But he turned them all down." Rachel said he'd been approached to be the star of the first season of the television series *The Bachelor*. He'd turned that down too.

Rachel handed me her phone. I looked at photos of Scott from the *People* magazine shoot. Wow! The guy was gorgeous, with sky-blue eyes, brown hair, tan skin, and a square jaw. He was also big trouble in a black leather jacket and maroon leather pants.

Absolutely not. This dude is going to be too much work.

I'd covered sports long enough to have learned that professional baseball players were a pain in the ass. Too many of them were complete egomaniacs—especially the pitchers. And baseball culture is rife with men who cheat . . . on their wives, their girlfriends, or baseball itself (by using steroids or other performance-enhancing drugs).

"I'm not interested," I said.

Rachel looked at me as if I were crazy. "You know who was interested?" She leaned in closer. "Julia Roberts. She was on the cover of the 'Beautiful People' issue. She saw his photo and called his manager to set up a date. Scott wasn't interested."

"Welp, this guy is not for me," I said.

Rachel shook her head. And that was that. Or so I thought.

A few days went by. My phone rang. It was an unknown number, but I answered it.

"Hi, Lisa, it's Scott Erickson. Rachel told me to call you."

He seemed under the impression that I had asked him to call me!

"I'm not interested," I said. Then I hung up.

Scott called back. He thought we had gotten disconnected. When it dawned on him that I'd hung up, he sounded startled.

"I think there's some confusion. Rachel thinks we should meet."

"I'm not interested in meeting."

And I hung up again.

Besides being a World Series champ, Scott Erickson was the most persistent man I'd ever met. It became a running joke. He'd call. I'd tell him I wasn't interested. A few days would go by. He'd call again. I think he'd gone through life never ever hearing the word "no" from any woman. When I said no, he was immediately interested.

"Don't hang up on me yet. We have friends in common. Let's just meet for coffee," he said.

"I can't. I'm busy."

One of Scott's friends was John Kruk, my *Best Damn* cohost. "I hear Scott's been calling you," he said. "Why won't you go out with him? He's a great guy."

That was the consensus. Scott Erickson was a great guy who was a team leader. He had a reputation for being a workhorse who never cracked a smile on the field. His nickname was Dr. Death. He wore black socks, black shoes, and a black rock-'n'-roll T-shirt under his uniform. He even used a black glove.

It seemed that everyone loved Scott Erickson. His teammates loved him. His opponents feared him but also loved him.

Still, I wasn't interested.

"I have an idea," Scott said over the phone. "Let's make a bet."

It was October 2002, and the Anaheim Angels were playing the San Francisco Giants in the World Series. This was the fourth time in the history of the series that two teams from the same state were playing against one another. Since Scott had grown up in Sunnyvale, a town outside San Francisco, he was a die-hard Giants fan. I'd grown up in Southern California and was rooting for the Angels.

He explained that the loser would fly out to the winner's city and take the winner to dinner.

Even if I lost, I would never fly to San Francisco to take Scott out to dinner. But I figured it was a way to stall the inevitable—at least until the series ended.

"Okay," I said.

Unfortunately, it didn't look very promising for the Angels. Going into game six, the Giants held a 3–2 series lead. I reported on the game at Anaheim Stadium for *Best Damn*. As I interviewed players, I ran into Barry Bonds.

"Did you go out with Scott yet?"

"Nope."

"You should. He's a great guy."

I didn't mention to Barry that I was betting against his team. It didn't matter. The Angels were poised to lose big. By the end of the seventh inning, the Giants had a 5–0 lead. They were going to win the club's first world championship in forty-eight years—and I'd have to welsh on a bet. But suddenly, the Angels rallied, stunning everyone with a 6–5 victory over the Giants. The next night, the Angels easily won the seventh game, 4–1. It was the franchise's first world championship. Even better, I didn't have to fly to San Francisco. I breathed a huge sigh of relief.

The phone rang.

"You pick a restaurant," Scott said.

I chose Katana, a sushi restaurant on Sunset Boulevard that was very close to my Hollywood Hills home. I figured I'd drive down the hill, have dinner, and leave. Quick in and out. We agreed to meet in the lobby of Mondrian, the hotel where he was staying, which was a few blocks from Katana. I parked my car with the valet and walked in.

As I waited, I started dreading the whole arrangement. A night out with an all-star, World Series, *People*'s "Most Beautiful" guy was a recipe for disaster. I braced myself for a couple of hours of epic boredom with a textbook narcissist.

And then . . .

The most beautiful man I had ever seen walked into the lobby. Scott Erickson did not even look like a real person. He was a walking statue of David dressed in a purple Versace silk dress shirt and jeans.

I also noticed that this perfect dude was sweating up a storm. He'd already pitted out his silk shirt. His face was clammy. I couldn't believe that this beautiful superstar athlete was nervous about meeting me. I found it completely endearing. Behind the all-star pitcher was a normal guy who was scared, just like everyone else. I had prepared myself not to like him. His sweaty armpits won me over.

In those few moments, I had an epiphany. I had judged this guy even though I didn't know him because I was scared too. It was easier to say no to him than to take a chance and be disappointed. How many times do we miss out on connections—romantic or otherwise—because of fear?

We walked toward the restaurant and stopped at an Irish pub along the way, where we ran into a baseball player we both knew. As the television above the bar reported on a story about a baseball player who'd gotten in trouble for saying he'd never play with a gay teammate, the guy nodded in agreement.

"I wouldn't want to play with a gay guy either," he said.

Well, that did it for me. I stepped into my *Best Damn* persona.

"Why wouldn't a gay man make a good teammate?"

"It would be terrible for team chemistry."

"I guarantee you have had gay teammates. You just don't know it."

"I would know it if I did."

"No, you wouldn't."

"I think I'd be able to tell."

"How?"

We spent about a half hour sparring about whether there were gay players in the MLB. Meanwhile, Scott sipped his beer and watched us. He didn't say a word. When it was time to go, the baseball player and I said goodbye.

"We'll agree to disagree," I said.

Scott was quiet as we walked the block to Katana.

"Sorry, I just get passionate about things," I finally said.

"Yeah, I can see that."

I waited for him to say something else, but he didn't. I thought I'd blown it big time. I'd gone into the date with a bad attitude, but I'd wound up liking the guy more than I had expected. And Scott had pursued me for weeks and weeks, but now he probably wanted to ditch me as fast as possible.

Dinner was pretty much the same. I did most of the talking. Afterward, we walked back to the valet and hugged. When he leaned in to kiss me, I moved the wrong way. It was a really bad off-the-mark first kiss. But that kiss summed up the date— awkward, embarrassing, and without connection.

I drove home, thinking, *That's it. I'll never see Scott Erickson again.* I felt a pang of disappointment because he'd turned out to be a sweet, soft-spoken guy who was nothing like the cocky jerk I had expected. As I pulled onto my street, the phone rang.

"I think I have to stay another night because I can't have that be our final moment. Can I take you to dinner tomorrow?" Scott asked.

"I'd love it."

The next night, we went to dinner and had an awesome time. The conversation flowed easily. We laughed and discovered we shared a similar sense of humor. We ended up making out in front of a cowboy bar on Sunset. And that was that.

Later, I called my dad. "I found the man I'm going to marry."

I could hear Dad's smile. "What? I've never heard you say anything like that before."

"Yup. He's really special."

When I laid down my gauntlet, Scott was fine with it.

"I don't want kids."

"Really? Me either!"

"Don't get me wrong; I like kids. I just don't want my own."

"Me too. I really like my friends' kids, but the kid thing is just not for me. After I retire from baseball, I don't want any responsibilities. I want to travel." (Put a pin in this one—it will come back to haunt me.)

And so began what was then the most important love affair of my life. In many ways, Scott was the perfect guy for me. He was comfortable and confident in his skin. He respected what I did. He certainly didn't worry about me being around naked jocks, especially since he was one of them. He was completely committed to his job, his teammates, and me. He was my biggest supporter, encouraging me to follow my dreams. When things turned sour at *Best Damn*, Scott had my back. He rented a minivan and helped pack up my office and dressing room.

"Trust me, you could get a job anywhere. You're talented, and the players respect you. You should have your own show," he said.

I was overwhelmed by the bigness of Scott's life. He was a multimillion-dollar athlete who lived large. When he invited me to his Tahoe home that he had designed, he referred to it as his cabin. He picked me up at the airport, and we drove up a winding mountain road through South Lake. I was confused when we stopped at a hotel.

"I thought you were taking me to your home."

"This *is* my home," he said.

I was floored. He'd spoken about it so modestly. This wasn't the cabin I had expected. It was a twenty-thousand-square-foot beautiful Italian villa built into the side of the mountain. The house had an indoor swimming pool, a disco, a huge gym, a Western-style bar, an elevator, and balconies on every level. Each room had enormous windows offering stunning views of the crystal-blue lake. When I walked around the house, taking it all in, I could barely breathe. The enormity of the place was overwhelming.

Most of our time together was spent visiting each other for a few short days, either in Tahoe or at my place in Los Angeles. We'd been dating only a few months when we started talking about marriage. I silently wondered if I could make a good wife. I wasn't doing any of the wifey things. I wasn't going to have children. I didn't know how to take care of a house. I couldn't cook. There were times I'd be in Scott's Tahoe kitchen and nearly have a nervous breakdown.

"I can't be a good wife to you because I don't know how to be a hostess in this big house. I don't even know how to cook. Don't you want a wife who can cook?"

Scott would smile. "I've seen your kitchen. I know you don't cook. You don't have to. I'll do the cooking. I'm very particular about what I eat, so I have to cook for myself anyway."

And he did. Scott was a great cook. He made the best spicy steaks I've ever had. Scott would pour me a glass of wine and tell me to relax while he prepared a meal. I'd sit at his enormous center island and oversee. Then I'd act as his sous chef, dicing vegetables or marinating. Little by little, I started cooking the meals too. Now my steaks are (almost) as good as his.

Any fears I had of getting married, Scott would quickly assuage. I was afraid I wouldn't be a good wife, but Scott assured me that he didn't want a traditional wife. I was afraid that my ambitions would have to take a back seat to Scott's, but he encouraged me to achieve my goals.

Looking back, I realize that after the fiasco with Hugh, I'd been terrified of relationships. That was why I had built so many obstacles during those early first dates with the guys in nice shirts. Because Scott was confident in who he was, he was able to get behind my facade and quell any doubts I had about commitment. It takes courage to share your life with someone, especially when you're thirty-eight and have become accustomed to being alone. It also takes bravery to be honest, to admit your limitations and your weaknesses, because you risk losing the person you love. But it's always better to expose them than to hide them and then have them exposed. I told Scott exactly who I was, and he did the same.

When I left *Best Damn*, my acting agent suggested I go on some auditions. I was cast in the independent film *The Play-maker* as a tough sports reporter opposite the gorgeous actor Boris Kodjoe. He played a football star, and our characters have a fling. I know, tough job.

Since Scott was recovering from surgery for a torn labrum, he had free time to join me on location. We set off to New Orleans to begin rehearsals and wardrobe fittings. Nearly as soon as we landed, we learned that the producers had lost their funding. As they scrambled for financing, Scott and I really got to know each other. One week turned into two weeks and then three weeks—and the producers still had not met their budget. Scott and I didn't care. This was the first time we'd spent more than a long weekend together. We explored the city, ate delicious meals, and relaxed. In some ways, it was like a honeymoon (except the producers were picking up the tab).

We discovered that we were really compatible. I'm low maintenance, and so is Scott. We both travel light (I can pack a week's worth of clothes in a carry-on). And we're both easily entertained. We were ready for any adventure, and we were ready to do nothing at all. We'd linger over lunches and dinners. We'd sit outdoors listening to the street musicians and buskers. We'd meander through cobblestone streets and poke around antique shops.

As we strolled through the French Quarter, we stumbled upon a psychic medium who did readings for $25.

"That's a hoot. Let's do it," I said.

When it comes to psychics, I'm a complete skeptic. Years later, when I joined *Inside Edition*, I investigated fake psychics and explained how they can extract information without their subjects realizing it. We walked in, paid our fee, sat down, and prepared for a good laugh. The psychic stared at me for a few seconds. Then she blurted out, "You lost your mother, didn't you?"

"Yes." I nearly choked.

"She's here, right now," the psychic said, pointing to a space next to me. "Your mother is always behind your right shoulder." The psychic cocked her head toward Scott. "She wants you to know she likes him very much. Very much."

Scott and I stared at the woman, our mouths hanging open. I thought I might faint. Her eyes darted from Scott to me.

"You are going to get married," she said.

Afterward, she gave us a cassette of the reading. If I didn't have that tape, I would think I'd imagined the moment. I like believing that my mother's watching over me, and now I feel that she is always with me and within me. In fact, I often talk to her about my trials and triumphs.

When we left, Scott said, "Now we really have to get married."

We continued our stroll and passed a consignment shop.

"And if we're thinking marriage, let's see what types of diamonds you like."

As days passed, we wondered if the movie would ever get funding. After years of working nonstop, including holidays and weekends, I loved this state of limbo, where we could spend endless days exploring the city and learning about each other. The producers would tell us they were a bit closer to financing, I'd say, "That's great." But I was silently thinking, *Just a little longer.*

One day, Kenny called. He sounded excited.

"You need to fly to New York next week. *Monday Night Football* wants to interview you for the sideline reporter job."

Monday Night Football? Wow!

But I was having the time of my life. I was cast in a movie. I had dreams of being the Barbara Walters of sports. Being a sideline reporter sounded like a thankless job.

"Kenny, no, thanks."

"Lisa, did you hear me? This is *Monday Night Football*, the most important sports show in the history of television! It gets thirty to forty million viewers each week—talk about exposure. With this platform, you can do anything you want."

Hmmmm . . .

I said yes, I'd fly to New York.

Scott began designing an emerald-cut diamond engagement ring.

I would soon become engaged and land one of the biggest jobs in broadcasting.

It sounded too good to be true. And, well, you know what that usually means . . .

10

Fumble!

I recently rummaged through some old boxes and found my VHS tapes from *Monday Night Football*. I debated whether I should look at them. Would they confirm that I was as horrible as the media had said? As I had come to believe for the last twenty years? When I finally watched, I nervously waited for that moment when I sucked.

I waited and waited.

It didn't come.

Instead, I thought, *I was good at that job! What was the media talking about?* When I finished watching, I broke down. I cried for my younger self, who had nearly been destroyed by the media's narrative of me. I also cried for my older self, who still carried around the humiliation of that experience.

Being a sideline reporter for *MNF* was both a dream job and a complete nightmare.

It didn't start out that way. The job would be a new take on conventional sideline reporting. That was what Freddie Gaudelli, the show's executive producer, said when I interviewed for the position.

He said he didn't envision me as a traditional correspondent. Instead, he saw me more as a sports-meets-entertainment reporter. He explained that I'd report from the sidelines as well as the stands, interviewing celebrities and fans. He even mentioned that if a couple decided to get married during a game, I'd officiate the wedding.

I loved everything about that job description. So I was thrilled when, a few days after my interview, I was offered the position. With close to forty million people tuning in weekly, this was the biggest gig a woman could get in sports broadcasting. I'd report on the game with Al Michaels and John Madden, two sports broadcasting legends. But not only would I be part of the American institution that is *MNF*, I would also be involved in its transformation.

When *MNF* debuted on ABC on September 21, 1970, with a game between the New York Jets and the Cleveland Browns, it was an instant phenomenon. Soon close to fifty million people would adjust their schedules to tune in every week. But *MNF* was more than a game; it was an event featuring colorful characters like broadcasters Howard Cosell and Don Meredith. (O. J. Simpson had a brief stint as a broadcaster.) Often their verbal sparring and antics during the game made more news than the game itself. When then President Richard Nixon visited the booth (*MNF* was that big), Don Meredith made national headlines by referring to him as "Tricky Dick." It was during an *MNF* game between the New England Patriots and Miami Dolphins on December 8, 1980, that Howard Cosell broke the news that John Lennon had been killed.

The show was so popular that other Monday events declined—movie attendance plummeted, bowling leagues rescheduled games for Tuesday, and rival television stations aired reruns. And even though the ratings have been on the decline since the 1970s, *MNF* is the longest-running prime-time sports program in American television history.

It was big news that there would be a new reporter on the sidelines for the 2003 season. The media covered it extensively and speculated about what woman it would most likely be. I was under a gag order until the reveal on ABC's *Good Morning America*. In late July, I flew to New York City for the official announcement. Charlie Gibson, who hosted *Good Morning America* with Diane Sawyer, introduced me. When he did, he sounded downright disappointed.

Instead of asking about my work on television, he referred to me as a former cheerleader. It seemed to me that Charlie didn't think I was qualified. But I smiled wide. "Well, Charlie, I was a cheerleader years ago. But I've been a sports reporter and anchor in Los Angeles for a decade, and I was on *The Best Damn Sports Show Period*."

He said he thought Melissa Stark was really good at the job.

Melissa Stark was the woman I was replacing. I kept the smile plastered on my face. "Everyone loves Melissa. She's great. But I'm really excited to be the new sideline reporter."

I waited for the next question. But Charlie wrapped it up and walked away. I stood on the studio's outdoor set at the corner of Broadway and West Forty-Fourth Street, feeling shell-shocked. I'd flown across the country for a few seconds of airtime.

After the interview, friends and family called, all with the same question: "What did you do to piss off Charlie Gibson?"

"Nothing."

The guy didn't know me and had never seen my work, but he already hated me.

I had no idea that this would be a sentiment shared by the sports media critics. Nearly as soon as my name was announced, the attacks began.

"Nothing but a teleprompter reader."

"A ridiculous new low for ABC."

"Another example of looks taking precedence over talent."

"A bimbo."

"A blow for women."

I watched on television as Keith Olbermann, then an ESPN superstar, said that Al and John should resign in protest.

What had I done to ignite such anger? I was stunned, hurt, and utterly baffled by the media's reaction. It was as if my accomplishments during the past ten years had disappeared. They didn't mention my recent sports reporting, anchoring, or exclusive interviews with top athletes. Instead, they mentioned what they called my "controversial past"—as cheerleader, actor, and model—decades before.

"They're just jealous of you," Scott would say. "You're an outsider, and you got the job they all wish they had."

Most of the mainstream sports media was based in New York City as well as in Bristol, Connecticut, ESPN's headquarters. If you weren't on their radar, you couldn't possibly have what it took. And then I showed up—a former cheerleader, actress, and model from Los Angeles. My type was already a punchline to their jokes. Yet I was the one who had earned one of the most coveted jobs in sports. And that was unacceptable to them.

To make matters worse, I'd done a photo shoot for *FHM*, a men's lifestyle magazine, which was scheduled to run at the beginning of football season. It had been a strategic decision to promote my brand and raise my profile with viewers while I was at *Best Damn*. But when the media got wind of the photos of me clad in black-and-white lingerie, it was more validation that I'd been hired at *MNF* for all the wrong reasons. When the executives at Disney, ABC's new parent company, found out about the shoot, they were irate. I wasn't the image they wanted for their family-friendly broadcast.

Apparently, the *MNF* executives really didn't know what they wanted me to be. They feigned shock over the photo shoot, yet after hearing about it, the publicity department tried to negotiate the cover for me with *FHM*. Then, for the show's promotional photos, I posed in a powder-blue blazer next to Al Michaels and John Madden. Yet the photos that made the cut, including a Times Square billboard, weren't from the official ABC photo shoot. Instead, without my permission, they super-imposed a photo taken from a modeling gig I had done years before. I wore a gold-sequined tube top and a come-hither look.

After the media attacked me, it seemed to me that Freddie's attitude toward me completely changed. It was his second year as the executive producer of *MNF*, so he was probably terrified that I would be his undoing. When he interviewed me, I think he was impressed by my credentials and believed we'd transform sideline reporting together. However, as we edged closer to the football season, ABC decided to forgo the revamp. Instead, I'd be a traditional sideline reporter—a job I'd never done and didn't feel qualified for.

Being a sideline reporter is a grueling, thankless job. Each week, you report on two different NFL teams—and you must know as much about each team as a beat reporter who covers the same team each week. Since you can't predict which players will impact the game or how, you have to prepare and memorize thirty stories a week, although only six to eight will make air. Researching, interviewing, and reading are the biggest parts of the job. It's as if every week, you have to cram for a final exam, but most of the stuff you study doesn't make it onto the test, and there are always a few questions you hadn't anticipated.

You'll also spend a few days before the game at the field, interviewing players, coaches, and offensive and defensive coordinators. The day of the game, you're at the field early, checking weather and wind conditions.

Then, once the game begins, you're everywhere, reporting on everything. You never stop running around the field, corner to corner, side to side, gathering information the broadcasters aren't privy to from their booth. You're the first to know what hospital an injured player is heading to as well as the extent of the player's injuries. You're the first to know if a backup quarterback is warming up to take the field. When it's halftime, you chase down both teams' head coaches to get their take on the first half. When the game ends, you interview the superstar player before the rest of the pack of journalists descends upon him.

You have to have a broad knowledge of each player so you can rattle off factoids when Al Michaels, the show's play-by-play commentator, throws to you. For instance, if a player is having a great game, you need a backstory prepared on the guy. You'll know where he went to school, what teams he's played for, and some fun tidbit like his favorite meal before a game. If a player is carted off the field and taken to a hospital, you'll know if this is a new or a recurring injury. If a backup quarterback is about to take the field, you'll have memorized a few items about him—hometown, family, and how he performs under pressure.

While you're racing around the field watching the game, flipping through your notebook, and gathering stories, you're also struggling to follow the directions your producers are yelling at you through your IFB. It's not an easy feat when there are 100,000 fans screaming and cheering behind you.

"Go to the other side of the field!"

"Go back!"

"Go to the end zone!"

"Get the head coach!"

"Find your camera!"

"You're going the wrong way!"

"Find your light!"

And all this work—weeks of research, miles and miles of endless racing around the field—boils down to a few "hits" (live reports). You're on air for less than ten minutes during a 180-minute live broadcast.

The first regular game of the *MNF* season—and my official debut—was a matchup between the New York Jets and the Washington Redskins. Since four former Jets had just been signed to the Redskins, it was a highly anticipated game, fueled by rumors of animosity among the players. The media called these former players "the Jetskins." Everyone was wondering if the ex-teammates would be civil to each other. Would a fight break out? Football may be a tough-guy sport, but it is sometimes as full of drama as any soap opera.

All the commercials, promotions, and billboards had been advertising this game for weeks. More than forty million people would be tuning in, including all of the sports media. A lot of eyes would be on me, judging me, writing about me, commenting on me. Any flub would be magnified. My outfit, makeup, and even lip gloss would be scrutinized. Freddie had already criticized an outfit during a preseason game. I'd worn a yellow top underneath a cream-colored blazer.

He said it was too revealing and told me to change into something else.

The shirt wasn't revealing. It didn't show any cleavage. But it was a bad omen. When I called Nola Roller, my wardrobe stylist, to tell her that I needed a less revealing shirt, she laughed.

"That top practically covers your throat. Gau-devil has lost his mind."

Gau-devil was the nickname Nola had given Freddie after she'd witnessed a few of his outbursts. Nola suggested that I change into the same shirt in a different color that she had packed in my garment bag.

"I bet Gau-devil won't even realize it."

I took Nola's advice. When Freddie saw me in the "different" teal shirt, he looked relieved. Nola and I had a good laugh over it. This was one of the few laughs I had during my tenure with *MNF*. During this game—my first preseason game in Canton, Ohio—lightning struck at halftime, canceling the second half. I should have taken this as the second bad omen. Another bad sign was Freddie's insistence on hiring a producer for me who had never produced live football games. He was fired quickly and replaced by another producer—who had also never produced live football games. This added to my stress.

But despite all the drama and all the naysayers, I was positive that I could turn the negativity around by being good at my job. I had spent the week before the season opener researching the teams. I was up to speed on the players, the rivalries, and the "Jetskins" controversy. I had written up my thirty stories. Then, before I headed for the game in DC, Freddie asked to see my work. He read it and explained that he would be rewriting my stories. He wanted me to memorize his words exactly. He told me I was not to improvise.

I believed I knew what was behind this request. Freddie may have been embarrassed by the media's depiction of me. I felt that he couldn't fire me because I was his first hire. Al and John had already joined the show during the legendary Don Ohlmeyer's regime. So instead of firing me, Freddie would micromanage me. Maybe he thought he'd be the brains behind the bimbo. He painstakingly revised every piece I'd written. He replaced my conversational tone with a formal style that didn't sound at all like me.

I was alarmed by Freddie's insistence on rewriting my stories in his voice. I'd been writing my copy for a decade, and I suddenly felt reduced to a ventriloquist's dummy. When I delivered Freddie's words, it was unnatural. It didn't sound like me. I felt like an actress playing a role that I wasn't meant to play.

There were critics who picked up on this. They would say I looked uncomfortable; that I glanced down at my notebook too much. I had been directed by Freddie to deliver his script verbatim. If I didn't, I'd get reamed out. So I'd sometimes rely on my notebook to remember exactly how Freddie wanted something said.

Today, when I speak to young reporters and journalism students, I tell them how important it is to speak in their own voice. "Imagine you're talking to a friend," I say. Looking back, I wish I'd taken my own advice and told Freddie that I'd write my own copy—after all, I prided myself on my conversational tone and storytelling ability. But I'd lost that confidence. I'd been so beaten down by the critics that I believed Freddie knew what was best for the broadcast.

When I reflect on this time, it often feels as if I'm talking about another person. I allowed my fear of failure to dominate me. I often wish I'd said to Freddie, *My gut instinct was to turn this job down. I never wanted to be a sideline reporter. But you told me you didn't want me to be a traditional sideline reporter. Then things changed. Let's both admit we make a mistake and move on.*

I'm not suggesting that you shouldn't take challenges. But sometimes you have to be brave enough to pass up an opportunity that may be prestigious but isn't right for you.

That first game ended without incident. I felt like I'd even proven my detractors wrong. But we were live for another ten minutes to do a postgame wrap. Al and John would impart their final thoughts while I would do a live "Horse Trailer Player of the Game," *MNF*'s term for the most valuable player. Since Washington had won the game, 16–13, I'd talk to Patrick Ramsey, the winning quarterback. Everyone wanted to interview him, but because I was *MNF*'s sideline reporter, I got first dibs, although other journalists would do their best to get to him first.

I watched as players and coaches trotted across the field to shake hands with their opponents. Some players also gathered in a circle to kneel down and pray. As Patrick headed toward the circle, I rushed toward him. Al would be tossing to me in twenty seconds, so I picked up my speed and galloped across a mud puddle, my cameraman right behind. I spied another reporter closing in on *my* quarterback. I didn't recognize the guy and figured him to be a local writer (no camera, just a tape recorder, potbelly, and what appeared to be a Members Only jacket). Media relations would normally run interference for me, but I had lost the guy in the mad dash to keep the player from the prayer. I cut in front of the writer about a yard from the quarterback just as I heard Al in my earpiece start to send his toss-down to me on the field.

I felt a crack on my left ear so hard that for a second, I thought I'd been hit upside the head with a shovel. During the broadcast, I wore an IFB in both ears to drown out the crowd noise and hear the crew in the truck and Al from the booth. I looked to my left and realized "the shovel" was the reporter's elbow smacking the side of my head and pushing my IFB painfully far into my ear.

"Cunt," he hissed as he brushed by me.

I headed toward the jerk. But Al's voice in my IFB reminded me that I had more pressing business. I grabbed Patrick and quickly collected my thoughts. Then I asked him about his pregame conversation with his former teammate Laveranues Coles.

Suddenly, Freddie was yelling at me through my IFB.

I was baffled by his outburst. What the hell was wrong with Freddie? What had I done to upset him?

That was when I realized that Patrick was looking at me as if he didn't understand my question. I replayed what I'd asked him. I'd asked Patrick about his *former* teammate. They were *current* teammates! I'd misspoken.

It sounds like a silly mistake—a mistake I immediately corrected on air. So what? But there was nothing silly about this mistake. I knew it instantly. In the eyes of the press and my bosses, I'd just confirmed everything that had been said about me. I'd provided all the haters with a reason to rant on sports radio or bitch on their blogs. I was that stupid bimbo, just like they'd said all along.

She's an idiot—she doesn't even know what players she's interviewing!

Freddie was still yelling into my IFB as I walked off the field. He wanted me to come to the production truck immediately. I took a few deep breaths. I pulled out my IFB and called Scott.

"That's it. I'm about to get fired."

"Don't be crazy. You just misspoke. You did a great job tonight."

But I knew better. I walked toward the production truck, feeling sick, my hands shaking. I swallowed hard. Then I opened the door and braced myself.

Freddie's head snapped toward me as he demanded an explanation for my mistake. Freddie is a short guy. But at that moment, he reminded me of a hulking, 'roided-out linebacker about to deliver a vicious hit that would send me off the field on a stretcher.

How do I explain making the biggest mistake of my career on live TV during the season friggin' opener of Monday Night Football?

I looked at the floor and closed my eyes as I tried to calm myself while formulating some kind of articulate explanation for my faux pas. I knew it was hopeless. There was nothing I could say to fix it.

"I had a brain fart."

Freddie's eyes widened. I'm sure my response must have infuriated him. I rushed out of the trailer and into the waiting car outside. The minute the door slammed shut, tears streamed down my face.

The driver shot me a concerned look. "Should I take you to your hotel?"

I nodded and continued to blubber during the fifteen-minute drive. Before we pulled up to the valet entrance, my driver handed me a box of tissues.

"Don't let the bellman see you like that. They know who you are, and they gossip. When I open your door, laugh like I told you something funny."

I was touched by his concern. "Did you see it?" I asked, hoping that someone removed from the debacle might give me an honest take on it. Maybe it wasn't so horrible.

"Yup," he said. "It was bad. And if you don't mind me saying, that color jacket doesn't look very good on you either."

When I got to my room, I dropped my bag on the floor. I took off the jacket and stared at it. The driver was right—the blazer was an ugly color. I tossed it into the trash. Then I headed to the toilet, where I threw up until there was nothing left in my stomach except a knot that refused to go away for the rest of the season.

11

Monday Nightmare
Football

I started having recurring nightmares shortly after that season opener. In one, it was the middle of the night when I stepped out of the limo after returning from another *Monday Night Football* game. As I headed toward my front door, a guy wielding a knife jumped out of the bushes and rushed toward me. I tried to scream but couldn't.

In another, I was naked on the football field. I was petrified, thinking that this was exactly the ammunition the media needed to prove that I'd been hired for my body rather than any talent. Freddie would definitely fire me. Worst of all, I couldn't remember anything about the teams. I didn't even know who was playing. Al Michaels threw to me. I couldn't speak.

Night after night, I'd jump up in bed, drenched in sweat, my heart hammering. I'd feel a pang of relief when I realized these were just bad dreams. But the relief would quickly be replaced by despair when I remembered why I was having such nightmares. Then I'd cry. I only slept for about three hours a night. I barely ate. I'd take a few bites of food but couldn't swallow it. I'd try to distract myself with a movie or TV show, but I couldn't follow the plot. I had absolutely no attention span. Even though I couldn't sleep, I didn't want to get out of bed.

Years later, when I relayed these symptoms to my uncle Dr. Jimmy Guerrero, a psychiatrist, he explained that I'd been suffering from a bout of situational depression. Looking back, it's pretty clear that something was wrong, but I was too exhausted and too anxious to even deal with it while it was happening.

After my season-opener gaffe, the media launched a new attack:

"Guerrero is offensive to any female with brains."

"Guerrero insults any male who not only loves the game but respects it in the morning."

"(Guerrero was) there strictly as eye candy for the predominantly male audience, and to pretend otherwise is to further insult whatever intelligence the audience may have."

"They don't call it the boob tube for nothing."

Those were the newspaper columnists. I was eviscerated by TV sports commentators and radio talk-show hosts. The radio guys were the worst. There was an ugly misogyny running rampant through sports radio airwaves—and I was their perfect target. They spoke in horrible hyperbole. To them, I was the worst. I was everything that was wrong with sports. I was everything that was wrong with feminism. I alone had set women back decades. They'd attack my clothes, hair (why was it so long?), lip gloss (I wore too much), even my nail polish (how dare I wear red—I must be a whore!).

Nearly every night, I had that recurring dream about the guy in the bushes. I assumed the lurker represented a football fan who hated me so much he wanted me dead. But my fans didn't hate me. *MNF*'s ratings actually went up that year for the first time in a decade. When asked about the increase in viewers during a weekly phone presser, Al Michaels called it "the Guerrero Factor."

Working with Al Michaels and John Madden was one of the few highlights of *MNF*. John is considered the greatest color commentator of all time, and as a coach, he was inducted into the Pro Football Hall of Fame. We'd both show up a few days before a game. He'd introduce me to the players and coaches and teach me about football from a coach's perspective. He hated to fly, so he was driven in his Madden Cruiser, a deluxe outfitted Greyhound bus, to all the games. Fans would recognize his vehicle and stalk him as if he were a rock star. But he was such a regular guy. I remember walking down a hotel hallway with him after a production meeting in a conference room. He swiped a cookie off a leftover room-service tray.

"Gross! That's someone's trash," I said.

He gobbled it down and smiled. "Yeah, but nobody took a bite out of it. Finders, keepers."

When we'd check into a hotel, hundreds of fans would be screaming and begging for autographs. When I joined *MNF*, I never imagined I'd be treated like a Beatle by rabid fans. Strangers would scream my name, hug me, and tell me they loved me. They had no idea that as soon as I reached my hotel room, I'd collapse in tears from the stressful night.

In the midst of all the controversy and bad press, I discovered an unexpected fan—President George W. Bush. He invited me to the White House that October to host the Hispanic Heritage Month reception.

"Lisa is the reason I watch *Monday Night Football,*" he joked as he introduced me to the room filled with Hispanic leaders in business, entertainment, news, and politics.

I had no idea about the growing support I had within the Hispanic community. I was shocked when they called me a role model. For the last few months, the media had painted me as the opposite of a role model. The warmth, acceptance, and praise that Latinos showered me with were unexpected. I was so overwhelmed that I had to sneak out of the event and retreat to the bathroom.

While there, I realized I had bought into the media's depiction of me. I'd thought I was failing miserably at my job and didn't deserve to be called a role model. I was so grateful for this group of people—my people—who seemed so genuinely supportive of my accomplishments that I burst into tears.

A woman in the bathroom saw me and asked what was wrong. As I started to explain, she stopped me.

"Do you know why they're criticizing you?"

I wiped my eyes and shrugged.

"They don't understand our culture. Latinas are comfortable with our sexuality. We embrace our femininity. They don't like that. Their criticism isn't your problem. It's theirs. Just by being true to yourself, you make them uncomfortable. But you keep doing what you're doing because we're proud of you."

She hugged me and disappeared. I shut my eyes and took a few deep breaths. When I opened my eyes, they landed on the mirror. I saw my mother's image looking back at me. I wondered what she'd think of all of this. What type of advice would she give me?

But despite what the woman in the bathroom had said, despite what the fans said, despite what the president of the United States had said, Freddie's criticisms ultimately obliterated all other sounds. After my blunder, he became even more critical. The media would obsess about how terrified I looked on the football field. They blamed it on how uncomfortable I was on the job.

Imagine having your boss yelling at you while TV cameras are on you, while your image is being projected into millions of people's homes. In retrospect, it's no wonder I looked terrified.

Looking back, it's hard to believe it was me. I was a woman whose self-esteem had been slowly chipped away for years. It had happened so gradually that I hadn't noticed. But I wasn't the Lisa Guerrero who'd sued Robert Kraft or who had told CBS executives that I was exactly what they needed. When had my confidence started to wither? Was it when I first walked into a locker room and was subjected to whistles, catcalls, and demeaning comments? Or when I had my ass grabbed by an anonymous colleague during a media scrum? Was it when I'd been taken off Super Bowl coverage because I wouldn't sleep with an executive? Or when the comedian asked on TV whom I'd fucked for my job? Every bit of this misogyny had worn me down until I lost my edge, my sparkle, my bravery.

The worst part about it was that I kept hearing the same thing: "You are the luckiest woman in sports."

How could I be depressed when I was the luckiest woman in sports? What was wrong with me? Being a sideline reporter for *MNF* was the top job for a woman in the sports television world. I was at the pinnacle of my career. I felt I should be grateful for this incredible opportunity that so many others desperately wanted. I decided that the executives and producers knew better than I did how I should look, act, and speak.

I wish I could have been more courageous. I knew if I quit, the media would say it was because I couldn't handle the job. I wish I'd said, "Freddie, I'm not going to let you talk to me this way. Don't ever yell at me again." No one should put up with their boss's anger. No one should cry before and after work. No one should be so scared of doing their job that they vomit, shake, and have nightmares.

How had I gotten to this place where I had lost my boldness, my bravery? What had become of the woman in the hot-pink suit who wasn't afraid to ask the tough questions?

I was so ashamed and humiliated by the mistake I'd made during that first game that I really thought I deserved the criticism and abuse hurled at me. Instead of seeing my mistake for what it really was—a silly flub—I believed the narrative that I'd made a colossal error. I couldn't let the negative press just roll off me. Instead, I absorbed each comment and allowed them to define me. These comments were all I thought about. They echoed in my head during the day and kept me up all night.

Truth be told, it doesn't matter how many awards and accolades I've won since that time; my experience with *MNF* still haunts me. Every day, my inbox is filled with messages from fans who love my *Inside Edition* stories. I can't tell you exactly what these people said, but I can recite verbatim some of the nastiest comments I received during *MNF*, even though it was twenty years ago.

The only explanation I can give as to why I allowed myself to be treated that way is that I wasn't Lisa Guerrero for that entire season. I didn't look like myself. I didn't sound like myself.

I was utterly lost.

Meanwhile, my friends and my dad were incredibly proud of me. Even Kenny had no idea that I was so miserable. It's one thing to grumble to your agent about some low-budget debacle like *Toughman* but quite another to complain about the Greatest Job Ever. Everyone I knew was thrilled for me. I didn't want to destroy the illusion. I usually told my dad everything, but I didn't want him to know about the dark place I was in. Scott was the only one who understood because he'd see me crying. He'd also been to some of the games, listened in on the headset, and heard Freddie yell at me. Scott's a calm person. As a professional athlete, he's accustomed to an environment where coaches, managers, and fans scream and hurl insults and curses. He's immune to the vulgarities of locker-room talk. But he was shocked and appalled by Freddie's language and disrespect. I've known Scott for twenty years, and I have never seen him as furious as he was when he heard how Freddie spoke to me. It was hard for him to rein it in. He wanted to storm the production van and beat up Freddie.

He saw how the job had changed me entirely. The smart-ass chick who'd given his buddy a hard time at the bar a year earlier had morphed into a sobbing mess.

"You should quit," he'd tell me. "It's not worth it."

Scott was concerned about my mental health. He saw me having a breakdown up close and in slow motion. He believed I could become myself again if left the job. He didn't understand why I'd want to remain in such a toxic environment, especially since I didn't have to be there. I didn't need the money. I didn't have to put up with the job, believing it would lead to better things. After all, this was the best job a woman could have in sports broadcasting. I appreciated Scott's concern. At times, the thought of taking his advice and quitting sounded appealing. I imagined relaxing in Malibu or Tahoe, taking long lunches with friends, and putting this experience far behind me.

But I couldn't. That's not who I am, and Scott knew it. I'd spent years working constantly to climb my way to the top. I couldn't quit in disgrace, which was what I felt it would be. I believed I would be admitting to my boss and the media that they were right—I couldn't handle the gig. I wanted to prove to everyone that they were very wrong about me. Besides, what kind of warrior quits when the battle gets tough?

During Thanksgiving, Scott proposed to me at his home in Lake Tahoe. He got on his knees on a giant boulder overlooking the lake at sunset. After I said yes, he popped open a bottle of champagne. I was completely in love with the guy and proud to be his fiancée. When I was away with him, I was able to compartmentalize. I could forget about the looming storm of *MNF* and focus on our romance. Until I met Scott, I'd never imagined I'd get married; I was thrilled that at thirty-nine, I'd found a wonderful guy to spend my life with.

But when I took a sip of the champagne, it was tasteless. One of the side effects of my depression was that food and drink had lost their flavor. As much as I tried to push *MNF* out of my head while celebrating with my fiancé, it was with me, taunting me. I gulped down the champagne and smiled, but I remembered what was waiting for me when I headed back to work after the holiday.

MNF announced our engagement during its broadcast that week. Anyone watching the live telecast would look at me, a big smile on my face, and be envious of my life—*a great job, lots of money, and a gorgeous fiancé*. But I was thinking, *Who decides to get married when they're also considering killing themselves?* That was how bad I felt. I was planning a wedding while considering suicide. Then, I would become even more depressed about being depressed at what was supposed to be the happiest time of my life.

I'd never thought about suicide before. Since my mom had died at twenty-nine, I had been convinced that I would not live past that age. That was why I tried to accomplish as much as I could. When I hit thirty, I was relieved. *Mom, I made it*, I thought. Since my mom's life had been cut short, I felt I was living for both of us. I was ashamed that I had had these thoughts, especially since my mom would have loved to have lived longer. But I wasn't thinking clearly. I was worn down from lack of sleep and nourishment. Besides Scott, I didn't confide in anyone. I was so consumed with *MNF* that I had become alienated from my friends. There were people at work who saw what I was going through, but we never talked about it. They weren't friends, so I suppose they didn't feel comfortable asking me if I was okay. This added to my loneliness and depression. But being the actress, I plastered a smile on my face and hit the road for the next game.

Al Michaels suggested that I have a destination wedding at the Four Seasons Hualalai in Hawaii. I took his advice because it seemed easier than planning something locally, where I'd have to be more hands-on. I hired the hotel's event planner, Kellie Berdon. I'm a detail-oriented person, but I completely checked out of planning nearly every aspect of what was supposed to be one of the biggest days of my life. Kellie would call me up with a suggestion, and I'd agree to anything.

"What do you think of the floral arrangements I suggested?"

"That's fine."

"What about the cake design I emailed?"

"That's fine."

"The DJ?"

"Fine."

Jacqui Bell, a good friend from my modeling days, took me bridal-gown shopping. She'd planned an entire day of visits to various boutiques in Beverly Hills. It seemed exhausting and overwhelming. I settled on the first dress I tried—a simple ivory silk slip dress with hand-painted ivory flowers by Monique Lhuillier.

"This is it. I'll take it."

"Absolutely not," Jacqui said. "We have appointments all day. No one picks their first dress. Wedding-dress shopping is an event."

How do you explain that when you're detached from life, you can't handle events? How do you explain that even though it has been thirty years since your mother died, her absence is felt in every bridal dress, every cake decoration, every wedding invitation? I missed her desperately. I thought about what that psychic had said and tried to imagine Mom next to me, her voice whispering advice into my ear.

Since the football season had started, I hadn't gotten my period. My periods had always been a bit irregular, so I didn't think too much about it. I chalked it up to stress, lack of sleep, and poor eating. But when three months went by, I wondered if my nausea and vomiting were more than just nerves.

I took a home pregnancy test. It was positive. Though Scott and I had said we didn't want children, I began to imagine a different life than the one we had planned. I loved Scott. We were about to get married. This pregnancy hadn't been planned, but maybe we'd make it work. Scott was a bit in shock. He thought the home test couldn't possibly be accurate.

"You have to get to a doctor first," he said.

I didn't need a doctor to confirm my pregnancy. As soon as the test came back positive, I realized I had all the symptoms friends had told me about. My breasts were swollen and painful. I felt queasy. Still, I didn't make a doctor's appointment. I wasn't ready to make it official.

* * *

It was during the first quarter of an *MNF* game that I felt some discomfort on the left side of my stomach. I took a few deep breaths, wondering if I'd eaten something that hadn't agreed with me. But I pushed through the pain and did my reports. By the second quarter, the pain had intensified. When I felt a dampness between my legs, I thought, *Oh, that's it. I got my period.*

And then I remembered that I was pregnant.

It hit me—I was having a miscarriage!

The second quarter was ending, and I desperately wanted to get to the bathroom. I could feel blood leaking out of me. I was weak and dizzy. But I had one more hit to do. I also had to chase down one of the head coaches off the field for a question for the first-half summary. I thought I could run to the bathroom and

be back in time. Before a game, I'd always scope out the officials'
bathroom because I'd only have a few minutes' break during
halftime. The bathroom was in the tunnel behind me.

"I'm going to the bathroom," I told my assistant, a young
guy whose job was to race around the field with me.

He looked at me as if I were completely insane. "Don't!
They're about to throw to you."

I delivered my live report. I was dizzy and nauseated. I don't
remember ever feeling more alone than at that moment when
I reported on the game to an audience of forty million while
surrounded by 100,000 football fans. Despite the pain, I even
reminded myself to stand up straight. During our Wednesday-
morning phone calls, Freddie would ream me out for bad
posture. I stared at the camera but could barely see. The pain
was excruciating. I heard myself mispronounce a player's name
and knew I'd hear about it later.

I was losing a pregnancy and worrying about a
mispronunciation!

As soon as I finished, I raced off to interview a coach. Then I
headed to the bathroom. As I sat on the toilet, I couldn't believe
the blood that was pouring out of me. It had soaked through my
pants. People banged on the door, but I couldn't move. I shoved
a bunch of paper towels in my underwear.

It never occurred to me to tell anyone. It never occurred
to me that maybe I should have gone to a hospital or called a
doctor or, at the very least, sat out the rest of the game. The only
thought that crossed my mind was that I could get through the
rest of the game as long as I buttoned up my long winter coat.
That way, no one would see the blood.

I've never talked about this devastating experience before. Only Scott and my doctor know about it. I didn't even tell my dad. Often my coping mechanism is to block it out, move on, and pretend it never happened. I haven't thought about that day in a long time. Some events are too painful to revisit. But looking back, I can't believe how utterly detached I was from what was happening to me. I was having a miscarriage—and I was worried about bloodstains being visible on television.

It's hard to believe that this was me. Today, when I confront a bad guy and get pushed or kicked, I do my job, but I don't jeopardize my health. I'll stop a shoot if I'm in pain, or I'll call a doctor if I need medical attention. But that day on the field, I was literally hemorrhaging, and I soldiered on, completely consumed by my job and utterly numb to what was happening.

It was as if I were on autopilot. I'd tell myself what I had to do and where I had to be. I pushed aside what was actually happening to me. *Get back on the sideline. Interview the coach. Listen to Freddie's directions.* That inner voice never mentioned that I should get to a hospital, call 911, or ask a coworker for help. I didn't see that I was on a dangerous downward spiral. I didn't see that I had become completely detached from my reality. I didn't see how sick I was—mentally and physically. I was completely checked out.

When the game ended, I was supposed to go to the production truck to talk to Freddie. Instead, I headed back to the bathroom.

I pulled out my IFB to mute him. Then I sat on the toilet. There was so much blood.

I never made it to the production truck. Instead, I got in the limo and headed to the Disney jet. I waited until Al had settled in his seat. Then I headed into the bathroom, changed my clothes, and dumped my underwear and pants in the garbage can. I looked into the mirror and didn't recognize the pale, gaunt, scared, and so very tired woman who stared back at me.

Later, as the plane ascended into the clouds, I thought about all I'd lost on those sidelines—my dignity, my courage, and now my pregnancy. There was nothing left to take. At that moment, I vowed to stop letting Freddie have so much control over me. Nothing he could do or say could be worse than what I'd just experienced, alone on the sidelines in front of millions of people.

The football season was coming to a close. During the last few games, I stopped memorizing Freddie's notes. I spoke in my own voice. I pulled out the IFB during my reports. That way, if Freddie was screaming at me, I would never know.

12

A Near-Deadly Detour
on Pacific Coast Highway

When the last game of the season ended, the *Monday Night Football* crew met up for a big dinner. For the first time in a long time, I felt good about my performance. I'd just had my most important moment as a sideline reporter when I'd interviewed Brett Favre. The football legend's dad had unexpectedly died the day before, and no one had thought he'd play. But he'd put on a surreal performance, leading the Green Bay Packers to a 41–7 victory over the Oakland Raiders. It was a thrilling, emotionally charged game that would be considered one of the most memorable in the history of *MNF*.

The Packers' media director said Brett was too grief-stricken to grant postgame interviews. But during the fourth quarter, I broke protocol and approached Brett from behind the bench. Since I'd interviewed him several times before and we had a good working relationship, he said yes.

When I called up to Freddie in the booth, he was skeptical. He said Brett wouldn't speak to me.

"Yes, he will."

The feisty part of me that I'd buried had clawed its way back to the surface after my miscarriage. During the last few games, I'd become a stronger, more confident reporter. It was because I'd pull out my IFB before interviews and reports. I spoke in my own voice. As I stood next to Brett, waiting for Al to toss to me, I quickly composed my lead and the questions I'd ask. I recalled how a few days earlier, the media's focus had been on whether Brett would play with a fractured thumb.

Al threw to me, and I began with this: "It's one thing to play with a broken thumb but another thing altogether to play with a broken heart."

Later, when I walked into the dinner party, Al was waiting for me.

"Lisa, that was one of the most beautiful openings to an interview I've ever heard," he said. "I wish I'd thought of it."

Throughout the night, people came up to compliment me on my performance and the interview. Even Freddie told me I'd done a great job. I'd ended the season on a high note. But when it was time to leave, I looked around the room and wondered if I'd be back for a second season.

A few weeks later, Scott and I were married in Hawaii. Our seventy-five guests flew to the resort for a four-day weekend filled with celebrations, including a welcome luau (Scott, who never dances, hula danced onstage to everyone's great delight), Scott's thirty-sixth birthday, and a Super Bowl party.

We were married on February 3, 2004 (we said we became one on 2/3/04). My uncle, a retired Salvation Army officer, performed the ceremony on the beach. When Uncle Herbie talked about my mom watching over the nuptials, everyone became teary-eyed, especially me. My wedding was a beautiful, perfect event. It was also bittersweet. Even though it had been thirty years, I missed my mother dearly.

Less than two weeks later, Scott and I moved into a small furnished rental home in Port St. Lucie, Florida, where Scott began spring training for the Mets. Since he'd missed the entire 2003 season due to labrum surgery, Scott was excited to work hard to earn a starting position in the pitching rotation.

I didn't have any friends in Florida or much to do while Scott was at spring training. I bought a bike and pedaled around town. I rescued a puppy that was about to be put down—a sweet little Yorkie that Scott named Cupcake (he thought I was holding a cupcake in my hand when I introduced him to the pup). I went to matinees. I read books. I honed my kitchen skills and began cooking dinners. I also waited for the phone to ring. Whenever it did, I breathed a sigh of relief that it wasn't Freddie.

Scott made a tremendous comeback and was named third starter in the rotation. In April, we headed to Atlanta, where he would pitch his first game with the Mets against the Braves. Since Scott had been out with an injury when we'd dated and become engaged, this would be the first time I'd see him on the mound for a game. I invited my uncle, aunt, and cousins who lived in Atlanta to cheer him on with me. We sat together up front, bursting with excitement.

I thought it was strange that Scott didn't warm up in the bullpen. Then, when he didn't take the field with the other players, I panicked. When another pitcher stepped onto the mound,

I grew frantic. A rumble traveled through the crowd. "Where's Scott Erickson?" "Where's Scott Erickson?"

I searched for Scott, but he was nowhere to be found. A ball boy ran toward me.

"Lisa, come with me. Scott pulled his hamstring."

I was stunned. Scott had worked so hard to recover and earn a starting position. I knew a hamstring pull could be a career ender, especially for older pitchers.

I raced down the tunnel and spotted one of the trainers. "It's really bad," he said, adding that Scott had pulled the muscle fifteen minutes into warm-ups. He'd been so amped up for the game that he hadn't stretched enough when he'd begun his tosses.

When I reached Scott, he was as white as a ghost.

"It's over," he said, shaking his head.

We didn't know it then, but it wasn't over. At least, not quite. Scott would be put on the disabled list and sent back to rehab in Port St. Lucie. In July, he would pitch six scoreless innings against the Florida Marlins. His incredible performance would earn him the cover of the *New York Post*'s sports page: "Great Scott!" But during his next start, he would last only two innings against the Montreal Expos. That game would mark the end of his career with the Mets. After that, he would jump from team to team, never again being the superstar player he had once been. It was devastating.

After his hamstring injury, we went back to Port St. Lucie. Once again, Scott threw himself into rehab, hoping to make that comeback that had eluded him. I was on my own with not much to do but think about my career. During the last few *MNF* games as a sideline reporter, I'd done a great job. Was this enough to prove to Freddie that I had the chops for another season? Plus, when the *MNF* season had ended, I'd been assigned a few other correspondent jobs as part of my overall contract with ABC. They had gone extremely well. On New Year's Day, I had cohosted the national broadcast of the Tournament of Roses Parade. In March, I'd covered the National Figure Skating Championships in Atlanta and the World Figure Skating Championships in Germany.

Those assignments had reminded me how good I could be when I wasn't entrenched in a toxic environment. The press had taken notice, writing positive reviews of my performance. As time ticked by, I started to feel more optimistic.

When my cell buzzed one afternoon in early May, I checked the number. I didn't recognize it, but I picked it up anyway. The guy introduced himself as a reporter for the *New York Times*. My first thought was that he wanted to ask some questions about Scott's rehab. I wondered how he'd gotten my number.

"Do you have any comment about being replaced by Michele Tafoya?"

"What?" The words didn't sink in. I had to replay them in my head a few times. I knew Michele was a correspondent for the NBA. But she'd replaced me? How could I have been fired without anyone telling me?

I was too dumbfounded to speak. Finally, I croaked out a "No comment" and ended the call. Then I dropped to my knees on the kitchen floor and sobbed.

Scott was rehabbing. Except for Cupcake, I was alone. I thought I was prepared for this moment, but being fired felt so much worse than I had imagined. What really hurt was that no one from *MNF* had respected me enough to tell me. Someone had leaked the story to the media instead.

I cried so hard for so many reasons. Freddie's silence was just as awful as his rants. It was as if he were saying, "You're not even worth a phone call!"

So I called him. He owed me an explanation. He didn't pick up.

My thoughts turned toward my dad, as they always do when I feel sad or upset. How could I ever break this to him? He'd been so thrilled when I'd been hired to report on the game I'd grown up watching with him. Throughout the season, he'd call me after every game. "You were wonderful. You looked beautiful." Even if I'd been eviscerated by the press or criticized by Freddie, I'd put on a happy face for Dad. He had no idea that my job had been in jeopardy because I had never mentioned the hell I'd been going through. When I called to tell him, he was completely floored.

"Why would this happen? You were so good at it. All my friends told me they loved you." (Such a Dad thing to say.) A lump formed in my throat.

Later in the day, Freddie finally called me back.

"We decided to go in a different direction. You're talented. But it's been like trying to put a square peg in a round hole. This was a bad fit."

(And they found someone else who was a better fit for the show. Michele Tafoya did a great job as the sideline reporter for *MNF* and later *Sunday Night Football*, where she worked with Freddie for sixteen years. In 2022, she quit the gig to pursue a career in conservative politics.)

While I waited for Scott to come home, my phone rang with calls from people genuinely upset that I'd been fired. A few players and coaches called. So did Al Davis, then the owner of the Oakland Raiders, who offered me a job with his Raiders TV network. I said I'd think about it, but how could I go from a national broadcast with millions of viewers to a local cable show? After I hung up with him, John Madden called.

"I'm so sorry, Lisa. I want you to know that nobody told me," John said. "I was never consulted. If I had been, I would have said that this is a big mistake. I'm really angry they did this to you. The players love you. The audience loves you. Fuck the media. Let me help you get another job."

I'll forever appreciate John's kindness. He even made phone calls and arranged some job opportunities in sports, but I was too devastated to consider them. I thought I'd hear from Al Michaels, but I never did. According to a *New York Post* article, he had pushed for my replacement. This was the ultimate betrayal. The man had danced at my wedding just a few weeks before I was fired. All these years later, this still hurts.

What would I do? I had no idea. I had spent years constantly striving to reach the next level. *MNF* had been the pinnacle of my career. I knew I'd never work in sports again. But who was I without sports? It was all I knew. Sure, I could probably get another sports job at a local television station somewhere. But how do you go from traveling on the Disney jet and reporting to forty million people to moving back home to become a weekend sports guy? ABC had asked if I'd be interested in covering figure skating for the network. I turned the offer down. While it had been fun as a side gig to *MNF*, it was a demotion—and anyone who followed my career would know this. It would provide more fodder for ridicule. Looking back, I should have taken the job and not cared what anyone thought.

The media had been cruel during my stint with *MNF*, but incredibly, it got worse. After I was fired, their comments became more vicious. They'd gotten what they wanted—I'd been replaced. Why were they still eviscerating me? I knew they'd be excited to report that I'd been fired. But I assumed that after a few days, my story would be over.

That didn't happen.

I wish I could say I ignored them, but it consumed me. Completely consumed me. I refused to watch any sports, but I couldn't help myself when it came to reading the sports page or listening to sports radio. It was like an addiction—I didn't listen to music while driving. Instead, I had every sports station programmed into my car radio. Out of habit and morbid curiosity, I'd jump from station to station, listening to the barrage of insults. Every market throughout the country had two or three guys who were desperately trying to be a shock jock like Howard Stern. I was their perfect target. They called me a bimbo. A pair of tits. A whore. I was a punchline to all their crass jokes. So much for the so-called Guerrero Factor.

My friends would email links to stories about me. Their subject heads would read, *Can you believe what this idiot wrote about you? It's funny how obsessed they are! This is nuts! Wow, this guy really hates you!*

Those friends didn't send me the articles out of cruelty. During the last few months, I was so embarrassed and humiliated that I hid my feelings from my friends and family. Everyone assumed I was this tough chick who didn't give a shit what the media said. My friends had no idea that each article pushed me deeper into what felt like an endless pit of despair.

I knew I should ignore the critics. But I couldn't. My heart would throb and my hands would sweat as I'd hit the link that opened yet another scathing criticism of me. But that was hardly the worst of it. Right below the article would be the comments section. I couldn't look away. Those anonymous trolls would write the most hateful, vile, devastating things about me. Each comment felt like another drop of poison slowly killing me. My friends thought that I'd get a big laugh out of the articles and move on with my day. Little did they know, I'd stare at my computer for hours as if I were watching some horror movie.

I thought the media would eventually grow tired of me. But months and months went by, and I was still getting emails and Google alerts. Anytime a newspaper ran a retrospective on *MNF* or sideline reporters or women sports broadcasters, I would be mentioned. I was always the worst mistake ever. As bad as someone was, no one could ever be as bad as Lisa Guerrero.

This was the most devastating part of all of it. In the short time I'd had with my mom, she'd taught me how important it was to be proud of being a Guerrero, a warrior. I had changed my name to honor her. And what had I done with her name? I'd brought shame and embarrassment to it.

I became the low bar. My name—Lisa Guerrero—was synonymous with failure.

When Scott finished rehabbing and returned to the Mets, we moved into a furnished apartment on Manhattan's Upper East Side. I'd sit in the wives' section at the ballpark—something Barry Bonds had warned Scott about before we had married.

"Keep Lisa far away from the other wives. Those vultures will peck her eyes out," Barry had said.

I wasn't worried about any eye pecking. I could definitely hold my own with the other "Diamond Divas," slang for those baseball wives whose status is determined by ring size, designer bags (the bigger the better), and how many nannies they employ. I had a career—or, I should say, once *had* a career. Also, there was this: I'd covered baseball; I knew too many secrets. I knew about the guys who had girlfriends on the side or groupies at the hotel (they called them "road beef"). Worst of all, the players knew I knew, and so did some of the wives. It was all a bit—well, more than a bit—uncomfortable for everyone.

I'd covered baseball for a decade. Now I was sitting in the wives' section. It felt like a demotion. Being in New York City— the sports media hub—was incredibly difficult. Some of the reporters at the games were the same guys who'd written nasty articles about me. The media was in the tunnel after the games, standing shoulder to shoulder with the players' wives, who were waiting for their husbands to emerge from the locker room. I'd catch them whispering and snickering. I wanted to be there for Scott. He'd gone from being a starting pitcher to a relief pitcher. He was stuck in the bullpen, waiting to be called to the mound as a replacement for the starter. He too felt demoted. When we weren't in New York or traveling for baseball, we divided our time between Tahoe and the house we had recently purchased in Malibu. It was a gorgeous, nearly ten-thousand-square-foot Mediterranean villa way up in the hills with walls of glass overlooking the glistening Pacific Ocean. Anyone who caught a glimpse of my life wouldn't possibly have understood how I could be miserable despite all this abundance. This was why my friends would send those emails. This was why my family wasn't worried about me. How could I be so affected by some newspaper reporter while I was living the dream?

Being the daughter of a social worker who didn't make a lot of money, I was aware of how lucky I was. I was extremely grateful for all my blessings. But despite the homes, possessions, and financial security, I was in a dark, dark place. I felt like I was stuck in quicksand, and every day, I'd sink deeper. My nightmares became filled with natural disasters like tidal waves, hurricanes, and earthquakes. It was always the same—I couldn't run. I couldn't yell. My voice was gone.

I thought I had moved past the miscarriage, but I had never processed it. It was as if I'd stored the fear and despair from that day and was experiencing those raw emotions for the first time. I hadn't mourned what I'd lost when it had happened. Months later, I was consumed by grief.

I had never been much of a drinker, but I started to down a bottle of wine every night. I'd tell myself it was to help me sleep—but I wanted to be numb. I drank to forget how much I hated myself.

Because I really had started to hate myself. I'd avoid mirrors because I couldn't stand what stared back at me. I was convinced Scott saw it too and would leave me any day. Why would he want to stay with someone so loathsome? I was being ridiculed everywhere. I knew Scott heard much more of it than he let me know. His friends heard it too, and I was certain Scott was mortified. When he'd fallen in love with me, I'd been at the top of my game. Now I was an unemployed, insecure mess. I wasn't the person he thought he had married. I wouldn't have blamed him if he'd left. I wished I could leave me too.

One day, I left my home to run some errands. As I drove along the twisting, cliff-hugging Pacific Coast Highway in Malibu, I did what I always do—turn on sports radio. I listened as the hosts cackled about something. As soon as one of them referred to the object of their hysteria as "she," I knew that they were talking about me. They were in the midst of reading an article that had appeared a few months earlier in the *Pittsburgh Post-Gazette*. The writer had called me incompetent, a liability, and the subject of water-cooler talks because of my frequent mistakes. It went on and on. Then the radio hosts started joking. "What does a bimbo do when she gets fired from *Monday Night Football*? She marries a baseball player and has ten kids." (Little did they know that at thirty-nine, and after suffering a painful miscarriage, there would be no children in my future.)

I clicked off the radio. I'd been fired months and months ago, yet I was still a laughingstock. After working so hard to earn respect for so many years, was this my legacy? To be a crass joke? I was so sick of all of it. I was sick of hearing about myself, sick of thinking about myself. I thought of the hundreds of cruel comments through the years, from everyone from Keith Olbermann to Christine Brennan to Freddie to all of the vicious, anonymous online trolls. It felt so personal. I couldn't understand how so many people who didn't know me could hate me so much.

The road was treacherous. It would be so easy to pull the steering wheel to the right and drive off the cliff. It would be over really fast.

During the last year, I'd thought about suicide, but in an abstract way, like the possibility was always there if things got too bad, but of course, I'd never really act on it. This time it was different. I visualized it happening. But before I acted on it, I found a turnout on the road and pulled over. I took a deep breath. Then I called my dad.

Throughout my life, I had felt an overwhelming urge to protect him from my problems. I had grown up believing he'd already reached his sadness quotient when Mom had died. During the last year, I'd hidden so much from him—how miserable I'd been during *MNF*; how depressed I'd become.

I thought I'd been brave by hiding my despair from my family and friends. I thought I'd been brave because I'd put on a sunny demeanor. As I spilled the details of the last year to my dad, including how I had just turned off the road to call him because I was afraid I was going to drive my car off a cliff, I realized I hadn't been brave. True bravery comes from honesty. True bravery comes from relying on others and asking for help. It takes courage to be vulnerable, to admit you have a problem.

Instead of confiding in family and friends, I nearly drove off the road. My first real step on my path toward bravery was when I took a detour and called my dad.

I'd never spoken so honestly about my mental health—it was terrifying, exhausting, and yet freeing. During the call, I revealed who I was instead of who I wanted my dad to see. Instead of pretending to be strong, I showed my vulnerability.

Dad didn't speak for a few minutes. I'm sure he was beyond shocked. I'm sure he was trying to process this version of me he didn't know. I heard him take a few deep breaths.

"Lisa, you're a great reporter."

"I will never be able to work in sports again. It's over."

"I didn't say anything about sports. You're a storyteller. It doesn't matter what the subject is. You could be a news reporter or an entertainment reporter. Who cares what the critics say about you? You may think the world revolves around them, but most people don't know who they are."

Until that moment, it hadn't occurred to me that I could do any other kind of reporting. Then I remembered what Hugh Downs had told me all those years ago.

Reach higher than sports. You could be a news reporter.

My dad pointed out that not everyone was a sports fan, and most people hadn't heard the insults and ridicule hurled at me.

"You need to get help. You have to talk to a therapist. And you have to stop listening to sports radio," he said. "Remember, there's a whole world out there that you haven't dipped your toe into yet. Reporting on a pulled groin isn't your destiny."

I got off the phone and wiped my tears. I felt a little bit better already. How could I have thought I'd done the brave thing by hiding the truth from my dad and so many other loved ones? If I had been more open, I would never have gotten to such a dark place. I vowed never to put on a brave face again because it was a facade. I learned that day that courage doesn't always come from within. Courage is like a battery that sometimes has to be charged by the people you confide in when you need help or advice.

And little did I know my opportunity to turn the tables would soon be waiting in the mail. It would be in the form of an invitation I'd thrown away every year for nearly twenty years. This year, it would change my life.

13

The Big F*** You

Every year, the offer to pose for the cover of *Playboy* magazine would arrive in the mail. And every year, I'd throw it away. But when Scott saw the envelope with the bunny logo in the garbage, he fished it out.

"What's this? I thought we weren't allowed to have *Playboy* in the house," he said, laughing.

"They want me to do the cover," I explained. "It's become kind of a joke because, of course, I always say no."

"What?" His eyes nearly popped out. "Why would you turn it down?"

I looked at him incredulously. "Why would I turn it down? There are a million reasons. It's porn. It's degrading to women. It's gross."

He thumbed through the glossy binder embossed with the Playboy bunny logo. "This isn't porn." Then he read through the letter. "They're offering you the cover and a ridiculous amount of money."

"Yeah, but . . ."

"But what? Look at some of the women who've been on the cover: Marilyn Monroe, Sophia Loren, Cindy Crawford, Halle Berry, Charlize Theron. They're iconic women, and so are you."

"Is my husband encouraging me to be naked in *Playboy*?"

"Have you even read this? They're not asking you to be naked, just topless."

"I'm not doing it. I'd never pose nude or even seminude."

"Okay," Scott said, sighing. "But you should think about it. Read their offer."

He handed me the binder and smiled.

Even though I'd been offered the cover for years (and before that, I'd been asked to be a Playmate, which weirdly embarrassed me), I'd never really looked at *Playboy's* proposal. I sat at the kitchen counter and read the folder's contents. I studied the photos of the past cover models. Scott was right. These women—Hollywood stars and legends—looked sexy and elegant. As I continued reading, I realized I'd be in control of my image. I could choose my photographer, and I'd receive final photo approval. Best of all, I could pick any place in the world to be photographed. *Playboy* would fly my team and me to the location of my choice. We'd travel first class, stay in luxury accommodations, and be wined and dined. And I'd earn hundreds of thousands of dollars for a few hours of work. Then, when the cover was unveiled, there would be an extensive media tour, which would include newspaper, magazine, and radio interviews as well as television appearances. I could promote my latest project. The problem? I had no latest project. I had nothing to promote.

I put the proposal down on the counter and thought about the offer. When I was in my twenties, I'd been a swimsuit and fitness model. I'd grown up on the beaches of San Diego and

Huntington Beach. As a Latina, I celebrated my femininity and sexuality in a less constricted way than most women in mainstream media. I'd always been comfortable in my own skin. But this was different—I'd never posed topless. And who was I kidding? I was forty-one.

Still, I was in good shape. I ran and worked out nearly every day. There was nothing I was worried about that a little airbrushing couldn't fix. What was the big deal? I'd find a fashion photographer who'd shoot photos with a vintage feel, like something Sophia Loren or Gina Lollobrigida would have posed for. And since I could pick any destination, I'd opt for Paris. I'd never been and had always wanted to travel there.

So, for the next few weeks, I fluctuated between thinking, *Why not?* and *Oh, hell, no!*

When I asked my friends, family, and business associates for their input, I became even more confused. Everyone had different advice:

"Darling, yes! This will be good for your acting career. You Americans are ridiculous about nudity."—Lorraine, my British-born talent manager.

"This could be a disaster. If you want to be taken seriously as a broadcaster, this is a mistake. Really think about it."—Kenny, my broadcasting agent.

"Don't do it. It's pornography."—Richard, my devoutly Christian brother.

"Oh, my God! A cover? At forty-one! That's so cool. You're beautiful. Do it!"—Deena Driskill, my best friend.

"I agree with Kenny—it could be a disaster. But I also agree with Lorraine—it could lead to great things. Write a list of the pros and cons and then decide."—Dad.

My dad's opinion was the most crucial to me. If he had told me not to do it, I wouldn't have. I assembled my list. And as I did, I realized that every reason I had to reject the offer had absolutely nothing to do with me and everything to do with how I would be perceived by other people, mainly the media. Less than a year ago, the media's attacks had nearly sent me over the edge—literally. Could I handle another onslaught? By posing in *Playboy*, would I be confirming my critics' harsh assessment of me?

That moment nearly a year ago on Pacific Coast Highway had been the lowest point in my adult life. Since that drive, I'd been on the path toward healing. I'd taken my dad's advice and talked with a therapist. I'd completely stopped reading, listening to, and watching sports news. I'd realized that my obsession with sports news was like cigarette smoking—a bad habit I had to break before it killed me.

The best cure for this addiction came unexpectedly when Jon Gale, an old theater friend, called. In my early twenties, I had played Sandy and he Kenickie in a production of *Grease* at the Westminster Playhouse in Orange County. He asked me if I'd be interested in starring alongside him in *Extremities*, a drama he and his partner were producing about a woman who exacts revenge on her stalker. In 1986, Farrah Fawcett had starred and received rave reviews in the television adaptation of the play.

I felt as if Jon was an angel sent to me to help me survive the upcoming football season. I immediately agreed. Scott and I rented a place in San Francisco near the theater. For the next few months, I rehearsed and performed in the physically and emotionally grueling production. There were brutal fight scenes, requiring precise choreography. I was able to release an enormous amount of pent-up anger and sadness. It reminded me of the theater therapy Dad had enrolled me in after Mom died. At the end of each performance, I'd be exhausted, bruised, and battered. But it felt cathartic. The dark clouds began to dissipate.

The best part of the experience was being surrounded by artists who had never watched *Monday Night Football* and didn't care about sports at all. Sports had been the center of my universe for as long as I could remember, and it was almost shocking to see how little they really mattered in most people's lives. There was a whole world out there that didn't even know who would be playing in the Super Bowl. Imagine that!

Theater and therapy had helped me rebound from my *MNF* experience. But as I pondered whether I should pose for *Playboy*, I knew I still placed too much importance on what the sports media would have to say about it.

I wondered, what if I didn't take their opinion into consideration at all?

Yes, if I posed, I'd receive some negative publicity. My critics would assume I was the person they'd always said I was. They could smirk and say, "Aha! We told you so!"

I had allowed them to define me for too long. But they didn't get the final say; I did. What if I took back my power by simply disregarding them completely? The thing that infuriates bullies the most is when they are deemed too irrelevant to matter. Sometimes bravery isn't putting your fists up and fighting. Sometimes bravery is tuning out, turning around, and forging your own path.

I thought about it some more. Could I turn this *Playboy* opportunity into my big fuck-you to the critics, the media, everyone who had ever said anything disparaging about me?

What if I flipped the script? What if I looked at this opportunity as empowering? I would be a fit and fierce forty-one-year-old brunette Latina in a sea of mostly twenty-something blondes. And since I had no movie, television show, or book to promote, what if I used *Playboy*'s media tour to simply promote what I hoped would come? I'd tell every media outlet that I wasn't finished—I still wanted a career in broadcasting. As Dad had said, I'm a storyteller. And there are a lot of stories out there that don't involve a football.

I called Lorraine. "Tell them I'll do it."

"Fantastic, darling! I always hoped one day you'd change your mind. I think this will lead to your next and best chapter."

Then I assembled my team. Since Scott was in spring training with the Texas Rangers, I decided I'd take a group of women to the shoot in Paris with me. I invited Lorraine, Deena, and Stephanie, my mother-in-law.

I chose Stephanie because ever since Scott had introduced me to her, I had hoped we'd have a mother-daughter-type bond. But she didn't seem to like me. Scott had warned me that she was very protective of him and didn't trust any of the women he'd dated—ever. Still, I was hoping that since we were married, maybe she would eventually accept me.

"Taking my mom is a great idea," Scott said.

"She won't care that it's because I'm posing for a *Playboy* cover?"

He laughed. "My mom will love it. Especially if you tell her that you'll be jetting off to Paris."

When the four of us landed in the City of Light, I had a panic attack. What had I been thinking? Millions of people would see me almost naked. Most of the women in *Playboy* are twenty-something specimens of perfection. I'd gone through a year of avoiding mirrors. And I was going to pose in my altogether for anyone to see! Talk about extremes!

My crew, including the iconic fashion photographer Antoine Verglas as well as hair, makeup, and wardrobe stylists, calmed me down as only the French can do. They plied me with champagne and compliments.

"Look at you! You're beautiful. Women who are forty aren't old here. In France, you are chic forever. And what's the big deal about showing your breasts? You Americans are such prudes."

You Americans are such prudes became the refrain among my new French friends. They thought it was ridiculous how uptight Americans are over nudity. They thought it was silly of me to be worried about what people thought of my body. I learned that women in France and other European countries don't have an expiration date as they do in the States, especially in Los Angeles, where I lived. Women in France have sex appeal for life. Paris quickly became my favorite city. I loved everything about it— the people, the food, the wine, the architecture, the beauty, and especially the attitude.

The crew planned my shoot perfectly. They understood that I was nervous. They did everything possible to make me comfortable. On the first day, they shot the cover, which was very modest. I wore a vintage Dior gold brocade jacket with black lingerie underneath. The gold-leaf cover would come to be considered one of the more conservative in the history of *Playboy.*

By the next day, I was much more comfortable in my skin. I clicked back into my old modeling mode and decided to convey an image of a strong woman confident in her sexuality. But I also wanted to have fun with it. I asked an assistant to grab a newspaper, and I posed with the French sports page. The crew didn't seem to notice my nudity. They were more fixated on the lighting and my hair and makeup. It helped that there was plenty of champagne in the hotel suite where we were shooting. Lorraine was always ready to pour me a glass.

"Fuck the haters," she said as we clinked glasses. With her British accent, she had a way of making cuss words sound classy.

I felt my groove returning. I was reborn and reinvigorated. Even my mother-in-law had warmed up to me . . . a bit.

When I looked at the proofs, I saw so much of my mom in me. I wondered what she'd think of all this. I had a feeling she'd say, *Good for you, Lisita. Live your life on your own terms. Warriors never let the bullies win.*

The magazine hit the stands in January 2006. I met Hugh Hefner at an event at the Palms Casino Resort in Las Vegas. It wasn't our first encounter. Remember when I used to go to the Playboy mansion for movie night? One night, Hef had headed toward me as I came out of the bathroom and tried to plant an open-mouthed kiss on my lips. I turned my head to the left as he slobbered on my right check. When he pulled away, I saw a flash of anger on his face.

But that day in 2006, when I officially met him, he was gracious.

"I love that a forty-one-year-old brunette is on our cover," he said. "You look great." I didn't mention that I'd stolen food from the buffet at his mansion during movie night all those years ago. And I certainly didn't mention the wet kiss.

After the launch, I was interviewed by newspapers, magazines, and radio and television stations. Whenever a reporter posed the question, What's next?, I'd talk about my desire to work as an entertainment reporter.

"I'd love to work on *Inside Edition, Entertainment Tonight*, or *Extra*," I'd say.

Only one journalist seemed to think this was a ridiculous idea: Neil Cavuto, the host of *Your World with Neil Cavuto* on Fox News, said I'd never work in broadcasting again. I didn't let his comments faze me. Instead, I smiled at him.

(And his on-air prediction would be . . . fake news.)

Two days later, a crew from *Inside Edition* came to my Malibu home to shoot a story about my cover. It was beautifully shot (thanks to Eric Chin, a photojournalist for *Inside Edition*). When the correspondent asked me what I wanted to do next, I said I'd love to be a reporter for a news program like *Inside Edition*.

A day after my story aired, Kenny called me. He'd just gotten off the phone with Charles Lachman, *Inside Edition*'s executive producer.

"They want to fly you out to New York and meet you."

Next thing I knew, I had a two-year contract as a West Coast correspondent. One of my first assignments was covering the auditions for *American Idol* at the Rose Bowl. I jumped in line with the contestants and mixed it up with them. My spontaneous comments made it on the program.

After that, I regularly reported on *American Idol* as well as *Dancing with the Stars*. I became the correspondent for all the red-carpet award shows—the Emmys, the Grammys, the Oscars, and the BET Awards. It felt great to be holding a microphone again. And instead of shivering on a football field in the dead of winter, I was clad head to toe in designer gowns and dripping in diamonds in sunny LA. Instead of asking athletes about home runs and touchdowns, I was interviewing actors about movie roles and TV shows.

Did I make the right decision by posing in *Playboy*? Absolutely. Would I do it again? Absolutely not. It was a risky move. Luckily, the risk paid off. Additionally, the experience was empowering, exciting, and brave. I had no idea that interviewing celebrities for *Inside Edition* would eventually lead to a career as an investigative journalist. How many investigative correspondents have posed for *Playboy*? It's safe to say I'm probably the only one.

After all, *Americans are such prudes.*

For years, this was how I told my *Playboy* story. I'd laugh about it. "Hugh Hefner is a funny old man," I'd say, explaining that I loved being part of his iconic brand. After all, posing topless for *Playboy* had been an empowering experience that had led me to my next chapter with *Inside Edition*.

However, I recently hosted *Secrets of Playboy*, a ten-part docuseries on A&E that revealed the dark side of the Playboy empire. Now I view my experience with *Playboy* through a much different lens. As I listened to the women—former Playmates, Bunnies, Hefner's ex-girlfriends, and women who had been employed by the brand—I understood that Hefner was not a funny old man. I now believe that he was a manipulative predator who used his power to control and sexually abuse women.

As these women recounted their traumatic stories, I thought about those years when I had attended movie night at the Playboy mansion. There had been so much heavy drinking and drugs around me, but I had never participated in any of that. In fact, my instincts had told me to get the hell out of there. I'd load up my bags with food, search for the fabled orangutan who lived in their zoo, and leave just as everyone else retreated to the screening room.

After spending time with these women, I wondered, *What if?* I felt as if I had dodged a major bullet. I have an enormous amount of respect and empathy for these survivors who weren't as lucky as I was. How incredibly brave of them to come forward and share their experiences. They are true warriors.

14

Between a Jock and
a Hard Place

As much as I loved covering red-carpet events for *Inside Edition*, I was ready for a new challenge. I reached my breaking point a year into the gig when I received a frantic, middle-of-the-night call from a producer. She wanted me to race to the San Fernando Valley salon where Britney Spears had shaved her head. An hour later, I scooped up Britney's hair extensions from the salon floor. I held them in one hand and a microphone in the other.

After I left the shoot, I sat in my car, feeling terrible. As a West Coast correspondent, I'd reported on real news stories, like the Malibu fires and courtroom dramas. But lately, much of what I was assigned to cover involved scandals surrounding young female celebrities. A few days earlier, I'd reported on Paris Hilton exiting a limo without panties.

What I really wanted was a different, more challenging role. From the moment I'd started working for *Inside Edition*, I'd been intrigued by the investigative unit. I'd worked on a few assignments with them and loved it. Once I was sent to Dallas, Texas, to report on hotel chains that had hired convicted sex offenders as night managers. I grilled these guys, interviewing one in an elevator and chasing another through a parking lot. My producers were impressed and surprised by my aggressive style. But it was a natural reaction to the alarm I felt when I thought about the single women travelers who were unaware that rapists and child predators had access to their hotel-room keys. Because of our report, the hotels changed their policy. I became hooked on this kind of journalism that really made a difference.

And when the investigative reporter retired, I begged Charles, our executive producer, to consider me for this job. "It could empower women to see other women doing badass things," I told him.

A few months later, I was named *Inside Edition*'s chief investigative correspondent. I was sent all over the country to report on consumer fraud, corruption, crime, child abuse, and sex trafficking. I had my own style—boldly questioning and interviewing suspects and openly weeping with victims. I remembered myself as the little girl who would chase imaginary bad guys around the house. I felt I'd found my destiny. And the best part? My chyron read, "Lisa Guerrero." Young Latinas could see me doing a job they could aspire to. The pride in my name—the name that honors my mother and my heritage—was back.

As my career started taking off again, Scott's baseball career was winding down. He was now an older player in the league and had been struggling for years after a series of surgeries and injuries. The last few seasons, he'd moved from team to team, hoping for a comeback that had never happened. After signing with the New York Yankees in February 2006, he was released from his contract just a few months later in June. In 2007, he officially retired after a solid sixteen-year career that included a World Series championship.

I thought when Scott retired, we'd finally spend more time together. We'd both traveled a lot for work and had never really been home, just the two of us. But Scott found it extremely difficult to be in the same place for more than two days at a time. Looking back, I realize he'd always been up-front about his desire to travel. I guess I hadn't been listening. When we first dated and agreed that we didn't want children, Scott said that when he retired, he planned to travel all over the world.

Still, I couldn't understand why he didn't want to be home with me. He said it wasn't that he didn't want to be with me, he just didn't want to be home. "Come with me," he said.

In between my assignments, I'd meet Scott at whatever latest adventure he was on—a celebrity golf tournament, an all-star poker game, a ski holiday. We'd head to New York for Broadway shows. We spent a lot of time traveling to Las Vegas for charity events.

I'd travel around the country as well as in Europe, South America, and New Zealand. Scott loved to visit new countries and have new experiences. Wherever we went, it was always first class. He knew how much I loved Paris, so we visited the city a couple of times. Scott introduced me to luxury cruising, and we'd stop in ports throughout Europe. During a visit to Barcelona, I fell in love with Antoni Gaudí's whimsical architecture, especially his mosaic design technique. I was intrigued by his process of finding broken ceramic tiles, plates, and cups and combining them to create his art. I could relate to that feeling of brokenness and the need to be whole. Since that trip, creating mosaics has become one of my passions. I've dedicated a studio in my home to my artwork.

On these trips, I would have fun, but they were exhausting. I was always ready to get home and back to work. But Scott was always looking for the next good time. He was like a shark who had to be constantly in motion. I love traveling, but I couldn't live on a permanent vacation. He and his baseball buddies were truly Peter Pans. Some had lots of money, so they never had to work. Many were divorced, so they had no obligations. They could do what they wanted when they wanted. And they wanted to golf at the best courses, ski the best runs, play poker at the best casinos, attend celebrity tournaments, and party all night.

After the disaster that was *Monday Night Football*, I felt I'd been given a second chance with *Inside Edition*. I didn't want to blow it. I was working hard and traveling over one hundred days a year to shoot my investigations. When I wasn't working, I needed to be home recovering and researching for my next assignment. I was resentful that Scott was partying while I was working. I'd be on the road in some small town, sitting on surveillance for hours, sometimes days, while my husband would be in Vegas with a bunch of knuckleheads. I'd wonder, *What is he doing on these trips? Is he cheating on me?* I couldn't understand why the guy known as the hardest-working player in the league didn't want to work at all.

While I was between assignments, Lorraine called and asked if I'd be interested in auditioning for a role in *A Plumm Summer*, an independent film set in Montana in 1968. I loved the script, auditioned, and was offered the part of Roxy Plumm, a mom of two boys who is struggling to save her marriage. But nearly as soon as I was cast, financing for the film fell through.

I was really disappointed. I had been drawn to the family drama, which reminded me of the Disney movies I'd watched as a kid. It was loosely based on a true story about a boy who becomes obsessed with the "kidnapping" of a beloved TV star—a frog marionette. Scott, who was a movie buff, had read the script and liked the story too. We thought, *Why not produce it ourselves?* Scott had talked about producing films when his baseball career ended, and the perfect opportunity had literally fallen into our laps. Besides, this would be a great way to spend time together while creating a beautiful film.

Everyone warned us against it. "You'll lose all your money!"

We didn't listen. We believed in the project and were certain it would resonate with audiences. We felt that *A Plumm Summer* would fill a much-needed void in the family entertainment niche. Plus, we had A-lister Hugh Jackman on board to play the adult version of Elliott Plumm, the little boy the story revolves around. Hugh was friends with Caroline Zelder, the director, and Frank Antonelli, her writing and producing partner. He would bookend the movie, appearing in the first and last scenes. With this kind of star power, we were told we'd receive wide theatrical distribution.

We knew Hugh Jackman would be box-office gold—he was at the height of his career. We had a verbal agreement from him, but Scott and I wondered if we should get a contract.

But Hugh had given Caroline and Frank his word, and they trusted him. We weren't concerned. Besides, Scott had already proven himself to be a successful investor in real estate and some other endeavors. We'd make the perfect team—he'd be the money guy, and I'd handle the creative end. Working with Caroline and Frank, we assembled the cast, which included Billy Baldwin, who played my alcoholic husband, and Henry Winkler as the TV host whose marionette sidekick is "frognapped."

When we weren't shooting the film and I wasn't away on assignment, we'd explore the beautiful Big Sky Country of Montana. Scott would fly-fish with Billy and Henry. We all took a rafting trip down a gentle river and had a picnic lunch on its banks. It was truly a magical summer.

Working together on the project had strengthened our marriage. Best of all, it seemed that Scott had discovered his second act. We imagined that *A Plumm Summer* would be the first of many movies produced under our shingle, Home Team Productions. We were already developing ideas for a sequel. Scott talked about branching out into television too.

Hugh Jackman was supposed to shoot his two scenes in New York City over a weekend. Nola Roller, my friend and wardrobe stylist (we'd worked together on *MNF* and other projects), began preparing the outfits he'd wear for his scenes. But a few days before Hugh was scheduled to shoot, he backed out due to a scheduling conflict with *Deception*, a movie he was starring in alongside Ewan McGregor. Since we only had a verbal agreement, there was nothing we could do. If we'd had a contract with him, he would have been obligated to shoot the scenes. We were devastated. Caroline and Frank blamed themselves since they had believed Hugh's word was as good as a contract. But Scott and I should have insisted. I suppose we were so excited about this project and its heartwarming message that we overlooked some important details. Still, we remained optimistic that we'd be able to get decent distribution without him. If the movie had a strong first weekend in limited release and received good reviews, maybe it would lead to a nationwide rollout.

Despite a rave review in *Daily Variety*, the movie was released in only a few theaters in four markets. The irony was that the small audiences that saw the film loved it. It went on to win seven family-film awards and honors. Even with an advance from Paramount for video distribution, we never made back the money we spent. To make matters worse, Scott hadn't set up an LLC, a corporate entity that would have protected us from being personally pursued for repayment of debts and liabilities.

To sum it up, when the film didn't make its money back, we lost millions of dollars of our own money.

Nothing made sense. It was like watching a slow-motion train wreck. Every day, we'd receive more bad news about our financial situation. We lost the dream home that Scott had built in Lake Tahoe. Then we lost the beachfront Malibu home we had designed together. Then we watched our bank accounts dwindle. It seemed that every day during 2008, the phone would ring with more devastating news.

All these years later, it still makes me sick to my stomach. I can't begin to describe what it felt like going into our Malibu house to pack up. We'd just moved in two years earlier. Every space in our beautiful Spanish-Moroccan-styled home had our imprint. My pieces of Gaudí-inspired mosaic art were installed throughout the house—an Aztec sunburst kitchen backsplash, a matching fireplace surround, a mosaic pizza oven on the back deck. Even the address plate at the entrance featured a mosaic— one of the first I'd ever created. I walked from room to room like a zombie, trying to make sense of what had happened. When I walked out, I felt like I was saying goodbye to the person I had been, to the couple we had been.

When we moved into a rental condo in Playa Vista, Scott completely checked out. His attitude was *I'll never see that money again. Those were dream homes, and now they're gone. But there's nothing I can ever do to get it back. It's gone forever, and it sucks. I'm going golfing.*

Scott was depressed, and I didn't blame him—I was too. If Scott hadn't liked being in one place before, he loathed being in our rental. This nondescript townhouse was a constant reminder of all we'd lost. We were in a really bad place. I blamed myself, and I knew Scott did too. Had I never suggested that we invest in the film, none of this would have happened. I even blamed Lorraine for bringing me the script. It was ridiculous to play the blame game, but I couldn't help myself. I dwelled on all the mistakes we'd made. To get out of my head, I threw myself into my work even more, believing that if I worked hard enough, I'd one day recoup the money.

I was on an assignment in Portland, reporting on a shocking story about a paramedic who sexually assaulted women in the back of his ambulances. It was a tough, emotional few days. Scott called when we were wrapping up. He suggested that we unwind with dinner and movie. He told me to pick whatever I wanted to see. He asked me what time exactly I'd be flying back.

I thought we'd been burglarized when I entered the condo a few hours later. I could tell things were missing, but I couldn't figure out exactly what was gone. Scott wasn't home, and our dogs—Twinkie and Cupcake—were barking in the kitchen. I rushed in to make sure they were okay. That was when I noticed that Scott's stuff wasn't on the counter. He always left a few things there—keys, mail, his phone. I ran upstairs to our bedroom and swung open the closet. His clothes were gone.

Scott had left me.

I looked around the room for a note, something. I checked my phone for a message. There was nothing. I replayed the last few days before I'd left for my assignment. I hadn't stormed off. We hadn't had a fight. When I'd said goodbye, there hadn't even been a hint of acrimony. Everything had seemed fine. Yes, I knew he was depressed. Yes, I knew he was devastated that he'd lost so much. But I also thought we'd somehow get through it together.

So what had happened? I decided he must have left me for someone else. It made perfect sense—that was why he was always traveling; that was why he never wanted to be home. He was in love with another woman. This had always been my worst fear, and it had come true, just as I had known it would.

For the longest time, I lay on the floor sobbing and couldn't move. When I finally stood up, I felt dizzy. I found my cell and called Scott. It went straight to voicemail. Scott had turned his phone off so he could ignore me, probably to be with this new woman he was in love with. I kept calling. He owed me an explanation. Finally, Scott picked up.

"What is going on?"

"Lisa, I'm sorry," he said. "I just didn't have the courage to face you. I knew it would be a horrible scene. You'd probably throw something at me."

"I don't understand."

"I just can't handle it anymore."

"Handle what? Scott?"

There was a long silence.

"Scott!"

"I want to do what I want to do when I want to do it. I want to travel. I want to golf. I want to be with my friends. And I don't want to be questioned about when I'll be back."

There was a long pause. I couldn't speak.

"Lisa, I don't want the responsibility of being married. I don't even want the responsibility of feeding our dogs."

My head spun. I couldn't absorb what he said. It was too much. The words were a foreign language. I struggled to decipher them.

"Do you not love me?" I asked, my heart throbbing.

"Lisa, I still love you."

"But you're in love with someone else."

He sighed. "No. I've never cheated on you. I'd never do that to you. I don't love anybody else. This has nothing to do with anyone else. I'll always love you. I just don't want to be married. I'll never get married again."

And that was it.

At first, I was shocked. Then I was furious. Then I was depressed. I missed having him around. But when I started thinking about what happened, I realized I'd been questioning our relationship for the last few years. As we got older, our differences became more pronounced. We argued a lot. I chalked up our recent problems to the financial devastation we'd just gone through because of our bad business decision. But if I was being honest with myself, our marriage had been a series of rough patches from the very beginning.

I thought about how stunned his friends had been when Scott had gotten married. No one had expected him to ever settle down. He had been the last guy at the bar or the strip club. He was the dude who was always ready to party. When we married, baseball wives would tell me they were relieved that Scott would no longer be a bad influence on their husbands. I'd smile, but I'd be thinking, *He's the same guy he always was. He's not going to change for me or anyone.*

I was right. Scott never changed. He was still the guy who wanted to party all night. But I barely recognized the person I'd been when I'd met him. I had a completely different career now. Instead of obsessing about sports, I had become a fierce advocate for victim's rights. I had become politically active. I was passionate about my mosaic art. I loved being home, working on my latest creation. Scott couldn't stand being under the same roof for more than two days. We were so different, and we wanted such different things.

After I recovered from the shock and pain of Scott leaving me, I was almost relieved. A lot of my friends echoed this sentiment. "You've been unhappy for years. Scott just beat you to the punch."

After a few weeks, Scott called to check up on me. Was I okay?

No, I wasn't. I was angry, hurt, and lonely. But after a few months, I began to feel empathy for him. I knew he was battling depression. The townhouse had been a constant reminder of all the things he'd lost, and he'd found it unbearable to be there. When he was traveling with the boys, being wined and dined and treated like a celebrity at tournaments and events around the world, he could live the life he always had and forget all he had lost.

I didn't want to throw away the happy parts of our history together. Despite our differences, we had truly enjoyed each other. We'd traveled the world. We'd lived on the beach and in the mountains. We'd loved each other and in many ways still do.

People I knew were shocked that we remained friends. But we'd been through so much together. Scott was there for me and so supportive of me when I went through my dark periods, especially during *MNF*. He was always on my side, telling me to ignore the haters and pushing me to pursue my dreams. If he hadn't encouraged me to pose for *Playboy*, I wouldn't have discovered my next chapter. I owe a big debt of gratitude to my ex-husband for my new career. So why wouldn't I want us to remain friends? If we didn't, it would be like erasing a big part of my past and disregarding the role he played in my present. It takes courage to forgive, move on, and forge a new relationship with that person.

At first, it was hard to live by myself. After a while, it felt freeing. It's brave to be comfortable being alone. It's empowering to go into a restaurant and say, "Table for one." A lot of my friends are mortified to do it. Often women feel that by sitting alone, they're announcing to the world that nobody wants to be with them. Who cares what anyone thinks? It's important to enjoy your own company. I have dated several great guys since Scott—and one or two not-so-great ones. I hope there comes a time when I'll meet someone who I can share my life with, but I wouldn't want to settle just because I don't want to be by myself.

Six months after Scott left, I began looking for my own home. The townhouse had never felt comfortable, more like a place in between moves. I searched Trulia for Spanish-style houses. I found the perfect place—an oasis in the city with a garden filled with orange, lemon, lime, and peach trees. When I toured it, I could feel that this was my home. In many ways, it reminded me of Casita Encantada, my first house in Hollywood Hills. After living in mansions with Scott, I'd returned to my much more modest roots. I called Scott up when I found the place, and he checked it out with me.

When I wasn't on assignment, I was busy renovating my home. It had great bones, but my 1924 casita needed attention. One of the benefits of living alone is that you get to make all the decisions on how you decorate. I decided to fill my home with my grandfather's woodwork, my dad's photography, photos of my family, and my mosaics as well as paintings and sculptures from my travels around the world.

When I was a little girl, my favorite aunt, Sonia, and my mother would say to me, "Can you hear the jungle drums, Lisita?," which means, Can you feel the pull of your heritage? I chose art, colors, and furnishings to reflect my Hispanic origins. It's completely my vibe. When I walk into my home, I feel embraced by my mother, my family, my culture. I definitely hear the jungle drums.

I love my casita, but I'd be an absolute liar if I said I didn't miss my house at the beach. I hope to make it back to Malibu someday. But that is for another love and another chapter.

15

Armed with a Microphone
and Lip Gloss

With an average of five million viewers per night, *Inside Edition* is now the number-one newsmagazine in syndication. And one of the most popular parts of the program is my investigations. Our television viewers—many of whom are women around my age—enjoy my tough investigative style. They love to see a fellow female chasing bad guys and giving them the business while wearing stilettos and fabulous lipstick. I get stopped on the street all the time. "You're a badass," some will say. Others legitimately worry about me. "Be careful. Don't take so many risks." For some reason, I'm often stopped at airports by concerned viewers who tell me they pray for me. Once a cute old lady grabbed my arm and hugged me. Then, she started loudly praying for me right at the Delta terminal in Denver.

I think people understand the importance of my stories and feel connected to me. They believe I'm watching out for them and their families—and this makes me grateful beyond measure.

What's funny is that no matter where I am—at a restaurant, hotel, or shop—people assume I'm doing an undercover story and that there are hidden cameras somewhere. A restaurant manager once asked me if I was doing an investigation on his place. I laughed and asked him, "Should I be?"

As the chief investigative correspondent for *Inside Edition*, I get to expose the bad guys for a living. Armed with nothing but a microphone and lip gloss, I interview criminals, scam artists, crooked politicians, and suspects in assault, rape, and even murder cases. Our news program has millions of fans. When they meet me, one of their first questions is "How are you so brave?"

Well, I wasn't always.

This job *is* dangerous. As I mentioned, I've had guns waved at me. I've been struck by cars. I've been kicked, pushed, hit, stalked, and threatened. I've been scolded by cops. I grab my *microphone* and pursue the truth to help others—just like my childhood idol, Wonder Woman.

Most people avoid confrontation at all costs, but I thrive on demanding accountability from someone who owes answers to a victim. It's the best feeling in the world. And I'm never scared. But when it's over, I'll head back to my hotel, shake my head, and scold myself while considering all the things that could have gone wrong.

Every morning, it's the same routine. I wake, feed Cupcake, and have coffee. Then I pour a second cup of coffee, sit in my kitchen, and spend two hours combing through the news online. I'm drawn to stories about women's issues as well as crimes against the elderly, the marginalized, children, and animals. I'm always looking for stories with *Inside Edition* angles.

I'm fortunate to work with the best and bravest investigative unit in the country. My producers and crew are professional, thorough, and committed to telling our stories fairly and honestly. When you see me on camera, remember that there is a group of hardworking journalists on the other side of the lens. Each investigation is a team effort. I'm so grateful to work with a group of pros whom I also consider pals.

#MeToo and Tom Arnold

A few months ago, Tom Arnold called to pitch a story he thought would interest me. It involved a sweeping lawsuit alleging the mishandling of sexual assault allegations against Liberty University, one of the largest Christian universities in the country. A woman who said she had been raped by another student wanted to tell her story and go on camera for the first time but was nervous about how a television show would handle the story. She had been interviewed in print and on a podcast but not on camera.

"I told her that she could trust you."

I couldn't help but smile. If you had told me during the *Best Damn* days that Tom Arnold would one day become a big advocate for women's issues, I probably would have laughed. But after years of sobriety as well as the demise of the show, he remarried, had children, and started using his vast social media platform to promote social justice causes.

We had reconnected a few years earlier. He said he'd been troubled by the way I was treated during *Best Damn*. I told him he'd always been a friend and had nothing to apologize for. Since then, he's been very supportive of my career, often retweeting my stories and connecting me to other journalists and media personalities.

Tom explained that the lawsuit accused the university, founded by Jerry Falwell Sr., of mishandling allegations of sexual assault and punishing women who tried to report them. Tom had been in touch with one of the "Jane Does," a former student body president.

Since 2010, I've investigated and reported on at least one hundred sexual abuse stories, including campus rapes, child predators, and sexual misconduct by coaches, doctors, professors, teachers, and driver's ed instructors.

And while I've earned a reputation for my confrontational style, I feel that empathy is my real strength. For a survivor, there's nothing harder than being in front of the camera with lights blazing while you tell a stranger about the worst thing that has ever happened to you. I believe my subjects, who are mostly women, open up to me because they can feel my empathy. As the interview progresses, my empathy builds. I sometimes become emotional along with these women. Oftentimes, I'll stop the interview so we can regroup or hug or go for a walk outside. I'll hand them a Kleenex and tell them we're not in any rush. That's a benefit of taped interviews. I'm able to give these women time to process the experience. Later on, they'll get in touch with me through social media or email and tell me that talking to me was part of the healing process.

Tom's contact, Chelsea Andrews, known as "Jane Doe #7," and I texted back and forth. Often, especially with these types of stories, I spend months texting with a potential subject. I'm never pushy about getting them on camera. Usually, it's just the opposite. I'll say to them, "Before you agree to talk to me, think about the ramifications, because if you come forward, it's a life-changing event. Everyone will know. Five million people will see you on the show—and then ten million will watch you on YouTube." Chelsea told me she was filled with anxiety, but she believed her story had to be told so others would feel comfortable coming forward. When she was ready to speak on the phone, I called her.

Universities across the country have faced scrutiny for their handling—or rather mishandling—of sexual assault cases. But Liberty brings it to another level. The college requires all students to sign a code of conduct called the Liberty Way. It's a strict honor code that calls for disciplining students for drinking or engaging in premarital sex. Because of this code, the university has created a climate where it's impossible to report rape without being accused of breaking a rule. That's why most of the sexual abuse there goes unreported. The punishment for drinking is the same as the punishment for rape. Complaints are often dismissed, or the accusers are held responsible and even fined.

Chelsea was concerned that because my segments are only a few minutes long, we wouldn't be able to accurately capture her ordeal.

"Our stories are short, but they're impactful. We get right to the heart," I explained.

She thought about it, watched some of the stories I'd covered on sexual abuse, and agreed to sit down for an interview. And then another woman came forward. Chelsea and Heather Wendel appeared together.

When the report aired, it blew up on social media. The response from our viewers was complete outrage at the university.

Before the interview, Chelsea and Heather had been afraid of the public's reaction and worried about the blame-the-victim mentality. The women wound up being so proud of their report that they retweeted it. Since it aired, more former and current students have come forward to share their experiences, and they've filed lawsuits against the university.

These women told me that by appearing on the show, they had discovered unknown depths of bravery.

"I realize how important it is to speak up because the floodgates open nearly every time," Chelsea told me. "I inspired other women to come forward."

This investigation and reports like it are some of my most important. Over the years, I've interviewed hundreds of women who have shared stories of sexual abuse. Most of the time, my investigation is the first time their name and face will be in the news. This is why I believe it's so important to have a woman fronting these investigations. In general, women feel much more comfortable revealing their trauma to another woman.

These investigations can take a long time before they're ready to air. Sometimes it will take weeks, months, and occasionally years. Some women decide to back out or wait until their kids are in college or their husband retires from a job or they leave the workplace. I never push anyone to do these stories. When these women agree to do it, it's because they trust me. They know our program will treat their account with respect. This is such an honor. I believe that the more victims speak out against their abusers, the less this abuse will be tolerated. I think when survivors like Heather and Chelsea feel comfortable tweeting their stories, it really demonstrates how much times have changed. Instead of hiding in shame, they're exposing the wrongdoing.

By shining a light on sexual abuse, we're showing other survivors that they are not alone, that they can come forward and be taken seriously. Before movements like #MeToo and TIME'S UP, women were terrified to speak about their traumas for fear they wouldn't be believed or they'd be blamed for dressing a certain way or drinking too much. Also, people are coming to understand that just because a woman doesn't report an incident right away doesn't mean it didn't happen. These types of stories are changing attitudes. Hopefully, those who commit these crimes will realize that they can no longer get away with them.

That's the beauty of our particular brand of accountability journalism. I report on crimes with the hope that they won't happen again. And that lawsuit against Liberty University? After our investigation aired, the school settled the case with the Jane Does, and the president of the university announced an $8 million increase to campus security and a revision to the university honor code so that future victims of sexual harassment and assault would no longer be blamed or punished.

The Wolf of Wall Street

Our Jordan Belfort investigations were important and memorable to our millions of viewers and, most importantly, to his victims.

This convicted felon was glamorized and immortalized in the blockbuster movie *The Wolf of Wall Street*. He was played by Leonardo DiCaprio, who shockingly endorsed him in a video that enraged Belfort's victims.

"Jordan stands as a shining example of the transformative qualities of ambition and hard work," DiCaprio said.

In the 1990s, Belfort ran Stratton Oakmont, a stock broker-age firm that would hard-sell clients into buying penny stocks designed to fail. Those artificially inflated stocks would then be "pumped and dumped" by Stratton Oakmont, resulting in hundreds of millions in profits for the company—and the loss of life savings for some of its clients.

In 1999, Belfort pleaded guilty to stock fraud and money laundering. He was sentenced to four years in prison (he served twenty-two months) and ordered to pay $110 million in restitution to his former clients. But he'd blown the money he'd swindled on his luxury lifestyle, which included yachts and beachfront homes as well as prostitutes, cocaine, and gambling. Belfort's victims were mostly working-class people, some of whom lost everything. One of the conditions of his release was that he was ordered to repay his victims in full. But Belfort's payment plan was only a few thousand dollars a month. It would take more than sixteen hundred years for his victims to be fully paid. Meanwhile, he wrote a book, which was turned into the film and developed a cult following because of it. His speaking engagements—in the United States and abroad—generated up to $100,000 a day. He was reportedly living in an oceanfront home, driving a $140,000 Mercedes, and traveling around the world, often on private jets.

And his 1,513 victims are still waiting for their money.

In 2014, I trailed Belfort through an airport in Toronto after he'd just finished a speaking engagement. I brought along Brad Johnson, who was one of Belfort's victims. I caught up with Belfort and his entourage as they were unloading luggage in front of the airport.

As I raced up to Belfort, a member of his entourage put out his hand to push me away.

"Don't touch me," I said as I edged closer to Jordan and turned toward him, microphone in hand.

"You are living this life of luxury, yet you owe your victims over $100 million. How do you explain that?"

He had sunglasses on and wouldn't look at me as he spoke.

"Actually, this is going to be a great year. I'm doing a US tour that I announced, and I'm giving a hundred percent of the profits to pay back the victims."

I asked the crucial question: "When?"

He said he'd begin paying his victims in the fall. Then I introduced him to Brad Johnson, but Belfort wouldn't acknowledge him.

"Can't you take your sunglasses off and talk to one of your victims?" I asked.

He rushed off with his entourage. We followed close on his heels.

"I was not a wealthy man. That was my life's savings. That was a big deal," Johnson said.

But Belfort wouldn't answer and disappeared.

Well, he finished his tour, but he didn't pay back all the money he told me he would pay his victims. Instead, he was again busy jet-setting and living in beachfront mansions. This guy was still living large while some of his victims were living in squalor.

I couldn't let this report go. My producer and I tracked his whereabouts. In 2017, we followed him to London, where he was speaking to an audience of 3,600 people. As soon as he opened the event for questions, I raced up to the microphone.

I'm sure he was expecting a question from some fawning fan. Instead, he got me. And I wanted answers.

"In 2014, you promised me you would pay back all of your victims that year. It's three years later, and you still owe your victims $100 million."

When the crowd booed and hissed, I raised my voice.

"When are you going to pay your victims back?"

Security ran up to me, grabbed the microphone out of my hand, and escorted me out. A few moments later, a shaken Belfort abruptly left the stage.

Demon Tube

Of course I can't write a book without mentioning the interview that amassed one billion views. It was with Kenneth Copeland, a wildly successful but controversial televangelist.

The irony of this report is not lost on me. When I was a young sports reporter, I was attacked by the mainstream sports media, who considered me "just a pretty face." And in this report—which went viral and earned me a reputation as a skilled journalist—you barely see my face. The entire interview is shot from behind me.

It was April 6, 2019, and I was spending three bleak days in Branson, Missouri, on an investigation that we'd been working on for months. I was in search of my "white whale"—Kenneth Copeland, a wild-eyed televangelist.

Kenneth Copeland has achieved astronomical wealth (estimated at more than $300 million) by preaching what is known as the prosperity gospel, an interpretation of the Bible popular among some evangelical preachers that equates Christian faith with financial success. According to this gospel, if followers donate their hard-earned money to his Kenneth Copeland Ministries church based in Tarrant County, Texas, God will enrich them in return.

As we sat there waiting, I thought about Bonnie Parker. I'd interviewed her daughter, Kristy Beach, who had told me that her mother had had breast cancer. Instead of seeking treatment for the disease, Bonnie had sent all of her savings to Copeland. She believed he'd cure her of cancer through prayer. When she died, Kristy couldn't even afford to bury her.

When people ask me why I'm so brave, I explain that it's because of people like Kristy.

I had questioned Copeland years earlier for part of a segment called "Rockstar Preachers." I was able to interview him before security escorted him away. We'd also rented a helicopter in Fort Worth to provide viewers with an aerial tour of his eighteen-thousand-square-foot mansion, complete with the Kenneth Copeland Airport, where he kept his fleet of planes.

This time, I was in Branson as part of an investigation on Copeland as well as one of his buddies, fellow megabucks TV preacher Jesse Duplantis, whose bodyguards manhandled me when I approached him at a book signing. They yanked me so hard that I had bruises on my arms, ribs, and shoulder.

I wanted to talk to Copeland about his lavish lifestyle and ask him about a comment he'd made in 2015 that he didn't want to fly in commercial planes because he refused to "get in a long tube with a bunch of demons," thus justifying his penchant for private jets.

We'd asked for an interview with Copeland, but he wouldn't return our calls. He's rarely seen in public, but we had discovered that he was doing a paid appearance as part of the Branson Victory Campaign at the Faith Life Church. Media wasn't allowed in the conference, and Copeland was usually ushered through a back door at events and into his waiting Cadillac Escalade.

So my producer, my cameraman, and I devised a plan. We'd wait in our SUV in the front row of the parking lot near the back door while Copeland was inside the church. Then, when he exited the building, we'd furiously race the twenty yards to the building to interview him while he took those five steps from the door to his car.

For two days we sat in the SUV outside the church, hoping for a glimpse of him. It was boring. We smelled bad. We were tired. On the third day, we began to wonder if this mission had been a bust. I headed back to the hotel to shower, rest, and escape the claustrophobia for a few hours. Back in the room, I started to dye my roots (every ten days, I've got to get the gray out). As I was applying the formula, my producer called.

"He's here! He's here! Get back here now!"

I quickly rinsed my hair out, threw on the only clean shirt I had left—a white sweatshirt—and topped it with an animal-print scarf. I tossed my wet hair into a low ponytail.

When I got back to the parking lot, we spotted a few of Copeland's security guards coming out. Then came his driver, his wife, and more security detail. Finally, Copeland emerged.

"Let's go!" I yelled to my team.

My cameraman was behind me, while my producer was to my left as we tore out of our SUV for his Escalade.

I greeted Copeland with a smile and identified myself.

"Why have you said you won't fly commercial? You've said that it's like getting into a tube with a bunch of demons. Why do you think that?"

At first, he was calm. He smiled at me. "If I flew commercial, I'd have to stop 65 percent of what I'm doing; that's really the main reason."

"Isn't it true that you don't fly commercial so you can fly in luxury? How much money did you pay for Tyler Perry's Gulfstream jet, for example?"

His smile tightened. There was a bit of an edge in his voice.

"Well, for example, that's really none of your business."

"Isn't it the business of your donors?" I shot back.

"I know, I know, give me a chance here," he said, showing off his pearly whites. "Oh, and I love your eyes!"

Then came the part of the interview that sparked worldwide attention.

"Do you really believe that human beings are demons?" I asked again.

In a flash, the old man's demeanor changed. For a few seconds, he looked completely unhinged.

"No! I do not!" He pointed his right ring finger in my face. "And don't you ever say I did!"

His hand was shaking with rage, and his crystal-blue eyes were ablaze. He glared and pointed at me before speaking again.

And then his personality completely changed—again. He calmed down and quoted a Bible passage: "'We wrestle not with flesh and blood, but with principalities and powers.'"

I kept waiting for Copeland's security team or a member of his staff to step in. They stood there, helplessly watching as Copeland quoted scripture, lectured, and flirted with me. Then he wrapped it up with one of his typical fire-and-brimstone flourishes.

"When you go back to the Bible, it's full of wealth. And it's full of miracles, and signs, and wonders," he said, staring into my eyes. "And it's full of meanness." He gritted his teeth. "And it's full of hell on earth. Those are the demons, not the people."

Then he grabbed my hand and prayed over me.

"Father, God bless Lisa today. . . . Thank you for giving me the opportunity to know her and her team, and I pray and believe her piece will be successful. I love *Inside Edition*. I love the people on it, and it thrills me to get the chance to have my face on it."

He kissed my hand. "I love you, girl!" Then he ducked into his car and was gone.

That. Was. Bonkers.

And it was also TV gold.

In a twelve-minute span, Copeland had showed every character trait imaginable—and we'd gotten it all on camera.

A couple of sound bites from the interview ran as part of a segment we dubbed, "Jets for Jesus." But I kept pushing my producers to post the entire interview uncut on our YouTube channel, which we'd never done with my investigations. Finally, on May 20, the show posted the full interview online.

Nothing happened. I thought the story had run its course. Then, a week later, the political action group Occupy Democrats shared an edited version on their social media platforms: *Megachurch pastor gets SHREDDED by brave reporter.*

Two days later, a British broadcaster named Jeremy Vine (he's kind of like the Anderson Cooper of the UK) tweeted out the entire interview to his one million followers and tagged me.

He called it the "doorstep of the year."

At first I thought "doorstep" was an insult, and then I found out it was a huge compliment. "Doorstep" in England refers to a journalist confronting a subject with tough questions on their own doorstep.

Within hours, my phone, email, and social media feeds blew up. After a few days, the full video had racked up more than a million hits. Eventually, clips of it were seen nearly one billion times worldwide.

Networks, cable news, radio shows, and newspapers were talking about it. Clips of my investigation were being shown to journalism students. "This is how it's done," professors were telling them. I was being praised for asking tough questions while remaining calm and collected despite how crazy Copeland appeared.

Who is this Lisa Guerrero? they wondered.

Even though it had been years since I'd weathered media attacks after getting fired from *Monday Night Football*, I hadn't ever completely shaken off the pain of that deep humiliation. I was in complete joyful disbelief that I was now considered a "credible journalist."

Dirty Super Bowl Motels

I may be a credible journalist, but that doesn't mean I don't sometimes crawl on dirty floors in search of roaches, condom wrappers, and drug paraphernalia to get a story. Our viewers love my annual exposés on dirty Super Bowl motels. This is a series of stories I hate with a passion. Every year, my crew and I head to the city hosting the Super Bowl to investigate the motels that raise their rates by hundreds of dollars due to high demand. We check in to a room for a few hours and tear it apart. We pull off bedsheets and couch cushions. We move beds and sofas. Then we get behind the couches and underneath beds. We crawl around the floor with flashlights. And we find all kinds of disgusting things—live roaches, dead bugs, mold, used condoms, cigarettes, fingernail clippings, used syringes, hair, and even blood.

I'll call management and ask them to come to our room. Usually, when they see me with my microphone and camera crew, they run. Our investigations have resulted in some motels reducing their rates and others deep cleaning the offending rooms. When I was first assigned this story—during Super Bowl 2014 in New Jersey—I dressed in my regular clothes. But I learned my lesson. I once brought bedbugs home from one of these stories and woke up covered with bites. I had to throw out my mattress and my clothes and hire a company to fumigate my house. Now I wear disposable clothes as well as gloves and booties. These stories always go viral. But I get itchy just thinking about them.

Smash-and-Grabs and the Kingpin of Bike Thieves

Other fan favorites are the investigations where we use bait to snag a bad guy. We'll put a GPS tracking device into a laptop or a bike or a handbag. Then we wait.

One of the most memorable stories we did was a few years ago in downtown Portland, where there had been a rash of bike thefts. We purchased a $2,000 bike, making the theft a felony. Then we fitted it with a tracking device.

I rode it up to a post and locked it. In less than ten minutes, a guy broke the lock and pedaled off. We tracked his whereabouts on an app in our car and followed him. When he disappeared under a bridge, we got out of our car and followed him for blocks—me in heels. I had to hop a chain-link fence and run through a homeless encampment. People looked at me like I was insane. They started yelling at us. "What are you doing? Get out!"

It certainly occurred to me that what we were doing was incredibly dangerous and possibly stupid, but I wanted to track down the thief and recover our bike. We found a chop shop under the bridge and a guy who had our bike, which had already been disassembled. He was different from the dude who'd stolen it, presumably trading it for drugs or cash. We called the cops, and they arrested him. We discovered that he was a wanted criminal with a long rap sheet who was known as the "Kingpin of Bike Thieves." The arresting officer congratulated us on catching him before admonishing me, "You could have been killed." Getting scolded by cops is definitely part of my job description.

Another time, we traveled to San Francisco to report on "smash-and-grab" crimes that were on the rise, especially in the renowned Alamo Square, where tourists flock to take pictures of the famous "Painted Ladies" row of Victorian homes. I parked our bait car, which was rigged with hidden cameras. Then I left a visible Michaels Kors purse along with a $250 speaker, equipped with GPS tracking devices, inside. Within minutes, a crook and his accomplice smashed the car window, reached in, and snatched the purse and the speaker—all in broad daylight.

Then the couple ran down the street and jumped on a bus. We activated our GPS units and pursued them by car through the city. When they finally exited the bus, I took off on foot after them, chasing one of them down the stairs and into a subway station. I caught up with the guy holding our speaker.

"You broke into my car," I said.

"What?"

"We've got it on camera," I said. "Five million people are gonna see you steal that. So you can choose to give it back or not."

He refused and pushed our cameras.

"You know what? I'm just gonna call my mother," he said.

I was stunned and amused—he was calling his mother on me!

"You should call your mother; that is awesome," I replied. I asked if I could speak to her.

"No." Then he dropped our speaker and ran.

In all my years, I'd never before had a criminal threaten me with his mom.

Animal Avengers

Most of the time, the threats are a lot more dangerous than a call to Mom. For instance, *Inside Edition* received a tip from an animal activist about illegal cockfights in Mobile, Alabama. My producer, my cameraman, and I headed to a remote area off a dirt road for an undercover investigation. I'd never been to a cockfight before—and wow, they are brutal! Bird owners strap razor blades to the trained roosters' legs, which are used to slash and stab their opponent until one of the birds dies a painful death. Meanwhile, spectators—including children—gamble on the outcome. Often both roosters are killed during a fight. And while cockfighting is illegal under federal and state laws, Alabama has the weakest anti-cockfighting laws in the country, with operators receiving a maximum fine of $50.

I'm an animal and bird lover (as a kid, I adored Tweety, our yellow canary), so this was especially horrible to watch. These poor birds are sliced to death. There are blood and feathers everywhere. Worst of all, it's considered "family entertainment." Kids are with their parents, cheering and applauding as the birds suffer. I even saw some small children playing with a dead carcass. There was a concession stand too—as if this was just a normal sporting event.

When we discovered who was in charge, I raced up to a large man clad in a red Alabama sweatshirt with my microphone in hand. My cameraman followed close behind, his camera rolling. "Get out of here!" the guy yelled. Then he headed outside. As I was peppering him with questions in the dirt parking lot, I happened to turn around and saw about a dozen good ol' boys following us with shotguns. My producer directed us to get into the car. It was a scary moment. We were in such a remote area that if they'd killed us, I don't know if anyone would have found our bodies. (Probably buried behind the barn along with a bunch of bloody birds.) But the investigation really opened my eyes to a world I hadn't been exposed to before. Since it aired, a bunch of cockfighting rings in Alabama have been exposed and shut down.

As hard as it is to report on stories of animal abuse, those reports bring awareness to issues and spark change. For instance, I received a tip about a filthy RV in downtown Los Angeles that was crammed with chihuahuas. Besides covering the report, we rescued the dogs. All forty dogs were spayed, neutered, vaccinated, and adopted, thanks to the amazing Ellen Ballon Dante and her team at Deity Animal Rescue. I once reported on a story about a cat hoarder. The house was so filthy that I had to wear a hazmat suit. The good news is that after the story, all one hundred cats were adopted—and *Inside Edition* completely cleaned and disinfected the owner's home.

Although I've won dozens of awards and accolades, my greatest accomplishments are the stories that make a difference. Those differences come in many shapes and sizes. It can be as big as an arrest or a change in laws or company policies. Or it can be as simple as a hoarder walking into a clean house or a puppy finding a loving home.

16

#BeingBrave

When *Inside Edition* began posting stories on its YouTube channel, teens and twenty-somethings started binge watching my investigations. Every day, I'm bombarded with emails and messages on my social media platforms from men and women of every generation. Regardless of their age, they all want to know the same thing: "How are you so brave? How can I be brave?" Women seek advice on dealing with husbands, friends, in-laws, coworkers, and bosses. They want the courage to ask for raises, be taken seriously at meetings, and stand up to abusive spouses. The teens and preteens want advice on dealing with bullies, teachers, and parents. They are desperate to see justice served. That's why they love my segments. I don't settle for the standard "No comment." I pursue and interview the bad guy. If he walks away, I follow. I demand answers. I hold him accountable. Usually that only happens in movies. No wonder my youngest viewers think I'm the real-life Wonder Woman.

In 2013, I guest cohosted *The View*. When Whoopi Goldberg introduced me to the audience, she described what I did. Then she looked at me incredulously. "Why?"

I explained that it is empowering for women to chase bad guys and demand answers. But broadcasting legend Barbara Walters took issue with my approach. She asked if it was really fair to stick a microphone in someone's face. "Don't you ever feel that maybe it goes too far?" I told her no. "Once you speak to a victim, you feel you owe it to them to get answers." I wish more journalists would hold politicians, scam artists, and crooks accountable.

I started speaking about bravery at schools—including my own. Recently, I was inducted into Edison High School's Hall of Fame. Remember Q-Tip? The insecure and shy girl in high school? She would have been shocked to discover that four decades later, she'd be speaking to a roomful of seniors about the concept of being brave.

This message resonates with kids. But I realized that adults wanted these tools too. I started my #BeBrave initiative and took my message to women's groups, nonprofit organizations, and corporate audiences.

I think people assume that brave people are born brave. That bravery is somehow wired into certain people's DNA. I tell them that I may do brave things now, but there were times when I was the opposite of brave. It took all of my life experience and the obstacles I've told you about for me to get to this point—and the things that I do are things that other people can do too.

Lisa's Four Steps to Bravery

Research

Before I ever pick up a microphone, I pick up my reading glasses. Behind every three-minute investigation I do for *Inside Edition*,

I spend hours, days, sometimes weeks researching. I read as much as possible to better inform myself about the background of my investigation. Google is my friend. By the time I go on camera, I understand the elements of the story, backward and forward. This fills me with the confidence of knowing that I'm thoroughly prepared for any situation or question.

And while research is the foundation for journalism, it is also the foundation for bravery, no matter what your profession or situation. If you have to talk to a boss, a client, a professor, or an employee and know as much as possible about the subject or problem you're addressing, you will be prepared for anything they throw your way. Preparation is the key to confidence—and confidence is the key to bravery.

Unbeknownst to me, I used this technique way back in the day when I auditioned to be a Rams Cheerleader. I wasn't the best dancer by a long shot. But during my interview, I knew more about football than anyone expected. That was likely why I was picked over women who were better dancers. And since then, I've used it over and over again. People have constantly underestimated me, had low expectations, judged me, and called me names. The best way for me to overcome that was to be as well prepared as I could possibly be with information, knowledge, and the right questions to ask. Yes, I still make mistakes here and there, but I never walk into a situation without doing the work in advance to be fully prepared for whatever might get thrown my way.

Perspective

Before I interview my subjects, I put myself in their seat. I imagine how scary it must be to have a camera and lights in my face while I'm recalling the most traumatic moments of my life to a complete stranger. This step is really about listening. It sounds obvious, but you'd be surprised how little people actually listen to each other. More often than not, people are waiting for their turn to speak. This even happens in journalism. Reporters come to an interview armed with questions. They become so focused on what they want to say that they don't really hear what's being said to them.

For me, the victim's perspective is crucial. This step is important because I'm listening to their concerns, fears, and frustrations. Many of them have lost their life savings, their homes, or a loved one. They're relying on me to tell their story honestly and with integrity.

Think about your relationships. We talk to our bosses, coworkers, friends, spouses, significant others, children, and parents, but do we really hear what's being said to us? When a conflict or issue arises at home or work, we come prepared to tell our side of the story. We often know exactly what we're going to say. Often, we visualize how we're going to get our points across. Our focus is always on winning the argument or being right. We rarely think about how the other person is going to receive our information and how they'll feel about it. It sounds so simple. But it's really hard because it contradicts our instincts, especially when we believe we're right and that we have the answers. For us to gain another's perspective, we have to get outside our bubble. This means dropping ego and judgment. We have to ask ourselves, what is this person going through, and where are they coming from?

So many of my friends were shocked that I was eventually able to move past the hurt and become friends with Scott after he left me. It wasn't easy. But eventually, I viewed the situation from Scott's perspective. When I did this, my anger dissolved. I was able to forge a new relationship with him.

If you adjust your ears to really hear what's being said, you will not only understand and solve problems better, you will develop empathy, which will lead to bravery.

Empathy

Empathy is the direct result of understanding another person's journey, problem, or trauma. Once you've gained their perspective and connected with them, you will become filled with compassion. It's not possible to have empathy until you've truly listened to the person.

After listening to my subject, I sit with their anger or frustration and absorb it into my body. Sometimes I cry on the way home from an interview. Other times, I'll cry in the room with them. I let it affect me. I draw on that anger and frustration for the final part of the investigation, which is the confrontation. Because I'm armed with the righteous anger of the victim, I can act on their behalf.

It's really an amazing transformation for me. When I interview a bad guy (and yes, I call them bad guys. There are times when being an unbiased journalist is plain ridiculous, especially when you know a victim's story), I am no longer myself. I am a victim too.

My Kenneth Copeland interview hit one billion views because I kept my cool while asking the same question over and over. This allowed Copeland's personality to be on full display. When people talk about this interview, they marvel at how I remained so calm in the face of Copeland's condescending retorts. My answer is simple. His comments didn't affect me because I was no longer Lisa Guerrero. I had become one of the marginalized people who had given their life savings to this man. I was a vessel filled with the victims' energy, anger, and frustration. I was intent on getting them some kind of answer.

If you're a woman, you probably have this gift of empathy but may have been trained not to rely on it. Women are told to divorce themselves from their emotions. I say bullshit to that! Men are often guided by their heads instead of their hearts, but our empathy is our secret weapon. This will help you in every part of your life—as a girlfriend, wife, mother, partner, coworker, employee, or boss. Instead of stifling them, let your emotions guide you. Use those emotions to propel you into making courageous choices on behalf of those around you.

Action

I am brave because my audience expects me to be brave. And by audience, I mean the literal audience that will watch me on TV as well as my bosses, my crew, our staff, the victims, my family, my loved ones—and me. We all expect me to be brave because I've done it before—that's what I do, and that's what I expect of myself. By the time I interview the bad guy, I've gone through the first three steps. This makes the last step, physical action, the most natural.

Once you've been brave, it becomes expected of you—and you expect it of yourself. The pressure of knowing that others are relying on you to make courageous decisions will propel you into making courageous decisions. Basically, once you become brave, you can't stop being brave.

From the moment we're toddlers, girls are told to smile, be nice, don't talk back, don't be confrontational. When a girl is confrontational, she's labeled a bitch. And a boy? He has leadership potential. We have to undo years of society's training. It's not easy.

How can you reverse what has been ingrained since childhood?

When I talk to audiences, I tell them to find an opportunity to commit a random act of bravery every day.

At some point every day, there will be an opportunity where you can step outside your comfort zone, even though your instincts will pressure you to ignore these moments. Often people hear #BeBrave and think big, like you have to rescue someone from a burning building. I like to think of bravery as a muscle that needs exercise to become strong.

For instance, I travel a lot. I'll eat dinner by myself in a restaurant. But for years, the thought of eating alone at a bar unnerved me. One night, I forced myself to sit at the bar instead of a table. Now I do it all the time. I've met so many amazing people. Plus, the bartenders always know the best places to visit. I can't believe that for years I missed out on this experience because I feared the unknown.

Sitting alone at a bar pales in comparison to some of the brave stuff I've done as a reporter for *Inside Edition*. But it forced me out of my comfort zone and made me braver. If I didn't work on these little moments of bravery, it would be much more difficult to tackle the big ones.

I believe it's these small and not-so-small gestures that lead you on your path to bravery. After all, you can't start exercising your muscles by bench-pressing one hundred pounds. You may start with a five-pound dumbbell and then work up to heavier weights.

Find one small thing every day to build your bravery muscle. It could be as simple as wearing that thing in your closet that you felt too timid or old to wear—maybe it's an attention-grabbing hat or a sexy dress. Maybe it's changing your hair color or getting that haircut you've always wanted. Maybe it's wearing that bright red lipstick that you felt was too bold for you. It sounds silly, but these small gestures shake you out of your pattern—and that pattern is all about being safe and secure.

Another way to step out of your bubble is to be the first at something. At work, you can force yourself to be the first individual in a sales meeting to pitch an idea. Or you can be the first person in a conference room to disagree with the boss. Most people opt to keep quiet, get along, and not offend. I challenge kids to raise their hand first in class or be the first to sit next to a lonely kid at lunch whom no one else talks to.

Years ago, I attended a charity event in Bowling Green, Kentucky, where I was surrounded by a bunch of professional athletes and country artists. Joking around, I said, "How hard can it be to write a country song?" Well, this producer bet me $20 that I couldn't do it. I told him I'd have one finished in twenty-four hours. I'm sure he thought he'd never hear from me again. But I was determined to accept the challenge, even though this would be a first for me. The next day, I handed over my lyrics for "The Comeback," a song about people searching for their next chapter.

I collected my $20 and thought that was the end of that. But the producer handed my lyrics to Keith Burns, a Grammy-nominated country-music artist and songwriter. (He was a founding member of the country band Trick Pony.) Keith asked if he could take a crack at the song. Two weeks later, he emailed me a tape of my song put to his music. That email sat in my phone for a decade until one day I rediscovered it. I decided to track Keith down, unsure whether he'd remember me. He did. I asked if we could record the song in a studio.

One week later, I was in a Nashville studio singing backup along with rising stars Presley and Taylor, a sister act, on the recording of "Everybody Loves a Comeback," produced by the legendary James Stroud. After recording the song, we performed it several times—for a music video in front of a live audience and at the iconic Bluebird Cafe. Singing on a Nashville stage was something I had never in my wildest dreams imagined. It was scary, exciting, and very rewarding.

I love what happens when you boldly attempt the unknown. It may seem like incredible opportunities find you, but you're really the engineer behind those moments.

When you push yourself every day, little by little, you become a little more courageous. Soon you're not thinking about it—you're just doing it. And then when you're confronted with a big moment—if you see someone being bullied or treated poorly—you'll speak up. I believe that with each small act, you chip away at the shell you've been living inside. The little cracks become bigger until you're no longer inside that shell. You wake up with your inner badass unleashed. And you're ready to face every single challenge head-on and without fear.

Most people don't have the ability to leap to someone's defense because they haven't built that muscle through these small acts. But once you do, it becomes a reflex. I guarantee it. You will see injustice in the world and act on it. You won't be able to help yourself. If you're a brave person, you're not going to stand by and watch someone get hurt.

Helping people figure out how to be brave is one of the most gratifying parts of my life. I used to be a little girl who was mesmerized by brave heroines like Wonder Woman or the Bionic Woman or Emma Peel. I wanted to know their secret to being a badass. It took me years to realize that my mother's small act of bravery in Pier 1 held the answer to my question.

Commit a random act of bravery every day—no matter how small. I promise you that big, sweeping change will be the surprising and gratifying result.

17

Embracing
My Inner Warrior

"LISA GUERRERO!"

I heard my name screamed as I walked into a restaurant in Los Angeles. I looked around and spotted Erin Andrews and Charissa Thompson waving at me. I had only met them each once, years earlier. The Fox Sports broadcasting superstars raced toward me and embraced me. They asked me to join them at their table for a glass of wine.

As we sipped our drinks, we talked a bit about the sports broadcasting industry. These two beautiful and talented women were kicking ass in the business and making the kind of money I never could have dreamed was possible when I started in the '90s.

"I remember watching you interview Brett Favre after his father died," Erin said. "My dad paused the television and told me, 'Watch this woman. Look at how good this interview is. She's having the moment of her career.'"

"Thank you for being so kind to me years ago when I came to your home for an interview," Charissa added. "And thank you for paving the way for us."

I was speechless. I really don't think Erin and Charissa had any idea how much their words meant to me. All those years, I thought sports media despised me because I was an embarrassment to the profession. Looking back, I realized that hadn't been it at all. They simply might have realized that I was the face of things to come. Maybe they thought if they could shame and humiliate me, the next Lisa Guerrero would be too afraid to pursue a career in television sports journalism.

But the haters didn't deter Erin and Charissa. And now there's an army of women covering sports locally and nationally. They're on the sidelines, in the locker rooms, and at the anchor desk. And they're here to stay.

* * *

In the midst of the pandemic, I received a phone call from a name that sounded familiar: Andrew Marchand. He was a sports media columnist for the *New York Post*. He'd interviewed me years ago when I was on *Best Damn* for an article called "Fox's Guerrero, More Than Just a Pretty Face." He'd also wanted to interview me several times during my *Monday Night Football* days, but ABC would not allow me to talk to the press. Fast-forward to January 2021. He'd heard about my career as an investigative correspondent and was interested in talking to me for a *where-are-they-now* type of column. He wanted to know what had really happened to me back then.

This was my opportunity to set the record straight.

But how could I tell my story without dredging up that incredibly painful time?

Only my family and a few close friends knew about my depression, miscarriage, and suicidal thoughts. I really didn't feel like opening the old wound that was *MNF*. Actually, it was so long ago, it was no longer a scab but a scar. Yet as much as that scar had faded, it hadn't disappeared.

I thought about it for a bit. I could probably talk to Andrew about my work with *Inside Edition* and gloss over the stuff that had happened when I was a sideline reporter. Maybe I could even toss in a fond memory or two of that time.

Then I thought about the interviews I conducted with victims and their families. When these people spoke to me, they revealed the most heartbreaking, devastating, and private details of their lives. As a journalist, I relied on their honesty in telling their story so that I could help them share it with the world in all of their vulnerability.

Was I being a hypocrite by not demanding that same honesty of myself? Was I being a phony by speaking of bravery but acting like a coward?

So I called Andrew back. Throughout the long conversation, the truth gushed out of me. I told him about the verbal abuse, the humiliation, my depression, and my suicidal thoughts. By the end of the phone call, I was in tears. It was the most difficult interview I'd ever given. I truly understood what it must be like for victims when they share their trauma with me. When I finished speaking, there were a few seconds of silence. I think Andrew was in shock.

"Well, I'll have to talk to my editor. I think this is a much bigger story than I was originally going to write," he said.

Boy, he wasn't kidding.

The two-page spread ran on February 2, 2021, with the headline "Ultimate Warrior."

The first sentence read, "Lisa Guerrero wasn't sure she wanted to live anymore." The story detailed my *MNF* experience along with my drive along Pacific Coast Highway, when I contemplated suicide. The story revealed the entire traumatic ordeal and how I overcame it with therapy, time, and the relaunching of my career as an investigative journalist. It was an emotional comeback story and the first time I'd ever seen the entire arc of my life and career in print. I wept when I read it.

Minutes after the story appeared, my phone buzzed with calls and texts. My social media inboxes were flooded with messages. I heard from almost everyone I knew—friends, relatives, colleagues, former coworkers, cheerleader alumnae, teachers, and classmates, people I hadn't spoken to in years. No one had any idea what I'd gone through and how it had affected me. Good friends called, saying they were shocked. "I thought your life was perfect" seemed to be the consensus.

Then athletes and coaches texted their support. Sports media people—newspaper, TV, and radio hosts around the country—also contacted me. I didn't know who some of them were, but a few actually apologized for bullying or slut-shaming me back in the day. I heard from other people who had worked for Freddie and shared their similar experiences with me.

Andrew Marchand would text with updates: "This story just hit one million views." "It hit two million." "Lisa, it just hit three million."

Between the online and print versions of the *Post*, several million people read the story. I think the piece hit a nerve because it was relatable to so many people. It opened the door to conversations about bullying, harassment, toxic workplaces, depression, and mental health in sports. I had no idea there would be so many people who felt the way I had. Strangers messaged me sharing similar stories. "Thanks for your honesty."

"I'm bullied at school." "My boss is verbally abusive to me." "I've thought about killing myself." "I've suffered from depression for years." "I don't feel so alone now."

And then I got a text from a name I recognized. Even though it had been nearly twenty years, the number was the same. And despite the happy place I'm in today, I reacted the way I had all those years ago—I felt sick to my stomach. I couldn't believe I was still terrified of him. I thought about ignoring it. But I responded and agreed to talk to him by phone.

After all, I had to face my demon, my Gau-devil.

Freddie is now considered one of the most influential people in sports broadcasting. He was recently inducted into the Sports Broadcasting Hall of Fame.

"I'd like to clear the air," he said.

"Okay."

I thought he was calling to apologize, and I was ready to accept it. In the *Post* article, Freddie didn't deny the verbal abuse. He told the reporter, "I did my best to support and encourage her. I'm disappointed to be hearing about this for the first time, 17 years after we worked together on 'Monday Night Football.'"

Unfortunately, he hadn't called to apologize after all.

Instead, he told me that I had misremembered my experience with *MNF*. He said he had never yelled or cursed at me. He told me he had done his best to support me and was disappointed that I had said otherwise to the media. (He later followed up with a letter repeating this and added that there were others who said the verbal abuse "just didn't happen.")

On the phone, the sound of his voice transported me back to the football field, listening to him through my IFB. And instead of feeling insecure this time, I felt disgusted and angry.

I took a deep breath. I was no longer that insecure reporter. I was a seasoned journalist who demanded the truth for victims. Shouldn't I demand the truth for myself too?

"You and I know exactly how you treated me," I said. "You yelled at me. You cursed at me. You humiliated me. But you know what, Freddie? I'm not that same young woman anymore. You're no longer my boss, and I'm not afraid of you."

He was speechless. Finally, he said something. But he refused to acknowledge how he'd treated me, and we ended the conversation. But I realized that I didn't need anything from him—an apology or an admission of the truth. He may be one of the most powerful men in sports, but he no longer has power over me. I am a Guerrero. I am a warrior.

Acknowledgments

When Richard and I were little, we spent part of every summer with the Guerrero family in Chicago, Illinois, and with the Coles family in North Little Rock, Arkansas. (I'm sure our dad needed a break and was relieved that we'd be in good hands with family for at least a month or so a year.) Cousins on each side would descend on the grandparents' houses as we played, performed dramas, and choreographed musicals. As the oldest cousin on each side, I took the helm as director and chief bossy pants.

One of the reasons I was driven to write stories was because of my Grandpa Coles's library. Along one wall was an entire bookshelf filled with red notebooks. They were journals that he had kept each day for over five decades. As a Salvation Army officer, he wrote down every single person he met, what their conversations were like, and how he could incorporate them into a sermon or testimony. I realized quite young that there was enormous power in storytelling.

So I began keeping journals. Throughout my life, I have kept track of important events and conversations. Those journals were the foundation for the early versions of this book, which took thirty years to bring to life.

Years ago, I wrote a column called "Notes from a Sports Chick" for a magazine in Los Angeles called *Street Zebra*. I simply pulled swaths of pages from my journals to submit to the editors. As those stories gained traction, they evolved into a TV pitch that was optioned by CBS a couple of years later. Although the pilot (written by Bruce Ferber of *Home Improvement* fame) was never shot, the interest in my story led me to begin writing "Between a Jock and a Hard Place," the first version of this manuscript.

As my career evolved from local to regional to national sportscaster, the book evolved along with me. What started as a series of essays became impossible to finish because my journey was just getting started. I was happy and busy, although I was so overwhelmed with juggling multiple assignments and shows that I couldn't find time to dedicate to writing. So the manuscript sat in my computer for years without a final chapter.

But then everything changed. In the span of eighteen months, I got hired by *Monday Night Football*, got married to a baseball player, got fired by *Monday Night Football*, got humiliated by every sports critic in the country, and got behind the wheel of my car with the intention of driving off Pacific Coast Highway to kill myself.

Years after recovering from that trauma, I pulled out my notebooks and journals. It was time to write my book. This book. Finally.

I am grateful to so many people who supported my vision, who believed in the value of my story and that it could help to inspire others.

Thanks to Kirsten Neuhaus, my agent at Ultra Literary, for your guidance and counsel. (And a shoutout to Jill Wesley for putting us in touch.) Thanks to Lauren Marino at Hachette for taking a chance on me and for helping me to craft a better book.

As Irene Zutell would say, she now knows me better than I know myself. This year of collaboration has been a joy and a healing process as well. Thank you for guiding me along this journey and for encouraging me through some painful conversations. So, so worth it!

Thanks to Michael Lewis, who helped me format and research an early version of crucial parts of this book, especially the segments about the Patriots and Fred Golder. And I am eternally grateful to Fred for his guidance back then and today.

Much of this book includes mentions of my first manager, Lorraine Berglund, who tragically passed away a few years ago, much too soon. I am so grateful to her for her unwavering belief in my talent and for being by my side during some incredibly challenging events.

To Kate Edwards, my friend and manager over this past decade, your support has meant the world to me. Our daily phone calls fill me with inspiration and intention. We are such a great team, and I love you dearly.

Thank you to Mike Liotta, Rachel Hosseini, Grace Topalian, and Emily Baird of PR Machine for your ongoing kindness, humor, and support . . . and for arranging this incredible book cover shoot! A huge bucket of gratitude to Diana Ragland, the immensely talented photographer; Nola Roller, my stylist and friend, who made me try on the men's suits, thank god; and the amazing makeup and hair artists, Veronica Arancibia and David Gardner, who helped me channel my inner warrior that day.

Thanks also to Ken Lindner, Melissa Van Fleet, Kristin, Shari, Karen, and the entire team at KLA for supporting me through our decades of partnership. Also to Jenna Yamaka and Jeff Ho of Tagawa & Ho, LLP, for your kindness, diligence, and guidance.

And to Lisa Bloom and her team, thank you for being warriors on my behalf!

So many folks gave me great advice through different stages of this writing process, including John Walters, Jeff Pearlman, Rebecca Aguilar, Byrd Leavell, Bob Costas, Benjie Kaze, and especially the incandescent, incredible Leslie Maxie. Thanks to all of you! I took most of your advice, but sometimes I didn't because I'm hardheaded like that.

Some of the people I worked with through the years were lousy, as is well documented in this book. But most were wonderful, supportive, smart, kind, and professional and taught me so very much. I'd like to thank the executives, producers, journalists, and most of all the talented and patient crew members I was lucky enough to work with at CBS-2, Fox 11, Fox Sports West, Fox Sports Net, ABC, Kingworld, ViacomCBS, Paramount, IPC, and A&E. Every time I step onto a set or out on assignment, the years of collaboration with all of you that have made me a better journalist continue to help me grow as a storyteller.

Which brings me to my friends and colleagues at *Inside Edition*. I want to express how much I admire and appreciate your talent and dedication to the show. Thanks to Charles Lachman and Deborah Norville for your guidance. Some of you have become dear friends, and our time together over my seventeen years at *IE* has been a joy: Nicole Ullerich-Kumar, Jim Moret, Sheryll Lamothe, Tony Coghlan, Les Trent, Kerry Maller, Megan Alexander, Kevin Harry, and Eric Chin.

And to the *Inside Edition* investigative unit whose members past and present are those who share some of my fondest memories and greatest adventures: I am grateful beyond measure to have worked with you, especially Filip Kapsa, Larry Posner, Charlie McLravy, Katie Taylor, Megan Lupo, Matt Troutman, Josh Bernstein, Will Evans, and our mentor, Bob Read (RIP).

To my friends who have put up with broken plans because of breaking news, weird texts too early or late from various time zones, and too many details of crazy assignments or even crazier Bumble dates, thanks for putting up with me. I am so grateful for my girlfriends, too many to list here because God has blessed me with precious sisterhoods during every step of my journey.

But I need to mention some of them specifically. Especially my Rams sisters: Denise Peoples, Carrie Myklebust, Tracy Elefante, Teri Newman, Karen Leibrick, Lydia Donaldson, Keiko Kelly, Lynn Ravner, Kim Espinosa, Mandy Ellen, Pennie Creager, and Mary Cromwell.

From the Falcons, Patriots, and around the NFL, especially Mickey Crawford-Carnegie, Carla Johnson, Kelly Stewart, Katrina McGee, Patty Darrah, Linda Drueding, Angela King, and Chie Smith.

Among my Los Angeles pals, who are unsurprisingly blonde and beautiful and have much better eating habits than I do, I send my love to Ellen Ballon Dante, Michelle Gillette, Paullie Chandler, Megan Garrett, Jacqui Bell Weiss, Lisa Marie Wilkinson, Suzan Hughes, and Deena Driskill. And to Monique Marvez, Elisa Gaudet, Victoria Goodman, Jillian Barberie, and

Janie Bryant because badass brunettes need to stick together and support each other like we do.

And to Priscilla Garita Cuzzocrea and Kam Heskin Maby. How did a villainess like me end up with two beauties like you? Thank you, Aaron Spelling!

Recently I owe a debt of gratitude to someone who has helped me begin work on my next and best chapter. Thank you, David Sheriff (XO).

My family is small but mighty, and their support and love through the years have helped me to survive, thrive, and share these experiences with you. Thanks especially to my brother, Richard Coles. I am so proud of you! To Pam Coles and Jenna Lillard for adding so many blessings to my life. To the memory of Matthew Coles . . . the sweetest spirit. My kind and caring cousins Katy (Gidget) Woods, Elizabeth Johnson, Elisabeth Cunningham, Jennifer Woodard, and Yvette DeGeorge. I am grateful for all of my aunts, uncles, and cousins and my remarkable, resilient, devout, and devoted grandparents. The fond memories I have of Evan and Myrtle Coles and Raul and Sara Guerrero are a constant blessing.

No words can express the love I have for the mother I knew for only eight years. Lucy Guerrero Coles lives in me and around me, and I know she'd be incredibly proud of this book . . . especially its title.

And finally to my father, Walter Coles, who is my mentor and friend and whose character is my constant inspiration. My mother told me that I was born to be a warrior. But my father taught me that the bravest and boldest warriors lead with love.